In Ireland

The author on an Irish hireling at the meeting of the Meath Hounds

In Ireland

With Margaret Cabell Self

SOUTH BRUNSWICK

NEW YORK: A. S. BARNES and CO.

LONDON: THOMAS YOSELOFF LTD

A. S. Barnes and Co., Inc.
Cranbury, New Jersey 08512

Thomas Yoseloff, Ltd
18 Charing Cross Road
London W. C. 2, England

6718
Printed in the United States of America

To that combination of cat, kangaroo, and mountain goat—the Irish hireling, whose courage, agility, and patience are equalled by few and exceeded by none.

FOREWORD

This is an account—as accurate and truthful as I can make it—of what happened when I, an American woman, went alone to Ireland to hunt. My hosts' extreme hospitality left me little time to make notes, so I hope I will be forgiven for any mistakes in names or dates.

I should like to thank all those who entertained me and the many who were so cordial and friendly on the hunting field. The Irish Tourist Bureau was most helpful, and I am very grateful to its personnel. Be sure that as soon as the opportunity presents itself I shall return to Ireland's beautiful shores, where I hope to hear again the scream of the hunting horn echoing over the hills.

MARGARET CABELL SELF

CONTENTS

I   Preparations   13

II   Irish Correspondence—The Trip—The Arrival   23

III   Adare—Fort Union Stud—Dinner with the Morleys   31

IV   On Hunting in General—A Day with the Limerick Foxhounds   47

V   Peg Watt and the Croom Harriers   59

VI   The Golden Vale   69

VII   A Dinner Party at the Dunraven Arms—Dancing in Limerick   79

VIII   Teddy Ryan and His Black and Tans   83

IX   Tea at the de Traffords'—A Farmer's Ball in Tipperary   91

X   Mr. Tillander's Collection—A Late Snack with Mrs. Hedderman—Paddy Punch and Family—Dancing in Adare   95

XI   Ballykisteen and Victor Studs—Tea with Tim Hyde   105

XII   Jack and Esther Maxwell—An Irish Cocktail Party—
On to Dublin   109

XIII   The Ballymanny Stud of the Aga Khan—The National Stud—
Dinner with the Laidlaws   121

XIV   The Ward Union Staghounds—A Chat with Stanislaus Lynch   131

XV   Ballykeane and the Mivilles   141

XVI   Hunting with the Meath   147

XVII   Dromoland—The Arrival of Sydney   155

XVIII   The Duhallow Foxhounds—Off to Kerry—The Beehive Huts
and Fort Dunbeg—Dingle—Over the Hills and Far Away—
Killarney—Dinner and Bridge at the Watts'   163

XIX   The Galway Blazers   177

XX   Sightseeing with Esther Maxwell—Doon Castle and the Sheelamagig—The Clonfinlough Stone—Clonmacnoise—Cashel—Mr.
Fraser, Tailor Extraordinary   183

XXI   St. Patrick's Day—The Limerick Harriers—Races at Limerick   189

XXII   An Irish Kayly—An Irish Point-to-Point—
The Midnight Plane to New York   195

Postscript   207

Index   211

In Ireland

I

Preparations

We ran into the Van Wycks at the Whitman's "Picken Chicken" party, which was given, ostensibly, to welcome Jeanne Reeve and her husband, Basil, who had unexpectedly appeared from Denver. Jeanne has been in the past and we hope will again be the conductor, instructor, and proctor of that noted organization, "The No Friends of Music." This is the only known group of musicians, amateur or professional, which will, without malice aforethought or, in fact, any premeditation, play any of the Beethoven symphonies except the Ninth (which involves a chorus) with only one instrument in each section! Furthermore, should the ranks be further thinned by the absence of a conductor, they'll carry on just the same without benefit of baton.

Although the party was really for the Reeves, the Van Wycks were also star attractions: it was their first pub-lic appearance since their return from a trip to Ireland. They were both even brighter and more starry-eyed than ever. Last year Spain had left them enthusiastic, but Ireland! Somehow Ireland had put something into their veins that gave them the bounce of two-year-olds let out of the stable on the first warm spring day!

Philip was the more voluble of the two. "Oh, Nonie, you'll just love it! You and Sydney just *have* to go. The people! They're the friendliest, most hospitable bunch. Of course they'd cut your throats if they felt it was for the good of the country. . . ."

"But they'd do it in a nice way," put in Katie.

"Absolutely! And the country! And the pubs! And the tweeds!" Sydney, a connoisseur of tweeds as well as of pubs, pricked up his ears.

"Why, look at this coat I'm wearing, made to order. Just feel the material! Look at the cut! Brooks couldn't reproduce it at three times the price." Sydney felt the material and agreed.

"And I have another one coming —a 'Poacher's Jacket' with a hidden pocket where you put the rabbits, or what have you. Wait until you see that one!" I could see Sydney beginning to drool. We both, however, refrained from asking what you put in the secret pocket if you weren't a poacher by trade. But Philip was off again.

"It was just marvelous. Why, we stayed with one old gal in a house just like yours—the furniture and woodwork were all scratched and scarred, dog hair all over everything. Just as soon as Katie and I saw it we thought of you and Sydney!" (How wonderful it is to have really honest friends!)

"And such a nice, relaxed atmosphere. I expected a horse to step into the parlor at any moment! Oh, you've just *got* to go!"

I suppose the desire to hunt in Ireland is deeply imbedded in the soul of every horseman. With me this desire has been accompanied by a calm conviction that some day it would be fulfilled. Each year, as far back as I can remember, I have brought the idea up out of my hidden cupboard of secret aspirations, dusted it off, looked at it longingly, and then reluctantly put it back again. But after the conversation with the Van Wycks, I gave it a more careful scrutiny than usual. Perhaps this was to be THE YEAR!

The children were all married and either settled or in the process of being so. Toby, my second son, who was manfully building his own house on our south lot after hours, expected to be moved in by the New Year or shortly after. Meanwhile his wife, Laura, and the two boys were with her parents. Gincy, my youngest daughter, her husband, Philip, and their little boy had just moved into their house. Skip, the oldest of the clan, Mary, and their two boys were settled in Niagara Falls and would presumably get along without any more immediate help. Of course there were Chips, my eldest daughter, her husband, Johnny, and daughter, Logan, who were living with us temporarily. Johnny had just changed his job and was looking busily for a house in Hartford. Logan, aged two and a half, and her mother were established in the big guest room, waiting for Johnny to close a deal on a house, and Chips was expecting a new baby in January. But unless the baby came awfully late she should have recuperated and be ready to move to her own home (if by that time she had a home) sometime early in February. The Spring Riding Circus, which we give each year for the benefit of the Foster Parents Plan for War Children, was planned for the 25th of April. But since only the officers of the New Canaan Mounted Troop ride in it, I could lay out a training program for Gincy (my assistant) and the student instructors to follow. Yes, the Troop, with its hundred-and-seventy-odd children, should get along well enough without me for a few weeks—it might be good for them. As for the stable, no one could be more reliable than our Texas cowboy, Red Sloan. I should feel perfectly at ease leaving everything in his capable hands.

There remained only two problems: how to persuade Sydney to go with me and how to find the wherewithal to pay for the trip. Regarding the first, I decided to let Philip Van Wyck's tweed coats break ground for further persuasive suggestions. For the second, I had always wanted to use Ireland as a background for future books. Perhaps my publishers could be won over to the idea also.

All of this took place early in November. Later in the month I was bidden by Lowell Pratt, chief and favorite of my publishers, to come in for a conference concerning some children's books about which I have been grossly negligent. As we were crossing Madison Avenue I brought up the matter.

"How about sending me over to Ireland to do some hunting and write you a nice book?" I suggested diffidently.

"Swell!" said Lowell, much to my surprise. "We'll make you an advance to cover the trip." (He knows my financial status only too well.) "You write me a letter and tell me what kind of book you plan to write and where you want to go and so forth and I'll see that it goes right through." It was as easy as that!

The next day I called Katie Van Wyck to see if I could get more information. They had stayed at Adare, in County Limerick, she told me. She didn't know how one arranged for hunting since they were not horse-minded to that extent and had made their trip in mid-summer, before the cubbing season. I tried some other friends, the Abernethys, who have Irish connections and are hunting folk but the telephone didn't answer. Perhaps I had just better stop off at the local travel agency and make inquiries.

So the following morning, at train time, I went in. But I committed a great *faux pas* in asking for travel information at such an hour. A gum-chewing miss, who neither knew nor cared to know anything about trips to Ireland for hunting-minded but indigent writers, was the only occupant. Between chaws, she advised me to come back after ten o'clock. I looked longingly at the posters on display, all to do with Southern cruises and holidays in Mexico, and came out.

Chips and Logan were in the car. I had not mentioned my hope as yet to the family, wanting the idea to be a little more jelled before presenting it, but Chips had noticed my exit from the travel agency and was hot on the scent in no time.

"What did you go in there for?" she asked.

"I was toying with the idea of going to Ireland to do some hunting and maybe write a book about it," I said.

"Oh, you lucky! Can't I go?"

I looked rather pointedly at the tightly fitting maternity slacks she was wearing.

"I know," she said. "But I can still wish, even if I know it's hopeless, can't I? Anyway, the Dress Box is having a sale of coats and you're going to need some new clothes, lots of them. Let's go right over and look at them!"

"But I'm not even sure I'm going yet!"

"That doesn't make any difference. You know Daddy's always trying to get you to buy yourself some clothes. Come on, Logan, we're going to buy Gammie a new coat."

Logan has the usual dearth of inhibitions of those her age. "I want to dinkle," she said.

"You see?" said Chips. "We have to take her somewhere, and it might as well be the Dress Box," and she was out of the car, towing Logan behind.

Now, the Dress Box is one of those snooty shops which require a bank balance of at least four figures before the trembling customer dares to cross their thresholds even to price a summer cotton. As for me, by the tenth of the month I am usually arguing with the teller as to whether my bank statement should be rendered in red or black. So I stayed in the car.

But Chips is unawed by the grandeur of the Dress Box. "Hurry up," she called. "I hear they're having a lulu of a sale!"

Logan now added her two bits. "I'm going to dinkle all over my pants!" she announced cheerfully. What could I do? I got out of the car and followed at their heels. Half an hour later we returned to the car,

with me wearing a really scrumptious gray affair that would be perfect over either hunting togs or ordinary clothes. Soft as chinchilla it was, with a snug collar that fit up around my neck. And it had been reduced from ninety-five dollars to twenty-nine fifty!

And with this auspicious beginning I started my Irish adventure.

Later in the day I stopped again at the travel agency. An affable young lady, who did not chew gum, rummaged about and finally produced a number of completely entrancing brochures. Two were especially enticing. The first, entitled "Hunting Holiday in Ireland," told me that, for a sum within the amount suggested by Lowell Pratt, my publisher, as a suitable advance, one was guaranteed two weeks of heaven, with all tedious details taken care of. Ten hours' flying time would find me in Shannon, said the writer of this lovely green leaflet. Once in Ireland, I could have a choice of hotel, inn, quarters with a private family, or what have you; type of hunting country, type of horse, valeting service for same and for my hunt equipment (the leaflet didn't say specifically that I might have a choice of type of valet and/or groom, but no doubt the omission was inadvertant). Even gratuities were to be included.

I could hardly bear to put this folder down in order to look at the second. This was called simply, "Hunting in Ireland," and it depicted the joys of same in flowing rhetoric and three colors. Again I read that one was given a choice, this time of variety of hunting. One could Fox-hunt, Drag Hunt, Staghunt, or go out with the Harriers. The respective sizes of the various type hounds used in each category were given, together with the gentle admonition that it was considered unsporting to interfere with their freedom. (Perhaps Mr. Stanislaus Lynch, who wrote the booklet, had read David Gray's famous tale describing a formal English hunt into which are introduced three American Indians in native dress, *i.e.*, loin-cloths. The story ends with one of the three outstripping Field, Master, Whips, and hounds, catching the fox by the tail, and presenting him to the Master for breakfast.)

Then I looked at the pictures. The jumps looked gigantic, enormous, completely impossible! I hastily turned the page and went on reading. Evidently Mr. Lynch had anticipated my reactions, for in the next paragraph he pointed out that though the natural obstacles which the Irish erroneously term "banks" (small mountains or cliffs would have been a more accurate description) appear large, one should remember that even little children on ponies negotiate them and that firm knees and a stout heart go far to render them innocuous. I inwardly hoped that all Irish horses had likewise read and profited by Mr. Lynch's remarks. Certainly any horse that I rode would have to have not only firm knees and a stout heart but knowledge and experience enough for us both. In America anyone who tried to jump an obstacle like those shown in Mr. Lynch's brochure would be at once adjudged hopelessly insane.

And certainly no self-respecting horse would think that a four-foot ditch filled with water, on the near side of a steep cliff some twelve feet high, was anything that *he* was supposed to take any interest in—at least not unless he was very thirsty!

I continued reading and learned that, in addition to the natural obstacles, one occasionally came across wire, which one naturally avoided, or, once in a while, a post-and-rail, also classed as unjumpable. I blinked! What kind of people were the Irish? Given the choice of a simple post-and-rail or a horrendous cliff-ditch-guardrail ensemble, was there a man or horse alive that would choose the latter? Evidently there was.

On the last page I was informed that those who preferred hunting without benefit of horse might still carry on with the beagles. The illustration showed green-coated figures scrambling merrily across ditches and over banks. But I was not tempted. Besides, I could always take out extra accident insurance. I decided that I must talk with someone who had had first-hand experience.

I tried the Abernethys again. This time Jane herself answered. She was delighted to hear of my projected trip and plunged immediately into a description of some people—connections of her husband, Sam, I judged—with whom they had stayed.

"It was the most fantastic place," she said. "Fourteen dogs and seven cats and the place a shambles, but the most marvelous food *and* service! It was a castle, or almost. We had a room way off where they had opened a window goodness knows how long ago and had simply forgot to close it, and the ivy had grown in and climbed all over the ceiling. Honestly, you'd have to see it to believe it! Our hostess said she hoped we didn't mind fleas. Luckily Sam didn't hear (you know how fastidious he is), and I said, 'Oh, no, of course not,' thinking she meant the fleas on the fourteen dogs and seven cats. But the next morning when we got up Sam was absolutely *covered* with little welts. They didn't itch, fortunately, and you couldn't actually *see* any fleas, so I said, 'Now, Sam, you know we were warned about drinking the local water, and this must be the result!' I had to think fast because I knew if Sam ever suspected it was fleas he'd have had me out of there before breakfast, and I was having too good a time to leave!

"Of course, we didn't do any hunting because it was summer, but we made friends with the horses. Our host had his own hounds and there was a good deal of ribbing about how he managed to afford them. His friends claimed that the only way he was able to keep them in such good condition was by means of his 'evil eye'—they said that as he rode through the country he'd look over the animals grazing in the fields, pick out a nice fat work horse, and give her the eye treatment. The next day she'd be dead, and he'd go back and buy the corpse.

"Well, I wish I had time to tell you all, it's a wonderful tale, but we'll get together again before you go . . ."

I thanked her and hung up. I could hardly wait to meet up with Sam's connections and their menage. Could they be the same as Philip's "old gal," whose dog-haired and scratched floors and furniture had reminded him so poignantly of us? But I had still to locate someone who had actually hunted in Ireland and lived to tell about it.

Then I thought of Jean Slaughter. Jean is a young thing who started her riding career under my tutelage. I remembered that she had recently spent a year in England and several weeks in Ireland, so I called her. Like Jane Abernethy, she was overjoyed to hear that I was contemplating such a trip. Could I have luncheon with her at the Red Barn so she could give me all the gory details? I said I'd be delighted.

Over our pecan waffles and tossed salad we got down to business. The country and its people had cast a spell over her, just as it had over the Van Wycks, and she couldn't praise Ireland highly enough. She, too, had centered her activities in County Limerick and said that the hunting country there offered the greatest variety. "The hunting there spoils you for any other forever more," she said.

"And the fences?"

"They're unbelievable. They're worse than anything you ever saw or dreamed of. You just have to take a firm grip on your martingale strap, shut your eyes, and leave everything to your horse."

"Just what I figured," I said.

"Oh, and I must warn you of one

thing," she went on. "The fields are small and the jumps come so fast you've hardly time to catch your breath and take inventory after one before the next rears up and snarls at you. But once in a while you do come to a big stretch of luscious green that tempts you to let your horse out and gallop. That's the time to really watch out, for there's sure to be a wide drain or even a full-grown river, completely hidden, sneaking its way through the middle." She went on to describe how she had come to just such a big open stretch when suddenly, without any warning whatsoever, her horse had taken to the air.

"I looked down over his left shoulder and all I saw was water. I just shut my eyes and groaned. Then I opened them and looked down over his right shoulder. The water was still there, and we hadn't even levelled off for a landing!"

Further conversation brought out the information that Irish "hirelings" (horses that are rented out for hunting) are universally intelligent and dependable; that falls are frequent but that the Irish mud is especially soft; that long-johns, flannel pajamas, and bed-socks are required items of equipment; and that I had better take along my own saddle, since the Irish ones, compared to ours, are just plain hell! All in all, a most satisfactory conversation. And that night I dreamed that I was jumping off a hundred-foot cliff on a bob-tailed hunter with a big, blazed face. I never did find out whether or not we landed safely because I woke up, cov-ered with perspiration from excitement.

The next step seemed to be a personal interview with the Irish Tourist Association in New York. Lowell Pratt arranged what turned out to be the first of several such meetings. He started by sending them copies of some of my books. This was a mistake, for it gave the impression that I, a complete stranger to Ireland, its horses, and its country (to a fox hunter the term "country" has nothing to do with scenery, meaning, rather, the type of obstacles and terrain over which one rides), had the temerity to think I could write a technical treatise on the hunting and horses of Erin. The gentleman to whom I was introduced politely welcomed me, then produced a copy of that excellent book *The Irish Horse* and showed it to me without comment. I got the point and quickly reassured him.

"This is not to be a technical book," I told him. "Far from it! I should never consider myself qualified to write such a book!" He looked relieved.

"But I *do* feel qualified to write on the American Fox Hunter (female) and what she sees and does while on holiday in your country," I continued. How many times during my stay in Ireland I was to make this explanation! And in every case the result was the same. Doubt and truculence would vanish, and a beaming smile would encompass the face of my interviewer. Write a critical book on Irish hunting? No! But on what happens to an American in Ireland? That should prove amusing!

So the Irish gentleman behind the big mahogany desk smiled warmly and drew up a pad and pencil. "I am so sorry neither Mr. Durnin nor Mr. Sheehy are here to meet you," he said, "they both being out of town. But I assure you I'll take the matter up with them most carefully. Meanwhile, what can I do for you?"

This question had me rather at a loss. Not having had any previous experience with tourist bureaus, I did not know just what their powers and duties were. So I merely said that I was sure this book would be valuable as a means of promoting travel in Ireland and that the more I could see and do the more valuable it would be. The gentleman agreed, and gave me a list of Irish hunts, with the names and addresses of their respective Masters and Hunt Secretaries, the number of couples of hounds, and the location of the hunts. I studied this all the way home on the train, wondering what pictures these now unfamiliar names would later bring to mind.

And now I began to think concretely and seriously of my trip. Until this point it had had the imaginary quality of a mirage. But gradually the conviction that it was a delightful reality took hold. I no longer said, "If I go to Ireland" but "When I go. . . ."

It became imperative to decide definitely on dates. Surely Chips' new baby would have arrived, accustomed himself to terrestial life, and would be ready to be taken to his (as yet undetermined) home by the seventeenth of February. If I returned by the twentieth of March I should still have time to polish up the Spring Exhibition of the Troop. So I took these two dates down to the Travel Agency and told them to cogitate upon them and come up with something definite.

Did I want to reserve one or two seats on the plane? "Two," I said firmly. "And if I can't persuade my husband to go, I'll cancel one of them by February first." This was agreeable, and so we left it.

There remained the riding clothes. I should need a bowler, cork-lined, at least two pairs of breeches, a melton coat in black or oxford-gray, two pairs of black boots, a wool hunting vest, sufficient shirts and socks, and such odds and ends as a hunting crop and a stock pin. I investigated my closets to see what the home front could produce. (It should be remembered that of late years my riding has been limited to teaching and show riding with the New Canaan Mounted Troop. For these occasions I wear the colorful Troop uniform: royal and cadet blue trimmed with scarlet and embellished with golden major's leaves. But this is hardly suitable for the hunting field. I also have informal riding clothes, but my hunting coat was loaned to a friend years ago and never returned.) I found one pair of good breeches, fawn-colored and heavy, with only one very inconspicuous mothhole tactfully located on a pocket. I found a very motheaten bowler, with the cork lining entirely gone, and another that was three sizes too small. And then, at the back on the shelf, I spied an unfamiliar hatbox. Inside a beautiful sight gladdened my eyes—a lovely new bowler —and it fit perfectly! Where could it have come from? Then I remembered that our friends the Lloyds had given me this treasure some months before. Mac Lloyd had insisted that it was a gift in the nature of a white elephant and that I was at liberty to refuse it. How glad I was I hadn't done so!

The boot situation was fair. I had one pair that would do, but I should need a second. And good boots are so expensive! Obviously second-hand ones, if they could be found, were the answer. So I went to New York to search for these, a coat, vest, and another pair of breeches.

As every horseman on the Eastern Seaboard knows, there are two places to go for riding equipment in New York: the Miller Harness Company and Kauffman's. Bitter rivals, they are almost next door to each other on East 24th Street. My good friend Joe Miller found breeches, vest, and coat for me and made me a present of a lovely hunting crop. And Mike Kauffman brought out a dreamy pair of soft, just nicely broken-in boots which fit perfectly in the foot and which he guaranteed to stretch in the leg so that they would go over the heavy cord breeches. At both establishments they wished me a happy trip and a safe and speedy return.

As for other clothes, I decided to take a warm suit with an extra skirt, several sweaters, a long evening skirt and appropriate blouses, walking shoes, and slippers that could be worn both for dancing and with the dressy type of wool dress I planned to wear on the trip. It would save me a great deal of weight if I had the nerve to travel in riding clothes, but I didn't.

There remained the luggage. I purchased two conservative, fly-weight bags and promptly made them most unconservative by putting wide stripes of red and yellow masking tape around them so that I could spot them easily in a pile of luggage. I splurged on a lovely red leather handbag with an accompanying passport case, address book, and engagement book, all lettered with my name in gold. I found a fine brown briefcase in which to keep papers, and, with various documents and two repulsive passport photographs I persuaded a lady official to issue me a passport.

Vaccination is necessary for re-entry into this country. Five minutes with a doctor and two days later a faintly pink, almost undiscernable spot above my knee took care of this.

Meanwhile the travel agency came through with two dates—February 22 for my departure, March 19 for my return. My biggest problem remained to be settled: How was I to persuade Sydney either to come with me or to meet me over there? So far I had been able to get nothing definite out of him. Every time anyone asked him if he were going along on my proposed trip he looked unhappy and wondered audibly what in hell he could possibly find to do in an Irish village while I was out hunting!

II

Irish Correspondence—The Trip—The Arrival

Christmas came and went with the usual excitement. Immediately afterward I started corresponding directly with Ireland. On the list provided by the Irish Tourist Bureau I checked the names of the Honorable Secretaries of the various hunts which Mr. Stanislaus Lynch, in a specially prepared itinerary, had recommended. I also checked their fixtures and the type of country over which they hunted. I found that the County Limerick Hounds hunted on Mondays, Wednesdays, and Fridays over country near Adare, where I planned to go first, and that some of the country was stone walls. I wrote to Colonel Conyers, their Honorable Secretary, telling him of my plans and the purpose of my trip. I described my experience in riding—and my lack of experience over banks and ditches — asked whether I might hunt with his pack on Wednesday, February 24, the

day after my arrival, and requested him to find a nice reliable horse that would take good care of me.

I got a prompt and most courteous reply from Colonel Conyers saying that the Irish banks were not nearly so terrifying as people made them out to be, that none of them had guard rails, that once I was over the first one (and he was sure I would get over it) the others would be nothing, and that anyway on the 24th we would be encountering nothing more formidable than stone walls. How delightful! At least I probably wouldn't break my neck on the very first hunt! Colonel Conyers added that J. Fennell, of Main St., Rathkeale, would be glad to supply me with a horse and assured me that my hotel would be able to give me full information on point-to-point dates and would also arrange for me to visit the Fort Union Stud, owned by the Earl of Dunraven.

(I was to visit it not once but several times, each time with greater delight and appreciation.)

I also wrote to Mr. T. J. Kennedy, Honorable Secretary of the Golden Vale Hunt, asking if I might go out with them on Friday the 26th. Another cordial letter was immediately forthcoming. Mr. Kennedy wrote that he had forwarded my letter to Major General Wakely, who was now Honorable Secretary. Meanwhile he had arranged to borrow a horse for me. He hoped that while I was in their territory I would have the opportunity of meeting Mr. Tim Hyde, founder and former Master of the Golden Vale, who would be able to answer any questions I might have regarding hunting, racing, steeplechasing, showing, show-jumping, point-to-points, and breeding horses in Ireland. I took it that Mr. Hyde really knew his stuff.

Meanwhile Major General Wakely wrote in an equally cordial vein. He expressed his pleasure at my proposed arrival, confirmed the arrangement for my mount (Dr. Kennedy's horse, which General Wakely assured me, had never been known to fall), told me to be at Rossestown Cross (not on the map) at eleven o'clock on the 26th, and said he was sending a duplicate letter to my hotel with a hand-drawn map of my route to the meet! Without ever entering the country I was beginning to feel that I already had many friends!

Having arranged for my first two hunts, I now turned my attention to personal correspondence. I would start by staying at the Dunraven Arms, for it was near Limerick. Philip Van Wyck had insisted that I spend at least a few days at Dromoland (accent on the second syllable) Castle, a fabulous place (according to Philip) owned and operated by the Earl of Inchiquin. The Earl's family name, one of the oldest in Ireland, was O'Brian, and, like other very old family names in Ireland, it carried its own title. The head of the clan was known as *The* O'Brian" and his wife as Madame. The Castle, said Philip, had been rebuilt about a hundred and fifty years ago, so it could not be considered old in Irish terms, but it was full of family treasures and pictures. Here, if anything, was the bait with which to draw Sydney! A letter to Lord Inchiquin brought the usual prompt and cordial reply, together with a mouth-watering brochure showing inside and outside views of the Castle. Sydney's resistance melted like butter on a hot griddle. He immediately agreed to come over for at least ten days. Looking at the pictures, I was sure the Castle was full not only of antiques and early documents, but of ghosts, pookas, and banshees as well. And could I have foreseen my actual arrival there, in the blackness of a starlit night, the great castle looming over me, I should have been even more certain of meeting eerie inhabitants.

I also wrote to the Abernethys' hostess, Esther Maxwell, giving her Sam's and Jane's regards and hinting that they had said we must be sure to see her place. Mrs. Maxwell's letter was even more friendly than the others I had received, even though I gathered she led a somewhat hectic life. "At the moment," she wrote, "we are having a terrible freeze and my cooking ovens are full of half-frozen new-born lambs." In spite of this, she assured me, we should be very welcome. And did I *really* want a quiet horse or did I like one with a little spirit?

I hastily wrote her that my ideal in horseflesh was one that, as the French so aptly put it, would "obey the wind from the rider's heel." (I was to discover later that to an Irish horse the heels signal forward movement only!) I also told her of Sydney's fondness for old castles and pictures.

The busy Mrs. Maxwell promptly wrote again to say that her husband would immediately start looking for the kind of horse I had described and that she herself, despite the fact that she had a temporarily invalided child at home, would be glad to escort us around and show us old castles and pictures. She professed herself particularly well equipped for showing off Ireland's treasures since one of her uncles had been the painter Orpen and another was the famous historian of the same name. She did not tell me that, as I found out later, she was also a most delightful source of amusing stories and legends and a very gracious hostess. Nor could I foresee the two wonderful visits I would have with her and her husband.

The name of Harry Kenny was also on my list, and the usual prompt and friendly reply to my letters was immediately forthcoming. Mr. Kenny wrote that he would be delighted to show me around. On the day his letter arrived, Jane Abernethy called to say that she and Sam had also received a letter from Harry Kenny, who wanted to know who I was, whether or not I knew how to ride, and whether I was a blonde or a brunette. Jane was highly amused at these questions, since Mr. Kenny is in his eighties.

The next day I got a letter from the Tourist Bureau containing most welcome information—namely, that I would not be the only American hunting in Ireland. Apparently three of my countrymen, who came from Kentucky (Colonels all, no doubt) were also enjoying a hunting holiday, and it was likely that we would undoubtedly encounter one another. This good news was later corroborated by one of the Honorable Hunt Secretaries with whom I was corresponding. It looked as though I would not want for escorts.

But surely the nicest letter of all, in these days of busy international correspondence, came not from Ireland but from one of the dear No Friends. Ralph Wheelock, writing me concerning a firm from which I could get horse-show trophies, ended his letter with, "Have a wonderful time, Nonie, but take care of yourself and come back safely for we all love you!"

Things now moved apace. Chips and Logan came back on the seventh of January, and we settled ourselves to await the coming great event. This occurred as predicted on the 22nd, and, as also predicted, it was a boy. So I added Jonathan Cabell to my list of grandsons and banished the last doubt about the trip.

First it was "next month." Then, "in two weeks," and, almost before I could blink an eye, it became "tomorrow." In looking forward to a special date or event one tends to think of time as stopping at that point and going no further. So with me. Time stopped on February 22. I could plan up to then, but beyond that, nothing.

The day came, the last farewells were said, the last details attended to. It was a beautiful day, February 22, 1953, prognosticating a beautiful trip. It seemed that from the moment I had first planned this adventure, the gods were determined to make everything as pleasant and easy as possible. We piled the car with my two gaily striped bags, stuffed until they looked as though they would burst, and all my smaller bits and pieces.

Gincy and Darleen, one of my students, elected to escort me to Idlewild. We arrived more than an hour before departure time—none too soon, for when we had had coffee, checked out with the customs (it broke my heart to pay out thirty-five of my carefully budgeted dollars for excess baggage), gone up on deck and tried out the camera, etc., my plane—"The Flying Dutchman"—was waiting.

The plane took off on the dot, scheduled for arrival at three fifty-eight A.M., Shannon time. Presently we were aloft. I looked down past the broad wing and saw little islands below and then, immediately, a vast expanse of ocean. Too bad! I wouldn't be able to see "Sachem Hollow (pronounced "sock'em") on Block Island, where divers of the No Friends were spending a long weekend. (When Sydney arrived two weeks later he told me he had flown directly over Sachem Pond.)

The stewardess distributed a bulletin telling us that our Captain's name was Gruenveld (Greenfield, if I could trust my Dutch née German), that we were flying at an altitude of 13,000 feet, that the outside temperature was 12°F. and the inside, 68°. Next came an offer of chewing gum and a depressing little notice in six languages telling what to do in the event of an emergency landing. There was a picture of the passenger, his air vest in place, hunched over on his knees like a praying mantis, waiting for the Awful Bump. Then there was a picture of a round rubber dinghy with the same character reclining in it, apparently cheerful and comfortable. Evidently the bump hadn't been fatal. I was delighted to learn that every member of the crew knew how to manage the rubber dinghy, that it was self-inflatable, untippable, indestructible, and provided with all sorts of special equipment for a holiday weekend such as whistles, fishing tackle, water-purifying elements, and fluorescent chemicals. This all sounded too delightful and efficient for words, but I couldn't help hoping we wouldn't have to use it.

Luncheon was served almost as soon as we were airborne, and the menu, in the form of a postcard, was in French. I quickly took the opportunity presented to address it to the No Friends, care of Herbie Whitman, so that they would know I was being well fed. Sydney was the recipient of another postcard, courtesy of K. L. M. This was a fine color reproduction of a painting by Jan Stern entitled "A Couple Drinking." It showed a sheep-faced, straggle-haired man pouring out a drink for a plump lady who was obviously, to quote Peter Arno, somebody's "Bosom Friend."

There were only eight others in my section of the plane. An elderly Dutch couple, evidently on their way home, sat in front of me. Two other ladies, strangers to each other, one German and one American, sat behind me. We soon established a kind of camaraderie that one often develops with people one knows one will see once only. A lone man, who had left a weeping wife and a howling baby son at Idlewild, was across from me, and in front of him sat a woman with an accent I couldn't quite place and a young American girl. The snatches of their conversation which came to me over the roar of the engines was intriguing. I gathered that the younger girl was joining her fiancé in Europe and was to be married almost immediately. But she didn't seem too sure of how satisfactory a bride she was going to be.

"He's a great rider, of course," she said, "and I won't come up to his expectations in that respect. I don't know what to do about it. This is really my last chance, you know."

The older woman considered the problem and then came up with a solution. "Perhaps you had better persuade him to go in for sailing," she said. I could not catch the reply to this, but some time later I gathered that skiing had been decided upon as the sport at which the young lady could really hold her own. Before we landed in Shannon a complete honeymoon had been planned, down to the last detail. I have often wondered how it actually turned out, and whether the honeymoon was spent on skiis, on horseback, or in a sailboat.

We had now been out for about four hours. I looked out of the window and, through scattered clouds, saw a wooded, desolate countryside below me. There seemed to be little snow but many small, ice-covered ponds—Newfoundland, no doubt. We followed the coastline for some hours; now I could see it, now it was gone. Then I saw the ocean again, at intervals, covered with what must have been great ice-floes, looking like huge, curved, white beaches. We remained above the clouds, and soon we could see the stars and moon, just beginning to wane. There was no perceptible motion, and only by watching the slow sway of the edge of the giant wing forward of my window could I be sure that we were moving.

After what seemed more like ten minutes than ten hours, I looked down over a great ocean of clouds that reared their crests like gigantic breakers. Then this mysterious sea parted, and between steep white banks appeared the black ocean far below. And always the stars and moon accompanied me and the great wing swung rhythmically. Suddenly there were no clouds, and I saw what appeared to be a gigantic flat serpent swimming toward me in the black ocean. It was frilled all around with white and had a diamond eye blazing in the center of its head. I knew without asking that this was my first glimpse of Ireland.

Another half hour of steady flight and the lights of Shannon were below us. The wing tipped suddenly. The moon disappeared as suddenly, and then the lights were on a level with my window. The plane slowed to a stop. We had arrived.

All the passengers were told to disembark while the plane was in port, but since I was the only one "leaving them," as the stewardess expressed it, I was instructed to be the first one off. I was met at the gangway by a charming girl, dressed in an appropriate and becoming emerald-green uniform. I noticed that there were puddles on the runway, although we had had clear weather all the way over and it was not raining now. Bearing in mind Mrs. Maxwell's description of the freeze, I inquired hopefully, "How has the weather been?" "Worse," I was told. Later I was to find that, according to the Irish, there are only two kinds of weather in their country at this time of year: "bad" and "worse."

But to an American the climate is not disagreeable. What is cold to the Irish is quite warm to New Englanders, accustomed as we are to oc-

casional zero weather. The first few days I was in Ireland I experienced weather which reminded me somewhat of a person coming down with a heavy cold—drippy with an occasional sneeze. But brief sunshine gave hope for clear weather, and I soon learned that Irish weather bore out Mark Twain's remark: if one didn't like it, he had only to wait a minute. Later in my stay the weather became more settled. We had occasional days that were consistently gray or cloudy and some that were all sun. But though I had brought a raincoat and galoshes, I never put them on, and the brief showers that I was to encounter in the hunt field were foiled by my wise provision in having all my hunting clothes shower-proofed.

My guide took me into a low building, where the health and emigration officers awaited me. A tall chap, bearing a large handful of papers, introduced himself as Mr. O'Sullivan and told me that the papers had to do with my boots and saddle.

"Where are they?" I asked.

"They went on to Dublin by mistake and we can't get them back without your signature," he told me.

"When will they come back?"

Mr. O'Sullivan's face assumed that vague look which is the standard expression of all Irishmen when asked a question requiring a specific answer.

"Toward the end of the week—maybe," he said. My own face was now making the acquaintance of my shoe-strings.

"But I'm going hunting tomorrow and I need them," I told him, carefully not mentioning that I had another pair of boots with me and that I *could,* if necessary, ride an Irish saddle on one hunt. The innate gallantry of the Irish came to the rescue. "I'll just telephone Dublin and see if they can't be brought down on the afternoon plane," he told me, and hastened off to do so.

I now faced the customs men, who took my word for it that I was not importing liquor, cigarettes, plants, or pork products, and poked vaguely in one bag. Then my guide escorted me through a door into the main waiting room, where, to my astonishment, I found myself in the middle of a square dance! I felt like Alice in Wonderland! On one side, seated in a chair, was a lugubrious-looking fellow with long, dank, black hair, playing a tune on an instrument that was new to me. It was played like a flute but was of black wood, like a clarinet. It was at least four inches in diameter and sounded something like an ocharina. In front of the musician was a cleared space with a waxed linoleum floor, surrounded by tables and chairs, or all the world like a night club. There were two sets of dancers in tweeds, the men complete with berets or golf caps. There was no "caller" such as we have here: the dancers went through their steps from memory. There were no individual performances by each couple successively in a square, and the figures were not very complicated. Although there was a good deal of "swinging" at intervals, there was more ordinary round dancing in between than one would see in an American square dance. Each dance began with the traditional "eight hands around and circle left," but there was no promenading.

Later I was to learn that, next to riding and hunting, dancing is the Irishman's favorite pastime. Although there is only one riding school in the whole of Ireland, in every newspaper and on the bulletin boards of every hotel one finds advertisements for dancing classes and private lessons for both "beginners" and "progressives."

In one corner sat the parish priest with a few men friends. In another were three maidens, handkerchiefs in hand, and couples and men and women of every age sat at the surrounding tables. There must have been fifty or seventy-five people present. And all this at three o'clock of a morning at an airport! I was spellbound!

"Is this a regular custom? Do you always provide entertainment for incoming passengers at this hour?" I asked. The guide was horrified.

"It's only a couple of the boys are off to the States and they're after giving them a bit of a farewell party," she said, "and the place that littered up and all! Indeed, Madam, it's *not* always like this! Usually it's nice and tidy and quiet. But come into the dining room now and have a bit of breakfast. When you come out they'll all be gone and you'll have the place to yourself!"

"But I love it," I protested. "Can't I just sit here and enjoy watching them? My taxi isn't scheduled to get in before four forty-five, so I've plenty of time." My guide was strongly disapproving, but I was determined, so she finally left me and went to check on the arrival of my taxi.

The dance continued and I continued to enjoy it. Presently the P. A. system broke in on the music and announced the arrival of the plane for Gander and New York. The music started up again, and, after several weak attempts, the whole crowd united in what was evidently the Gaelic equivalent to "Auld Lang Syne." The three girls wept copiously and there was much patting of shoulders, kissing and shaking of hands; then the whole crew swarmed out onto the outer deck and the place was empty, as I had been promised.

I went into the restaurant, deciding that I might as well use up a bit of time though I was not really hungry. I was served very black coffee mixed in equal parts with hot milk, which is the Irish way (I was not to see cream served with either coffee or tea until I once more landed in New York), and a queer, crystal-like kind of sugar, Irish bacon (which is much like the Canadian variety), and fried eggs. Toast, ice cold, was delivered in a little rack guaranteed to ensure its remaining cold.

Having finished my breakfast, I returned to the waiting room, to be informed that the Shannon Travel Bureau, which was providing my taxi, had prudently telephoned before starting out to make sure that I had arrived. My cab was expected to be along in good time. It was now 5 A. M. A sleepy-looking lad was busy picking up the scattered papers and straightening the chairs. Presently a tall man in dark livery came over to where I was sitting, handed me a sealed envelope, and then discreetly withdrew to give me privacy in which to read it. I was somewhat mystified—I couldn't imagine who would be writing to me. The letter turned out to be an invitation to take dinner that night with a Mr. Morley of the Shannon Travel Agency. Mr. Morley apologized for suggesting that I go out so soon after my arrival but explained that he was leaving shortly for the States himself and wished to get my advice on certain matters before his departure. He would understand perfectly if I did not feel up to dining with him and would I please let him know by telephone from the Inn.

How delightful! I arrive in a strange country at three in the morning, am entertained by dancing and immediately invited out to dinner! Things were moving apace!

III

Adare—Fort Union Stud—Dinner with the Morleys

The night was velvet black as we started for Adare. The road seemed to have a good surface but was narrow. I could get little idea of the topography of country, catching only an occasional glimpse of high banks or thorny hedges. There were no other automobiles on the road, but we frequently passed people on bicycles. "At what time does the sun rise?" I asked the driver, hoping to get some idea of the length of the days. But I was foiled by the native reluctance to make any definite statement involving figures. There was a long pause, and then he admitted that he had no idea. "I see it so seldom," he said.

Presently I noticed that we were approaching the lights of a town or city.

"What's that ahead?" I asked.

" 'Tis Limerick," said the driver. He paused, then added, "The cities of Ireland, Madam, are like currants in an old maid's cake—few and far between!"

Limerick, even in the dull glow of the street lights, looked beautiful. The houses were of simple, Georgian architecture, red brick with fan lights over the doorways. They had no porches, but occasionally one saw white steps leading up to the front doors. We passed a row of houses set back from the street and surrounded by elaborate iron grillwork fences. I could easily have been in Baltimore.

A traffic light at an intersection provoked another few words from my taciturn driver. Traffic lights in Ireland are something special and were introduced only a few years ago. When the one which we were approaching was first installed, all the townspeople collected to inspect its operation. But no one knew just what the red and green signals meant. One of the first vehicles to go through was a small donkey cart driven by a young girl. When she reached the corner the light was red, but, knowing no better, she continued on her way. A traffic "guard" standing in the center of the intersection halted her and explained that she would have to wait until the light turned green. She halted willingly enough, and so did the donkey, but getting underway was another matter. The donkey folded his ears, went to sleep, and refused to be aroused. No small confusion resulted. Words and blows proved of no avail. Finally, the light having gone from red to green and back again several times, the guard called on the bystanders to assist. Disregarding the color of the light, they surrounded the animal, lifted him and his cart off the ground, and carried them to the far corner.

This same intersection was to cause me many puzzled moments. It was the junction of four important roads, one leading to Dublin, one to Tipperary, the third to Shannon and Ennis, and the fourth to Adare. Every time I set out from Adare I found myself sitting in my car at the traffic light in Limerick, trying to decide upon the correct road. It would have been quite simple were it not for the fact that there was no sign, route mark, or indication of any kind as to which road was which. So each time I would draw up to the side of the street and cogitate. "When I came back from Tipperary I turned left to Adare," I would say to myself, "and since I am now on the road from Adare I must turn right to go to Tip-

perary. But since I want to go to Dublin, I must either turn left or go straight. The question is, which?" Usually I ended by asking my way—a good plan, since the Irish always know exactly where every road leads. They can even tell you how to find a particular person's house even though it may be two or three towns away. Of course, their directions can seem a bit misleading. "Go straight ahead but keep turning" is a favorite.

It took about five minutes to go through Limerick and we were again in the country. We continued to meet occasional cyclists as well as grazing donkeys and cattle. After ten miles the driver drew my attention to a high masonry wall which seemed to go on forever on my left. "Lord Dunraven's estate," he said, and I knew we were almost at my destination.

We drew up in front of a long, low building—the Dunraven Arms. No light was visible, but the driver got out and rang a bell. Presently the door was opened by a young woman whom I was to come to know and admire. Her name was Kathleen, and she was maid-of-all-work at the Dunraven Arms. Kathleen, as far as I could see, was always the first one up and the last to bed. She woke me and built a fire for me every morning. She cleaned my room and was then to be seen on her knees scrubbing miles of painted floors in the long passageways. She carried suitcases, saw that my hunting clothes were delivered to the valet, helped wait on table when there were more than a few staying at the Inn, and answered my questions, no matter how odd they must have seemed to her, with perfect good humor. She built up my fire again in time for the room to be warm when I returned from hunting and, as a last service, turned down my bed and buried a beautiful, hot, hot-water bottle under the blankets. Nothing was too much trouble for Kathleen. Her cheerful voice was to be heard singing all day, from one end of the long corridors to the other. Because she had so much to do, she never walked a step. Instead she ran, her body slanted as though she were leaning into a strong wind. Although there were many other servants, including several men, it was Kathleen who was expected to get up before daylight to welcome me and show me to my room. She had been in such haste, in order not to keep me waiting, that she had put on no shoes but paddled ahead of me in her stocking feet, carrying my heavy bags as though they were full of feathers and chirping that she hoped my flight had been comfortable and that I was not "eaten up with the cold."

When I climbed into bed I made the first of two delightful and unexpected discoveries about Irish homes and inns: namely, that the beds are universally comfortable! The second discovery I was to find even more welcome: there seems always to be plenty of scalding hot water! The bathtubs are a bit strange, to be sure, being six or seven feet long, from eighteen inches to two feet wide, with a drop-jump on the landing side. The first time I got out of my coffinlike tub in the Dunraven Arms I did not expect the drop and almost fell. "It would be a fine thing to break my leg getting out of a tub," I said to myself. "No one, not even the No Friends, would ever believe I hadn't met with a hunting accident!"

Kathleen came back promptly at eight-thirty, armed with kindling and a scuttle full of coal and matches. The fireplaces in Ireland are not open as ours are. The face is tiled over, leaving only a small opening, perhaps a foot in width, eighteen inches in height, and eight or ten inches in depth. There is usually, though not always, a grate of some sort, no doubt the forerunner of the American Franklin stove, set in the opening. The fires are either of turf or of coal, which seems to ignite and to burn much more readily than our coal; a few slivers of kindling, a bit of paper, a puff or two from the bellows or from a pair of good strong lungs and the fire is going. It will burn for hours without further attention and gives out a steady heat that soon warms up a small room. Turf burns much the same way but is sootier.

Kathleen drew back the heavy draperies. "What is the weather like?" I asked.

"Sure, it's worse," she told me cheerfully.

While dressing I looked out onto the village street. Adare is a very "dressed-up" Irish village. The thatched cottages have more and larger windows than most, neat yards in front of them, and even an occaional sizable tree. It is almost like an

English village. The street was wide and filled with a continuous though thin stream of traffic going in both directions. First, foremost, and most common were the milk carts, which might consist only of a frame or skeleton of a body mounted on wheels, or of a proper body with low sides. The

A typical milk cart and driver outside the Augustinian Abbey at Adare

carts were drawn either by donkeys or by smallish, heavy-set, rough-looking horses. Spotted horses seemed to be very popular, which rather surprised me, since I had always thought of these as being a Western-American type. I learned later that "colored" horses, as they are called, are much in demand. Some of the drivers of these carts were women, who sat side-saddle on the shafts, dressed in voluminous brown wool skirts, black shawls, and "gum" boots, and who all looked older than God. The animals, when the driver was female, invariably moved at a snail's pace—so slowly, in fact, that one was tempted to take a sight against the horizon to be sure that they were moving at all.

The men were of every age but were universally tall and thin. In fact, I don't remember seeing a single really fat man in Ireland. They wore flat, peaked wool caps and heavy coats that hung to their ankles, emphasizing their height and thinness. They stood up to drive, balancing nonchalantly on legs spread wide apart and shouting cheerfully at their animals. Always in the cart was a pyramid-shaped milk-can, at least four feet high and wider at the base than at the top. These cans looked anything but hygienic, and every time I drank a glass of milk I thought of them, of the prevalence of tuberculosis in Ireland (which has the highest T. B. mortality rate in the world), and of the lack of pasteurization!

Naturally, I wondered at the number of the milkcarts. Later I learned that it is thus the small farmer makes most of his ready cash. He takes all his milk, each day, to the local creamery (every tiny crossroads of a village boasts a creamery), where the milk is separated. The farmer is paid for the cream, which is then made into butter and either sold locally or shipped to other markets, and the skim milk is returned to him for his own use and for feeding his pigs. Despite the number of creameries in Ireland, I was to see cream only twice while I was there.

Some of the carts, in addition to carrying the inevitable milk cans, were also loaded with school children, and many times a group of children ran along behind as well, holding on to the back. The little boys wore shorts, jackets, and berets. The little

Irish tinkers heading for the open road

They are a hardy race, some with gypsy blood, who make their living horse-trading and mending pots and pans.

girls wore dresses, long coats, and berets. It seemed odd not to see the inevitable blue jeans of the American rural school child. They all carried school bags strapped across their backs instead of in their hands or hanging over one shoulder. They looked rosy-cheeked, fat, and healthy, but statistics show that mortality among young children and infants in Ireland is deplorably high.

Occasionally a cart belonging to a tinker would pass, followed by a loose horse or two, a couple of goats, and perhaps another cart, pulled by a donkey. Underneath the main cart ran odd dogs and often a pig. Men on bicycles helped herd the loose animals while women, usually holding infants with pacifiers in their mouths, drove. The tinkers' carts are very reminiscent of the covered wagon of our colonial days. The canvas is stretched over a wooden frame and then mounted on a wagon body. A jaunty stovepipe sticks asymmetrically out the top, and the whole is painted in gaudy reds and blues. Some of the tinkers themselves are of pure Irish ancestry, but some have real gypsy blood in their veins. They prefer to live a wandering life, traveling through the countryside mending pots and pans and occasionally doing a bit of horse-coping. Since they own no real estate, they pay no taxes. They camp by the side of the road wherever it pleases them and fill their larders by means of forays on the local chicken roosts, going on their way only when the farmer who owns the land can stand their litter no longer. The children look filthy, though not underfed, and become professional beggars as soon as they can talk. The Irish seldom give them any money, claiming that many of them are fakers and will not accept a meal if it is offered to them or do even a small amount of work for the requested shilling. The tinkers haunt the fairs and point-to-point races. In summer they have two great "get-togethers," one at Killorglin, a little town in the southern part of Eire, the other at Galway. Each summer at Killorglin a platform is erected in the tiny square for the celebration of "Puck's Fair." The ruler of the fair is a large billy goat, who is dressed up and lifted to the platform, where he reigns for the duration of the fair. No doubt this celebration has pagan origins. The other big celebration is a horse fair in Galway, where all the tinkers and gypsies meet with their horses for several days' trading. Each bargain is sealed by a curious ceremony: the seller of the animal spits on one of the coins which he receives from the buyer, then hands it back to him. After the horse trading is over, the king of the gypsies announces the weddings which have been arranged during the week. The priest is asked to come and officiate, tables are spread with food, and all the village is invited. For several days the feast to celebrate the multiple weddings continues.

I was sorry that I would not be in Ireland to see these two festivals. But I saw the tinkers often on the roads and at point-to-points, and whenever I gave them a penny or so they were always most polite and promised that I would be remembered in their prayers.

My room, by now, was nice and warm, but the passageway was cold, and I was glad of my woollies. A delicious breakfast and warm inquiries from Miss O'Hare, who ran the Inn, and her two assistants put me in just the right frame of mind to go on with my plans. Did they think, I asked, that Lord and Lady Dunraven would permit me to come and visit their stud, Fort Union? I was assured that this could be arranged with the greatest of ease. A few minutes later Lady Dunraven was on the telephone, inviting me to luncheon.

Did they think, I asked, that J. Fennel, who had promised to provide me with a horse for my first hunt on the following day, would actually provide one? Another short interval and word came back that J. Fennel was expecting me and that my horse would be at the meet. All I had to do was get on him and ride off! Such service!

I examined the Irish telephone book with interest. I say "the" book since there is only one for all of Ireland. In it everyone with a telephone (and nearly everyone with either business or social activities has one) is listed alphabetically. Thus it is not necessary to know in what town or county a friend lives; his number can be found with no difficulty. If he lives within twenty miles of the inn or hotel where one is staying, nine chances out of ten the person putting through the call will know the exchange and probably the telephone number from memory.

I went into the small room off the bar which served as a lounge. There I was introduced to a charming gentleman in a pale blue hunting waistcoat. From his strong Southern accent, I rightly surmised that he was one of the "Kentucky Colonels" I had been told about. His name was Jack Rodes. When he learned that I was hunting with the County Limerick the next day, he invited me to share the taxi that he and his friends had engaged for their stay.

"Benny Supple, the driver, is invaluable," he told me. "He tells me how much and whom to tip, where to get horses and anything else I want. And he knows every by-path and road in Ireland. When we planned to come over we were told to hire Benny for our whole stay or not to come at all."

Soon we were joined by Messrs. Jack Bass and Bill Haggard, the other two gentlemen in Mr. Rodes' party. As it turned out, they were from Tennessee, but I still thought of them as the "Kentucky Colonels." They all agreed that they had been having the most wonderful time imaginable, that the hunting and horses were even better than they had anticipated, the people the most cordial in the world, and that I certainly need not worry about not having enough to keep me busy.

Presently Benny arrived. He was broad-shouldered, narrow-hipped, and of medium height, with sharp features and the usual Irish courtesy. The "Kentucky Colonels" packed their saddles and their luncheon sandwiches and were off. They had been hunting practically every day and planned to continue to do so.

Lady Dunraven arrived at twelve thirty. She was lovely to look at and had an easy graciousness about her. She was, I later learned, half American. After she had a short consultation with Miss O'Hare about the Inn, we got into her car and drove through the great gates into the estate. It was an enormous place, beautifully kept, with a river abounding in salmon running through it. She waved at a hip-booted figure who was fishing in the muddy waters, pointed out a beautiful old ruined castle, and then we drew up before a lovely Georgian house of yellow stucco. This was the "small" house, she told me; the Dunraven's had closed the manor house.

Lord Dunraven greeted me cordially in the library and offered me some sherry. He was the perfect picture of the English, or Irish, country squire—healthy and hearty looking, with a manner of assurance that comes of generations of overlordship. He plied me with questions about my trip and my purpose in coming. I had the feeling that everything I said was being carefully tucked away for future reference.

When the sherry was finished we went in to luncheon, where we were joined by the children's governess. The luncheon was delicious—clear soup, a fish course, and meat with salad and a desert, or "sweet." The service was incredibly smooth; we were waited on by two men who moved like shadows and anticipated every want. Such training is not perfected in one generation; through the ages the Earls of Dunraven had demanded and become accustomed to this kind of service, and through the ages men-servants from father to son had been trained to render it. Just when I was beginning to wonder if there was anything which would not be immediately forthcoming at the flick of an imperious eyebrow, Lord Dunraven asked if he might have cream with his sweet. Inquiry in hidden regions divulged that there was none. I allowed myself a secret smile. The noble Lord had his castles and his perfectly trained staff, but I, at home, with the co-operation of Betsy Browneyes, had all the cream I wanted!

After luncheon Lady Dunraven offered to take me around and show me the stud, since Lord Dunraven had a previous appointment. On the way to the stud, Lady Dunraven explained to me that since 1945 Lord Dunraven had been trying to provide the most perfect environment and routine possible for his horses in an attempt to

Courtesy of Time-Life, Inc.

Lord Dunraven and his dog

Each morning the pair come to the stables to discuss matters of importance with the head groom and to watch the veterinarian check the mares and foals.

prove that such care, though expensive, paid off.

For the benefit of those not familiar with such matters, a "stud" is an establishment that keeps one or more stallions, to which outside mares may be sent for breeding purposes. The mares usually come about six weeks before they are to be bred. Some are in foal; some, called "barren mares," are not, not having been bred the previous year. After they have been succesfully bred, the mares and their foals return to their owners.

In addition to these mares, the owner of the stud usually has some mares and foals of his own as well as some yearlings from the previous year. In October, when the yearlings are about a year and a half old, they are sent to the yearling sales in England. Here trainers bid for them on the basis of their blood lines, general conformation, and way of moving, etc. (these criteria must suffice, since the yearlings have never been bridled nor ridden). These yearlings are all destined to be trained for racing.

Unless the owner gets at least a thousand pounds ($2800) for each colt, he does not make his expenses, but many colts bring far more. Naturally, the large majority of the yearlings do not prove to be outstanding, but for one that demonstrates unusual speed and stamina on the track and, later, prepotence as a sire or dam of the new generation of yearlings and two-year-olds, the cash rewards are enormous. The most valuable stallion in Ireland's history, to judge by the amount paid for him, is Tulyar, sold by the Aga Khan to the Irish National Stud for the not trivial sum of 250,-000 pounds (about $700,000). Stud fees at the various establishments range from three to six hundred dollars.

In addition to the "studs" there are "stud farms," where the mares return, after they have been bred, to bring up their foals.

Fort Union, the Dunraven stud, proved to be a series of beautiful courtyards, enclosed by one-storied, slate-roofed buildings fronted with strong "dutch" doors spaced twenty feet apart. These doors opened directly into the spacious box-stalls, knee-deep in straw. We looked into several and saw mares and foals, some three or four weeks old, some newly arrived. Carefully kept graveled walks led from one courtyard and building to another. Broad expanses of lawn occupied the open spaces in some of the courtyards; smaller areas were planted in roses, each plant carefully tied up and the species tagged. Narrow borders of roses edged the paths and espalied flowering shrubs were trained on many of the walls. For breeding or for exercising the horse in bad weather, there was a circular

A novel way to carry a bundle of straw!

building with a conical roof and a deep sand floor, similar to what we call a "Hitchcock pen" over here, although Hitchcock pens are used mainly for free longing and jumping. In another oval building was a covered track, the center open to the sky and carpeted with closely clipped, green, green turf. Marble benches invited one to sit in the center and watch the yearlings being exercised, for Lord Dunraven believed in having

The Fort Union Stud at Adare

*This large and very beautiful stud belongs to the Earl of Dunraven, who is shown
here with his dog and two of the stable staff watching the grooms bring the mares
and newborn foals in from the fields. Note the circular building at the upper left. It
may be used as a breeding pen or in bad weather as an exercising pen for the stallions.*

Guersant

One of the two outstanding stallions at Fort Union comes out of his little play yard into his big one.

his young stock led at a walk for an hour each day rather than just turned out to play, and the covered track was designed to protect the men in wet weather.

The stallion barn was a separate little building with its own special paddocks. An enormous box stall, at least twenty feet square, occupied each end of the building. Each stall had one door opening into the main courtyard and another leading into a small paddock with high, solid walls, of the same yellow stucco as the buildings. This paddock, which could be used as a breeding pen, had a second set of doors leading into his majesty's private playground—a carefully tended green field, about five hundred feet square, which sloped gently away

from the stable and so was naturally drained. The field was completely enclosed by the same stucco wall, built in a series of descending levels to take care of the slope. Here the stallion might play at will; there seemed no way in which he could possibly hurt himself, and although he might catch a glimpse of the mares in the next field and become excited, as he approached the boundary of his territory his view would be obstructed by the high wall.

Each of the three double doors leading into the individual boxstalls had a padlock as well as heavy iron hasps. The stud groom had to unlock each padlock every time he went in or out. Lord Dunraven was taking no chances on having one of his valuable

41

sires escape. When the groom let one of the stallions into the pasture for us to see, we stood on little platforms provided for such purpose outside the high walls, at regular intervals. Every little detail had been thought out carefully to ensure the best of care and comfort to the stallions; yet the flowers, the walks, the color of the buildings, and their uneven roof lines took away any commercial effect and made the whole plant a thing of beauty.

The two occupants of the stud barn were stallions quite different in type. The first was a grand old chestnut, eighteen years of age, named Panorama. The second was a younger horse, a dark bay of French lineage, named Guersant. Most of the men interested in breeding Thoroughbreds with whom I talked agreed that there are three outstanding sires in Ireland today. Panorama is one, and Phoenix and Denturius, two syndicated stallions standing at Ballykisteen stud, are the others. The value of a stallion is determined by the amount of money won at the tracks by his get in a given year. In the past season the two-year-olds by these three stallions had been the most outstanding in their winnings, and many people thought that of the three Panorama was the best. His fee for a service was

The three outstanding sires of 1953-54 two-year-olds

   (a) *Old Panorama of the Fort Union Stud.*
   (b) *Denturius of Ballykisteen.*
   (c) *The Phoenix, Ballykisteen.*

three hundred pounds, and he was to serve forty-four mares. I saw him several times while I was in Adare, and each time I liked him better. He hardly showed his eighteen years. There was no dip in front of his withers to speak of. His lovely red coat, his beautiful quarters, and his crest put me in mind of our own Man O' War. The groom told me that he sometimes got a bit too playful, but there was nothing mean or dangerous about him.

Guersant was of a finer build. Lord Dunraven had bought him from Baron de Rothschild in January 1954 for fifty thousand pounds. He had a fine track record of his own; now it remained to be shown whether he could pass his talents down to his offspring.

A gray stallion called His Highness was the third standing at Fort Union, and there was also a youngster destined to receive only a few ladies, since he was completely untried. For his services no stud fee would be charged.

After I had admired these beauties, Lady Dunraven took me in to the office, where there were paintings of His Highness, Panorama, and other famous sires of former years. But the most unusual feature of the stud was yet to come: the graveyard in which old favorites were buried when the time came for them to go wherever good horses go. The graveyard was a quiet place, surrounded by a low wall, with daffodils blooming in clumps and flowering shrubs. Over the wall one looked out upon the beautiful

Courtesy of Time-Life, Inc.

The final resting place of an old favorite
This is the grave of Desmond, who lies in the quiet graveyard at the Fort Union Stud.

countryside, great, rolling green fields, the mountains behind, and in the distance the roofs of a tiny village. By way of headstones, each grave had a large cement horseshoe with the name of the occupant lettered in one-inch-square studs, arranged to represent nails. The beauty and peace of the place made me realize that Fort Union Stud was more than a commercial enterprise; the owners obviously loved their animals and took pleasure in ensuring the perpetuation of their noble and beautiful characteristics.

Surrounding the building were various grassy fields. In some, mares with foals cantered and frolicked; in others, the still-expectant mothers waited patiently. Sheep with their

The stables where the barren mares are kept while waiting to be bred
Some of the cats and pigeons shown here on the roof are made of French porcelain.

lambs occupied still others. A separate barn was used for the mares that had not been bred the previous year. Flocks of white pigeons wheeled above it, now settling on the roof, now walking in the courtyard. And on the roof, too, were two cats, crouched to spring. The pigeons paid them no heed; in fact, I noticed that several of the birds seemed phenomenally still, as did the cats. Then Lady Dunraven explained that these were made of white French porcelain and that she had put them there to confuse spectators. Apparently I was not the only visitor who had had a hard time distinguishing between those birds and cats which were alive and those which were not.

Having given several hours to my entertainment, Lady Dunraven returned to the Inn, and I decided that I had better make further inquiries about my wandering saddle. A call to Shannon brought the good news that it was there. "But," I said, "I'm in Adare, and the saddle is in Shannon. Have you any ideas as to how it can be brought on here?" There was a further pause; then another voice took over and assured me that my saddle would be delivered that night.

I had tea with the "Kentucky Colonels," who told me they had had a fine day and looked forward to my hunting with them on the morrow. Then, at eight o'clock, Mr. Morley's car arrived, and I was driven five miles to his beautiful estate in Croom. I could just make out tall trees bending to the strong wind and hear the rushing of a river as we approached the house. Broad steps led up to the doorway, and when I entered I could hardly keep from gasping with delight. All the rooms were huge, with very high ceilings. The walls were done in muted "Williamsburg" colors and ornamented with decorative plaster moldings. The heavy draperies were floor length, completely hiding the big windows. Magnificent pictures, some modern French, some old, and such furniture as one rarely sees except in museums combined to make this easily the most beautiful house I had ever seen. Mr. Morley greeted me most kindly and introduced me to his wife, who is Belgian. I shall never forget the picture she made sitting on a mauve-colored sofa. She had coal-black hair growing low on her forehead in a "widow's peak" and drawn simply back. Her eyes were dark, her skin of the most beautiful texture and a pure ivory in color. She wore an ivory-colored damask hostess gown. The soft light of the coal fire threw a warm glow over her, emphasizing her lovely coloring and the design in the brocade. I could hardly keep my eyes from her. I never again expect to see anything as satisfying to the eye as that graceful figure in that beautiful room.

After a delicious dinner, Mr. Morley got down to business. He said that he headed the Shannon Travel Agency and that Ireland, as a country, needed American dollars. Tourists came in summer, he told me, but in winter, when the most unusual thing that Ireland had to offer—i.e., the hunting—was available, few came. Mr. Morley was going to the United States to try to interest American horsemen, via our tourist bureaus and travel agencies, in spending their vacations hunting the Irish way. What did I think of the idea? He said that one American had told him that since hunting was considered a strictly non-commercial sport in America, it would be difficult to get co-operation from the hunt clubs, and that, furthermore, the possibility of accidents might discourage many riders. "Do you want a funeral a week?" asked the American.

I told him that since I had arrived only that day and had yet to see the Irish country from the top of a horse I could give no opinion on the latter but that the "Kentucky Colonels" seemed to be making out very well. I also reminded him that the proportion of Americans who hunt is very low compared to Eire. He assured me that even an additional fifty visitors a season would make a big difference. As for the likelihood of getting co-operation from the hunt clubs, I said I felt this would depend a good deal on how the matter was presented. I added that I myself, when I considered coming over, was anxious to get accurate information concerning prices, availability of horses, etc., and that I was sure other prospective visitors would need the same kind of advice. I gave him some names to call and suggested that he get a list of American hunts and plan to see some of the Masters.

He thanked me, then asked how he could help me. I told him that I was gathering material for my book but that I was handicapped by the lack of a car and that I couldn't afford to go out and hire one by the day or week. He thought a moment, then said he would see what he could do about it.

Our conversation turned to other matters, and we discovered a mutual interest in music. He had an excellent record player and a fine collection of records, and I listened with delight to some unusual recordings of chorale singing. And then it was time to say good night, and I was driven back to the Inn.

My fire was burning brightly, my bed was lovely and warm, and I went off to sleep with all sorts of beautiful images of what I had seen on my first day in Eire dancing in my head.

IV

On Hunting in General—A Day with the Limerick Foxhounds

John Jorrocks, best known and best loved of all Masters of Fox Hounds, is famous for his pithy sayings. Perhaps the one most quoted is " 'unting is the sport of kings—the image of war without its guilt and only five-and-twenty percent of its danger." What a fine thing for mankind if hunting could be made a "substitute" for war! For Jorrocks forgot one thing: hunting imitates war in that there is excitement, but the hatred and vindictiveness are absent.

Many people think of fox-hunting as a sport for only the rich. Many think of it as just an excuse for a man to dress up in a pink coat and show himself off. Still others think of it as a barbarous sport in which one small fox is pitted against a hundred people and as many hounds. Few think of it as it really is, at least as it is in Ireland: namely, the most democratic sport in the world, where earls and farmers, doctors, priests, barristers, commercial travellers, grooms, and children rub elbows at the same gaps, catch one another's horses, and meet on equal terms. The plow boy who, hearing hounds coming his way, unhooks his horse, takes off the harness, and substitutes a bit of rope for the plow reins has as good a time as the lord in a high silk hat. And whoever knows the country best will lead the way, regardless of rank or wealth or position. Only the hunt staff has precedence, and that is because it is their job to hunt the hounds.

I know of only one other assembly of people as democratic—an amateur orchestra. Here one finds men and women from every walk of life and of every nationality sitting side by side with seldom any friction. I believe that this spirit of equality exists in hunting and in playing an instrument with an amateur group because in both cases the performer is there to enjoy himself. Furthermore, he is contributing whatever he has to offer in the way of skill, as a musician or as a rider. And there can be no bluffing. He can either play the notes or he can't; he can either get across the country over the fences or he can't. No one can substitute for him, he can't live on anyone else's reputation nor pay anyone else to do his work for him, and he is not in competition for pay or prestige. There are no slackers, and every person present has spent hours of hard work in attaining proficiency.

I made this analogy to someone (English, not Irish). She thought a moment, then said, rather hesitantly, "Yes, I suppose that's true, but somehow I don't think you'll find the Irish very musical!"

Hunting is one of the oldest of sports. In the early days each lord or baron organized his own pack with his servants dressed in his private livery and, several days a week, they went out to try to kill off the foxes that would otherwise rob the farmers' roosts. Today the picture is much the same. The Master of Fox Hounds, and his "whippers-in," try to catch the wily fox, with no modern weapons but only the noses of the hounds he has trained to aid him. The fox has a better than fifty-to-one chance of escaping, unless the Master feels that he must exterminate the vermin at all costs to keep on good terms with the farmers. Usually what happens is that the fox, who is stronger and faster than the hounds, runs until he gets a bit tired and then goes to ground in a hole or eludes the hounds by clever maneuvering. I hunted with nine packs while in Eire and ran six or more foxes on each hunt, but I saw only one kill. People who think of the fox as being so vastly outnumbered by his pursuers should remember that the members of the Field do not hunt him; they merely follow along if they can. Certainly any sport that gives the animal a fifty-to-one chance of escape, uses no modern weapons against him, and depends on the skill of other animals cannot be called very bloodthirsty.

For the benefit of those who are not familiar with fox hunting I will give a brief analysis of what actually occurs, or, rather, what may be expected to occur. A "Fixture" card is mailed each month to members of the hunt, telling them at what place and hour and on what days each meeting will take place. From fifteen minutes to a half hour before the appointed time, the Field (those who plan to follow the hounds that day) assembles. Some hack to the hunt, some have their horses brought to them in trailers or vans ("boxes," as they are called in Ireland), others follow along the roads in cars, catching glimpses of hounds whenever they are lucky and sometimes leaving their cars to go across country on foot. In addition, there are usually other people on foot who station themselves at likely points to see the fun, open a gate, or give information.

At the scheduled time, the Master, Whips, and hounds appear.

(There may be a few minutes' grace for latecomers, but usually everyone moves off on the dot.) By this time girths have been checked, last-minute instructions have been given to those following, and the Hunt Secretary has collected capping fees (fees paid at each hunt for the privilege of riding, usually collected in a small chamois bag). Subscribers pay only a small amount for individual hunts since they pay a regular yearly fee as well. Non-residents are asked to give from one to two pounds. The term "cap," or "capping fee," derives from the old custom of collecting fees in a hunting cap. Incidentally, in the old days, people who wore hunting caps did not have to pay a "hat tax," which is why the caps were so popular among hunters.

The Master, assuming that he is hunting his own hounds, knows from information received from farmers or from his own men where he is apt to find a fox. The fox's den is known and has been stopped up while Reynard was out. At a toot from the horn the Field sets forth to hack (ride) to the chosen covert. The Master, or Huntsman, if there is a professional Huntsman, goes first, followed by the hounds. On each flank and a little to the rear ride the two Whips, whose duty it is to prevent any riot (misbehavior) on the part of the hounds. When the covert side is reached, the members of the Field are told where they may stand. The Whips take up their position on either side of the covert to be drawn. Now hounds, encouraged by the Master, enter the covert (which may be a wooded patch or a patch of grass and undergrowth) to try to find Reynard and persuade him that he'll do better to run than to stay where he is. Only the Master carries a horn, but I was interested to note that in Ireland the Whips were equipped with whistles with which they can signal.

A tense silence falls as everyone tries to figure out from the whimpering that comes occasionally from the covert or by watching, checking the wind, and from experience just how the fox will break and where he will go. If he comes out near a Whip, the Whip must see that the fox gets well away and is not turned back into the covert and he must make sure that all the hounds, not just one or two, take up the pursuit. To guarantee the fox a good start, the Whip waits until the quarry is too far away from the covert to turn back before he blows his whistle and gives the "Gone-a-way-ay, Talli-ho!" for which the Master, hounds, and Field have been waiting. Then, aided by the Master's horn, which responds at once, he tries to hold back the first hounds until the bulk of the pack is on the line. If the fox chances to break out of covert where neither the Master nor one of the Whips is stationed, any member of the Field may shout the magic words, first giving the fox the customary period of grace and then taking off his hat or cap and holding it to point the way. Once the "gone away" is given and hounds are on the line, the hunt staff must make sure that they are on the spot at once in case the hounds should lose the scent. In such a case, the Master can often "lift" the hounds, leading them to another spot where he thinks they may pick up the scent again.

From the foregoing it is apparent that members of the Field must so direct their course and pace that they do not interfere with either the hounds or the hunt staff. They must not endanger another rider by cutting across his line or crowding him at the gaps, nor should they ride across newly planted land or across crops. Gates must be closed after the last rider so that cattle will not escape. If a rider has a fall and his horse runs on, the first person to catch him returns him to his owner.

Sometimes Reynard proves too wily for his pursuers and escapes after ten minutes or so. At other times he is strong—"stiff-necked," as the expression goes—and, running straight, takes the riders over many a mile before he eludes hounds, or, in very rare instances, is run down in the open.

This brief description of procedure in the hunting field cannot possibly convey the excitement, the variety (for no two runs are ever alike), the exhilaration that spells hunting! Take the pleasure to be derived from hard physical exercise; add the beauty of nature, as it can be seen and appreciated only from the back of a horse; add, too, the interest of never knowing just what is in store for you and the thrill of finding yourself alive and whole after successfully meeting and overcoming a series of

obstacles, any of which might prove your downfall (in the literal sense). Combine all these ingredients and remember, too, that all other thoughts and worries are, for the time you are hunting, momentarily banished. Then perhaps you will begin to understand the fascination that is fox hunting.

The meet, my first one in Eire, was being held at a little crossroads about fifteen miles from Adare. At ten thirty the three "Kentucky Colonels" and I assembled in the hallway of the Inn with our saddles and our lunches. Presently Benny appeared. He loaded up his car, and we started. The weather was fitful. The sun ducked in and out among the clouds like a porpoise. Sudden little black clouds would loom up from nowhere and there would be a brief spatter of rain followed by an equally brief period of bright sunshine. The air was chilly, but my "long-johns" and excitement kept me amply warm.

We were going out with the County Limerick Hounds. This pack is hunted by an Englishman, Lord Daresbury, and is reputed to be the best-disciplined pack in Ireland. Lord Daresbury is a very keen and thoroughly experienced Master, having hunted the Belvoir before coming to Ireland. He gives virtually all his time to one facet or another of his job, walking his hounds on foot, inspecting kennels, checking with farmers to see that any damage is promptly taken care of, keeping a close tally on the whereabouts of foxes, and, in short, providing the best sport possi-

The County Limerick Hounds at Croom House

ble. He has the aquiline features and the tall, spare build of the English hunting man. I am sure whoever designed the velvet hunting cap originally must have had just such a face in mind, for the two belong together as a cup belongs to a saucer. Being English, Lord Daresbury was a more formal man than some of the Masters I hunted with later. One felt that he was out there for one purpose only: to catch foxes.

The Limerick Foxhounds were organized by the local gentry in 1828 or thereabouts, under the mastership of Mr. George Fosbery. The hunt uniform is bottle green; evening dress is scarlet with a green collar. The Honorable Secretary is Lieutenant-Colonel C. G. Conyers, and the capping fee for non-residents is two pounds.

In the United States one may not hunt without an invitation from the Master, and it is considered very bad form not to present yourself to him on arrival at the meet and not to thank him for your day at the end. But in Ireland apparently none of this formality is required. Anyone who wants to hunt shows up at the covert side, and it is next to impossible to find the opportunity of carrying out the amenities. So I contented myself with thanking Colonel Conyers for his kindness in finding me a horse, hoping I would have a chance to meet and thank Lord Daresbury later.

My mount turned out to be a little bay cob named Shorty. A cob, in Irish nomenclature, designates any horse between the heights of fourteen-two and fifteen-two hands. Shorty was about fifteen hands, and I was more than delighted to find that I was not mounted on a seventeen-hander, as I had feared.

If I found the Master rather un-approachable, it was otherwise with my fellow Field members. There were about thirty of them, and nearly everyone made a point of speaking to me at some time during the day. What I found even more reassuring was that a good many of them knew Shorty, and one and all recommended him without qualification. Anyone who has had the experience of taking a completely strange animal over un-known country without the oppor-tunity of trying him over a fence first will understand my relief on being told that Shorty would and could take anything that we were apt to come across with safety and good judgment.

Hounds moved off on the dot and certainly proved the value of their training, for they followed discreetly at the heels of the Master, glancing neither to the right nor to the left, as well disciplined as a regiment of sold-iers on parade. We hacked for a mile or so, and I learned that Irish horses are expected to trot down the center of the hard roads, up hill and down. All the horses are shod with "Mordax" studs, which are tipped, I suppose, with borium, to keep them from slip-ping. This it certainly did, but I could not help wondering how good the hard jarring was for legs and tendons. Later I was to learn that when hounds are running the Irish think nothing of galloping on the tarmac (macadam). Since many of the horses I saw in the Field were no longer youngsters, and since I seldom saw splints or distorted tendons, I can only conclude that this treatment, plus whatever it is in the Irish grass and water that gives the Irish horse his size and stamina, must also increase the toughness of his tendons. I tried keeping Shorty on the grassy edge, which was plenty wide enough, but he objected strenuously, partly be-cause this edge was intersected at short intervals by shallow drainage ditches and he was forced to change his stride constantly in order not to stumble over them.

I now had a chance to see the countryside from that most admirable vantage point, the back of a horse. In driving a car one goes too fast to see much, and the pedestrian hasn't enough height to see over the banks and walls that edge the roadsides, but the rider can look around and enjoy himself to the utmost. The terrain was rolling, the fields comparatively small and separated from each other by delightfully familiar stone walls. But for the gorse, the occasional thorn hedges, and the absence of woodland, I might have been looking out over my own Connecticut.

We passed many little thatched cottages with tiny, hermetically sealed windows. Since the yards are usually a morass of mud and manure, it is not strange that the peasants do not go in much for open windows!

Shorty trotted along on a light rein and seemed willing to take my suggestions as to pace. Presently we turned through a gate into a field, where the hunt members stopped while the staff went ahead to cast hounds. The chosen covert was a big open field with a low growth of gorse intersected by cattle tracks. Regan, the first Whip, stationed himself on the far flank, with Miss Atkinson, the other Whip, on the near side. Hounds entered and immediately scattered and set down to business. A more thorough quartering of a field I have never seen, nor was there a babbler* among the lot. Every inch of territory was gone over as systematically as possible.

Soon we heard a whimper; then a hound spoke on the distant side. Three others honored his find and joined their voices to his. Immediately after came a whistle and a shout from the distant Whip. The Master's horn brought all the other hounds up in short order, and presently they were running, noses down, their beautiful, discordant cry proclaiming that Reynard was away. Every rider rose in his stirrups, and together we galloped along the edge of the field to follow the disappearing Master through a muddy gap. I could hear the suction of the horses, fetlock- and sometimes almost hock-deep in mud, ploughing along. I was careful to keep a little to one side of the rider in front since some of the clods thrown into the air

were large and heavy and would have been unpleasant to receive in the face or head. Shorty proved to have a good gallop. He had no difficulty in keeping up but was easily controlled in the snaffle and martingale with which he was fitted.

Another gap brought us to a gently sloping hillside. I could see a stone wall ahead and beyond that, the gorse, thick and high. Those in front of me were going for a low place, perhaps three feet high, so I pulled in behind them, expecting, of course, that the horses would fly it in stride and wanting to be sure that I did not crowd the rider in front. But what was my amazement to find that the horses of County Limerick do not fly stone walls, not even low ones! As he approached the obstacle, each horse came down from a gallop to a canter, to a trot, and then to a walk. At the point of departure, each horse first hesitated, then, jumping like a cat, landed on top of the wall, and, midst the rattle of falling rock, jumped off again and galloped on! Why didn't they break their legs? Why didn't they cut themselves to pieces? I have no idea. The stones were big and not smooth or rounded. By the time the first five horses were across, fallen rocks covered both the approach and landing, but this bothered the other horses not a whit. Picking their way, they took off and landed in the rubble, seeming to have eyes in each of their four hooves. An American horse jumping thus from a standstill would have given the rider a terrific thrust, but Shorty's take-off and landing were

* A babbler is a hound that whimpers or bays unnecessarily before he is actually on the line of the hunted fox.

as smooth and light as a feather. I hardly knew we were over until I found myself galloping up the crooked little cattle-track, dodging the thorny gorse and ducking under low branches.

I was surprised to see almost every horse equipped with a simple snaffle. Some time later, I heard the expression, "Fools and Irishmen hunt in snaffles." I was also told that an English artist who came over to paint an Irish hunt depicted all the riders in full bridles, which the Irish took as a great insult. This seemed an odd point of view to me, since it takes a much more sensitive hand to ride a horse successfully in a full bridle than in a snaffle, but I soon saw the wisdom in using snaffles, and my admiration for the Irish horse increased as the day went on. The Irish have the greatest hearts in the world, and firm seats, too, but they rather pride themselves in not riding "scientifically." They learn to ride as children on grass-fed ponies, and if they can't stick on, they fall off. Since it is always more comfortable to do the former, they soon learn to stick on. As a result, the horse, in jumping, must often be prepared to support his rider's weight on his loins and not to mind if his reins are sometimes used as lifelines. The Irish Hunter has learned to do this, and his agility, balance, and courage, be he cob, pony, half-breed, or plow horse, is incredible.

Our stout fox ran for perhaps half an hour before he managed to elude the hounds and disappeared. Meanwhile I had a chance to look over the Field. There was a wide variety of mounts and an equally wide variety of riders. There were two ladies riding sidesaddle, one, in a conventional habit with a silk hat, mounted on a tall gray; the other, on a chestnut or bay, wearing an ordinary "astride" habit although she rode sidesaddle. Several gentlemen in "pink" coats (the scarlet hunting coat is usually called a "pink" coat after a famous tailor) from outside hunts gave color to the panorama of riders as they streamed across the fields. Grooms in gaiters and flat caps and farmers in rubber boots were well represented, and I also noticed two little boys, evidently farm lads, riding scrubby ponies about thirteen hands high. One boy rode bareback. His bridle consisted of a leather crown-piece, evidently designed for a much larger animal, for the ends flapped down around his bit. One cheek strap was leather and the other of heavy cord; the browband was non-existent, but there was a throat latch, also of cord, as were the reins. The other lad was a little better off for tack. His bridle had a higher proportion of leather and he had a saddle, although there were more patches than original leather in it. But these two boys displayed a remarkable knowledge of the mind of the fox, the country, or both, for countless times, after a run up and down hill through brush and briar, we would come out onto a lane only to be met by the two little farm boys. Our horses would be blowing while theirs, in their rough coats, would be cool and unwinded.

At about two o'clock, having

found several foxes and had some fine runs, we dismounted on a road where all those following in cars, including Benny and the grooms who were in charge of my horse and those of the "Kentucky Colonels," met us. The grooms mounted and hacked off down the road while Benny opened the "boot" of the car and offered us welcome nourishment. Drinks, "Bovril" (a delightful concoction like a very rich consomme), milk, water, chicken sandwiches, and cake had been provided. One would think that three or four hours of hard riding would encourage a ravenous appetite, but such was not the case with me: one sandwich and one piece of cake was plenty. When we had finished we crowded into the car, our group augmented by the presence of an attractive girl in a navy hunting coat, whose name, appropriately enough, was Hunt. I had noticed her in the Field and used her as a pilot several times, for she seemed to know the country well. A few miles' drive brought us to the next covert, where the horses were awaiting us. I noticed that the hunt staff had new mounts, but my friend Shorty seemed as fresh as ever and I had no qualms about continuing on him.

Our next fox took us up into a hilly, gorse-covered, and shalley country known as "the crags." I found myself riding hard down muddy, narrow cattle tracks, my horse picking his way cleverly between rocks. Although many of the Field expressed the opinion that the country was far from ideal, I found it very similar to our rough Connecticut terrain. Occasionally a bright sun and a fast run would cause me to open my coat and take off my gloves. A moment later a squall would hit us, and I would button up my collar tightly against the slanting rain.

Once I found myself, with the Master, Regan, and two other hunters, skirting an impenetrable hilltop and listening anxiously for hounds that were after a fox somewhere in the gorse. We came out onto a railroad track—and when I say *on*, I mean just that, for in landing over a wall each horse twisted sideways to avoid stepping on the "sleepers" (Irish for railroad ties). On the other side of the track was a steep hillside, and a biggish stone wall two and a half feet from the rails blocked our egress. There was absolutely no place to take off, although after what I had seen the Irish hunter do, I would not have been surprised had Lord Daresbury, first balancing on a steel rail, sprung gamely at his obstacle. And I'm sure if his horse had been able to maneuver it successfully Shorty would have likewise succeeded. But no, at the Master's suggestion Regan dismounted and, with a hefty shoulder, proceeded to lower the wall. When he had it down to two feet Lord Daresbury stopped him, saying, "You don't need to take it all the way to the ground, Pat." Giving his horse a chirrup, he was over the remaining bit and up the hillside, with the rest of us following.

Presently we came out on a dirt road edged on both sides by high walls. Hounds could be heard some distance away in the heavy gorse to our right. We turned a corner and met, as was to be expected, the two little boys. Further along the rest of the Field waited, looking rather smug, beside a high iron gate. A moment later there was a hail, and an excited little man was bouncing up and down in the middle of the road, beckoning frantically to us. A man in scarlet, who up to that moment had proved a most reliable pilot, Miss Hunt, and I detached ourselves from the group and rode up to see what was afoot. The little chap was somewhat incoherent, but we understood him to say that Reynard had just crossed the road and was away through an open field. Since hounds and staff were drawing a heavy cover on our right, we settled ourselves to wait, thinking that hounds would shortly cross in front of us. But soon, to our consternation, we heard the irate voice of the Master raised in righteous wrath. Either the fox had not crossed or else he was on a different one, so we were in the act of committing the foxhunter's second most heinous sin: We had so placed ourselves that should hounds get their quarry out of covert we must inevitably head him back again. (The *most* heinous sin, of course, is to tread on a hound.) The air was a brilliant shade of blue for some time. I slunk back to my former position by the gate. The remainder of the Field looked even smugger.

After some time the music of the hounds changed to the den cry, with the pitch and cadence that indicates that the fox has gone to ground. The iron gates were opened and the hunt car, containing the terriers and the necessary implements for digging, went in and disappeared down a narrow track leading through the gorse. We followed, a few at a time, until all the Field was gathered in a cleared space in the gorse. The scene would have been a fine subject for a painting. On a little knoll, silhouetted against a tempestuous sky, were the Master, the two Whips, and several other members of the Field, both men and women, some in hunting pink, some in bottle green, and others in black, all on foot. The men were taking turns with the shovel and pick. A group of the foot-followers who always spring up from the bowels of the earth at such times were also watching the proceedings. Hounds clustered expectantly, some unable to restrain their exuberance and getting cuffed out of the way for their zeal, others sitting alert with wagging tails and only an occasional whine. One of the kennel staff was in the act of replacing a terrior which had been unable to bolt the fox. He was carrying the dog by the scruff of the neck, and the little creature hung perfectly limp, looking highly uncomfortable but not objecting audibly. A hundred yards away, against a background of big evergreens and the ruins of a stone castle tower, were a group of bay horses and their riders. In the foreground was the lady in the silk hat riding sidesaddle on the powerful gray and holding another gray. One had the feeling that the scene, with its beauty and drama, was an ageless re-enaction of a scene familiar at the time of the building of the tower, twelve or more centuries ago.

As an American and a woman, I was sorry that Lord Daresbury felt it necessary to dig out his fox and have a kill. I heard that this season he had accounted for seventy-one and a half brace. But, from a realistic point of view, one must remember that civilization has eliminated most of Reynard's natural enemies, that he is destructive, and that, in Nature's plan every race and breed needs a challenge of one sort or another to survive. The tradition of hunting the fox with hounds provides this challenge.

We had one or two more short runs before we heard the long call which indicates the end of the hunt. A hack of a short mile or so brought us to waiting cars and grooms. I dismounted for the first time (except for the luncheon respite) since I had mounted shortly after eleven. I was sorry I had not thought to provide myself with a tidbit with which to reward Shorty. As I turned him over to his owner and paid Mr. Fennell the five pounds that I owed him, I assured him that if every hireling I was destined to ride turned out to be as sturdy, reliable, and honest as Shorty I should consider myself very lucky.

As I dropped off to sleep that night I reviewed the events of the day, concluding that Irish hunting was everything and more than I had been led to expect, that Irish Hunters had the greatest hearts, the most wonderful dispositions, and the toughest constitutions of any horses in the world, and that compared with them our horses are just plain sissies.

V

Peg Watt and the Croom Harriers

Since I had nothing planned for the day after my hunt with the County Limerick Hounds, the "Kentucky Colonels" insisted that I come out with them and Mrs. Peg Watt, Master of the Croom Harriers. They promised me a good day and a fine introduction to the famous banks of Ireland.

Now, I had seen pictures of Ireland's banks in those enticing brochures at the travel agency. I had even seen them in the flesh, so to speak, from the roads. But I had not met them personally and I still did not know what it would be like to jump one. Meanwhile, I had done a bit of research on them. I learned that they were the direct result of the Irish farmers' constant battle with the climate. When the Connecticut farmer first cleared his fields, he realized that before he could grow anything he had first to get rid of the rocks. So he built

stone walls with the double purpose of dividing up his lots and disposing of the rocks. The Irish farmer discovered that his land was very wet and therefore untillable. To rectify the condition he dug deep, straight-sided ditches, or drains, to carry away the excess water. He piled the dirt parallel with the drain, topping it with sod "skinned" from the fields to make his ploughing easier. When he finished he had a very effective barrier to prevent his cattle from straying, and his fields were dry enough to till. Often he repeated the process on the opposite side of the bank so that he had a much higher and wider bank with a ditch on both sides, known as "double." Occasionally one runs across the opposite kind of formation: instead of a "double"—two drains with a bank between—one sees two banks with a drain between.

Some of the banks are wide and

solid, covered with turf and with little or no undergrowth. For obvious reasons, these are the most popular with hunters. Some, called "razor banks," are narrow at the top and slippery with mud. Most banks are of a variety known as "hairy," with thorn bushes, gorse, or small trees growing on them. The ditches, trenches, or drains have straight sides and range from three to eight feet in width. They are seldom less than four feet deep and many are more than twice that depth. In most ditches a swirling stream of muddy water leaves the actual depth to the imagination of the horseman. Certainly to an American-trained horse they would be a first-class nightmare. I had yet to see what an Irish-trained horse thought of them.

Since the Golden Vale country, where I had planned to make my bow to the bank country, was sixty miles away, I decided it might be wise to break my neck nearer home. Besides, harriers were supposed to be slower than foxhounds since the hare runs in circles. So I accepted the kind invitation of the "Kentucky Colonels" with pleasure.

Hunting harriers is slightly different from hunting foxhounds. In all areas where fox- and hare-hunting are popular, it is customary to divide up the territory. Each foxhound pack has the right to hunt its particular section, and no other pack may infringe on its rights without invitation. The harriers hunt over the same territory as the foxhounds and with the permission of the M.F.H. of their locality. Theoretically they never hunt foxes, so they are not permitted to draw the covers where they might disturb Reynard. Instead they start their quarry in the open fields. I say "theoretically," for in Ireland, if harriers *do* start a fox, everyone politely looks the other way, and no attempt is made to call off the pack. I was even assured on good authority that Mrs. Watt's harriers were unique in that they were the only pack in Ireland in which Master, Huntsman, Whips, horses, hounds, and fox all drove to the meet in the same "box." "But mind you," as the Irish say, "I've said nothing."

The three "Colonels" were delighted at my acceptance. "It's a wonderful country, and Peg Watt's a riot," said Rodes. "Besides, maybe we can get you Victor Cola."

"Who's Victor Cola?"

"He's supposed to be the best cob in Ireland. Belongs to a man named Harris. I've been trying to persuade him to let me hunt him ever since I've been here, but no soap. Harris will let him only to a lady. I bet Benny can arrange it for us."

So the faithful Benny was consulted. Presently word came back that Victor Cola was available and would be at the meet for me on the following morning.

Although harriers do not go out until noon, I left a call for eight so as not to waste an Irish morning. Promptly at that hour Kathleen appeared to start my fire.

"How's the weather, Kathleen?" I asked.

"Sure'n it's worse, Madam," came the usual reply. Over her arm she had my black coat and my boots, brightly shining from the capable hands of James, the valet. But she told me that my breeches had had to be washed and were not yet dry. Washed! My heart sank. My new canary-colored breeches, the pride of my heart and my greatest extravagance, washed! And they were already so tight that I felt, when wearing them, somewhat like the fop in "Handley Cross" who, in ordering new breeches, told the tailor that if they were big enough for him to get into them, b'gad he wouldn't take them!

With an effort I concealed my distress and told Kathleen that I had another pair. But all the time I was getting dressed I mourned my canary breeches. I needn't have worried, for James knew his job. Later in the day these same canaries were hung in my closet looking as though they had just come from the cleaners! Subsequent inquiry produced the information that it is perfectly safe to wash woolen breeches, even those with leather strappings (the chamois reinforcements at the knee), provided that they are washed with a good-quality glycerine soap in cold water and that more soap is rubbed into the strappings. They must then be pulled straight and hung on a hanger not too near the heat. No pressing is necessary. Live and learn. I could hardly wait to get home and try this method for myself!

Incidentally, all hotels and inns that cater to fox hunters always provide this valet service for hunting equipment. After each hunt, breeches, boots, gloves, hat, saddle, riding crop, and even vest and stock if desired are spirited away, to reappear next day in perfect condition, with all signs of mud and other stains vanished. There is a charge of about a dollar a cleaning for this service. Even with frequent cleaning it is best to bring at least two pair of boots and breeches and several stocks, and preferably an extra coat as well. James told me of an American gentleman who had had the foresight to send on *three* complete sets of hunting equipment, including three saddles, a month ahead by boat. "I could really keep his things proper!" said James, rubbing his hands in remembered satisfaction.

At ten thirty we collected in the hall. Benny appeared and stowed the tack and lunches, and we were off, accompanied by Major Raymond de Trafford, another member of the Field. When we entered the pub where the meet was held, I found myself in a little nook behind the bar. Mrs. Watt, her Huntsman, Mike Fitzgibbons, and a lady whose name I did not catch were having a drop of what warms and waterproofs from within.

Had Peg Watt lived at the time when Cruikshank was doing his famous illustrations she would surely have been one of his favorite models. She looked precisely like a feminine counterpart of Jorrocks, but with the cheerful, cherubic expression of Mr. Pickwick. Every sentence she uttered ended in a peal of laughter. She was about five-foot two or three, compact and square. She rode astride, usually on a very tall horse, but since her legs were not long and her thighs on the round side, she had a peculiar contraption, new to me, fastened to the pommel of her saddle to give her extra security. This consisted of a pair of leather-covered metal prongs, shaped like horns, mounted on springs and encircling her thighs. She could brace herself against them if she wished, but they would release automatically should she be thrown.

During the hunting season Mrs. Watt hunted four and often six days a week, going out with neighboring packs on days that she did not take out her harriers. Though she resembled Jorrocks in build and love of the chase, Peg Watt certainly did not resemble him in attitude toward jumping. For Jorrocks avoided jumping whenever possible, swearing mightily whenever fate decreed that jump he must, whereas Peg Watt sought out the stiffest and most terrifying banks and ditches that were to be found and plunged merrily up, over, or through them. The only type of fence which she really did not like, and avoided whenever possible, was a simple barway! I could have had no better preceptor for my first adventure over the Irish banks than Mrs. Watt, nor did I enjoy any day with hounds more than this day with her harriers.

Mike Fitzgibbons, the Huntsman, had one of the finest faces I have ever seen. His hair was gray under his huntsman's cap, and his skin was fine-textured, with tiny veins in his cheeks giving him the ruddy look of the out-doors. His nose was high-bridged, his eyes twinkling. He was so typically the hunting man of the sporting print that I was sure he had been born in a stall, weaned on mare's milk and a stirrup. He was in the midst of a story when I came in. I did not hear the beginning of it but it seemed to involve a trespassing fox hunter named Shamus, his son Pat, and an irate farmer with an ash plant.

"So," Mike was saying, "the farmer brings the ash plant down on Shamus's thigh, and him sitting there quietly on his horse. 'Be gob,' says Shamus, 'it's on my head he'll be laying it next!' And he drops off his horse on the far side the way the farmer couldn't get at him. Then as the old rascal is about to bring his ash plant down on the horse doesn't Shamus come up under the beast's neck and fetch the farmer one in the chin! It shook him up a bit, and just then Shamus, out of the corner of his eye, sees Pat going for his gun. So he ups with another one that starts at his boots and he catches the man in the middle and he stretches him out there on the turf so all he'd need would be a lily in his hand. Then Shamus hops back on his horse and nods to Pat. 'Let's be off before there's trouble,' he says, and away they go and leave the old chap to come to by himself. But wasn't it clever of Shamus to come off on the far side the way he could come up under the horse's neck without the farmer seeing him!"

We all agreed that it was most clever and everyone had a second (or perhaps third) drink on the strength of it. The lady whose name I had not caught was not in riding clothes. She was wearing tweeds with a kerchief around her head. She had the usual beautiful Irish complexion, somewhat marred by two wounds which were now in the process of healing but which must have been very deep to start with. I learned that, a few weeks before, her horse, falling in some rock, had stepped on her face and that she had also suffered an injury to her vertabrae. She was very much annoyed because her doctor would not let her hunt for another week or so. But she took great interest in telling me all the gory details of her accident, accompanied by much laughter both from her and from her audience.

"There I was," she said, "flat on my back with his great foot on my face" *(laughter),* "and I could feel my poor nose being pushed in" *(more laughter)* "and my teeth dropping all around me" *(shrieks of laughter)!*

The discussion went on to other accidents, and I learned that some riders took great pleasure in keeping track of the number of times they "bought a bit of real estate," as we would say over here. A prominent lady member of the County Limerick Hounds, for example, was reported to have run up a score of over eighty for the season.

Our thirst having been assuaged, it was announced that the time had come to get on to the more serious business of the day. I found Victor Cola and his groom waiting for me outside. Victor looked very like Shorty—the same size, build, and color.

I mounted, and a moment later we moved off. Peg Watt was riding a very tall dark bay. Major de Trafford rode a chestnut, as did Mike Fitzgibbons. Of the three "Kentucky Colonels," Bass rode a tall gray and the others were on smaller bays. We constituted the Field, and it appeared that that day's hunt was in honor of the "Kentucky Colonels." The hounds were not the perfectly matched and disciplined pack of yesterday—in fact, they were of every description and more interested in the world at large than might be considered ideal. I found myself beside Mrs. Watt as we hacked down a little side road.

"Your first visit to Ireland?" she asked.

"Yes, and my very first try at your Irish banks. I'm told, however, that this is an exceptional horse, so I'm planning to leave everything to him."

"Oh, Victor will take you over anything at all," she assured me. "And besides, he's got a mouth you don't often find."

We rode across a field, through a gap, then into another field. Fitzgibbons and the hounds that were ahead quickened their pace. "Hack on!" called Mrs. Watt, breaking into a canter. I followed. At the far side of the field was a bank covered with thorny undergrowth. My pilot galloped straight for it. Her horse stopped and hesitated. "G'wan!" shouted Mrs. Watt. The horse leaped into the air and landed with his front feet on top of the bank. For a moment I saw him perched there, his back feet under him, then he was gone. The next moment I found myself gazing over the steep sides of a precipice that seemed to have no bottom. Muddy water swirled beneath me, and the bank that rose on the other side was considerably higher than my horse's head. I couldn't see over the top of it. Victor Cola also hesitated, deliberating as to the best way of maneuvering this obstacle as though he were about to make a recommendation to the chairman of the board. Meanwhile Mrs. Watt was getting farther and farther away.

"G'wan!" I shouted, and took a firm grasp of the neck strap. Victor Cola hesitated no longer but hurled himself in the air, landing light as a feather, and paused only long enough to take the wind direction before springing a good twelve feet and clearing the even larger drain which edged the bank on the far side. Peg Watt's voice floated back to me. "Never look down," she said.

Almost immediately we came to another bank, and then another. Victor took them all, stopping for a moment at each—not, you understand, with any idea of refusing, but merely so that he might look the situation over and decide on the best possible strategy. On the top of each bank he also halted, no doubt in order to get a bit of air and decide for himself where hounds were apt to go next. But later in the day, when we got on what I am sure was a fox, Victor forgot his desire for meditation and took all the fences as they came with no hesitation, and with never a mistake.

Although he jumped from a standstill, and although he was so small that it was often necessary for him to give a mighty spring to clear a big drain, there was nothing rough about the procedure. I soon found that the neckstrap, on which I had decided to depend, was really superfluous as a lifeline and that if I just kept my weight out of the saddle, let my reins run perfectly free, and gave the necessary low growl to which all Irish horses seem to be voice-trained, Victor would carry me over any type of obstacle as smoothly as though he were doing a ring canter.

The three "Kentucky Colonels" were not so happy in their hirelings. Haggard was well mounted, but Rode's horse had a nasty habit of throwing his head and gave his rider a black eye before we had been out an hour. And the gray beast that Jack Bass rode pulled like a steer and was sticky on his fences.

Major de Trafford was the first to run into trouble. His sight was poor in one eye, and since, like 90 percent of the Irish, he rode the English hunting seat, with his head up and his weight thrown back, he was unexpectedly raked off under a low branch on top of one of the banks. This time one of the riders caught his horse and he was soon up again. However, before very long he was in difficulty once more. At one of the razor-type banks—a very high, narrow one, wet and slippery from the rain —his chestnut sprang and landed successfully, but the top of the bank crumbled under her and she slid back. The Major dismounted and, standing on top of the bank, urged the mare to exert herself. She, poor thing, had her front legs doubled up under her, and since a horse cannot rise unless his front feet are extended and level with or higher than his back feet, she was helpless. After a few attempts she gave up and lay back in the singularly fatalistic attitude of the cast horse. Being a newcomer, I did not like to give advice, and after a bit the Major turned her back, letting her slide into the ditch, then brought her out on the takeoff side.

Meanwhile, we had lost Bass. Presently we found our way through a muddy, mucky farmyard and onto a road. Fitzgibbons was ahead with hounds, which were not running at this point, so we paused to pick up the pieces. Haggard was all right, and Rode's black eye, although it looked painful, seemed not to be serious. But where was Bass? After some moments we saw him coming toward us through a gate leading into a large field. Furthermore, he was not alone. Pursuing him came an enormous herd of cattle, Short Horns (although the horns of some of them weren't so very short at that) and Herefords. Down the slope they charged, with Bass well in the lead and observed with great interest by two geese, two goats tethered together at the neck, and a small donkey. The sad part was that when he got to the end of the field, thinking he had successfully outrun his pursuers, poor Bass found he had it all to do over again: the fence was wired all around. We all shouted and yelled

until he saw us and finally guided him in the direction of the path we had taken. After a few minutes, the gray and his rider joined us once more.

I was the next to run into difficulty. I followed Mrs. Watt over an especially evil-looking double bank. The thorny growth through which we jumped was reinforced by the trunk of a fairly good-sized tree. As I ducked my head, to avoid the vicious thorns and also a dangerously low-hanging branch, I felt a strong, thorny branch rake my instep. When I landed on the far side of the ditch, my stirrup leather fell to the ground. There was nothing to do but stop, dismount, and put it back on. Hounds were running again, but Mrs. Watt, who was keeping a motherly eye on me, seeing me dismounted kindly came back and held Victor.

"Get on as slowly as you can," she said, "but don't waste any more time than you have to!"

This advice seemed a bit paradoxical, but I did my best to follow it and in a moment was mounted and galloping along, with the voice of my kind pilot floating back to me. "Hack on!"

We ran for some time, then hounds got out of sight and soon we found ourselves at the edge of a swiftly flowing river. It was too wide to jump, and the banks, which rose several feet above the water, were muddy and not too firm. Obviously we would have to ford it. With one accord we all stopped and looked at Jack Bass, for he was the tallest man in our party riding the tallest horse present. Unhesitatingly the noble chap urged his horse into the water, and immediately the animal was swimming. The stream, which I had supposed to be perhaps four feet deep, was probably eight! Since the banks on the far side were even steeper than those on our side, it was obvious that no horse could scramble them without first getting a foothold and we all persuaded Jack—only slightly waterlogged—to come back and climb out where he had gone in. The thorn hedge to our left, through which we must go if we were to catch up with the hounds, was firmly wired and unjumpable, but on the far side of the river this was not so. So, while Fitzgibbons and de Trafford, wire cutter in hand, attacked the wire at the gap, the rest of us scouted to the right with the idea of getting into the field there, crossing the river, which might be more fordable below, then doubling back on the far side. I saw Peg Watt and my fellow Americans making for a particularly repulsive-looking hairy bank, so thick that I didn't see how any horse could be asked to face it, and all the time just to their left was an enticing gap with a couple of thin saplings, not more than two feet off the ground, laid across it. Was there a law against jumping timber in Ireland? Maybe Victor didn't understand about fly jumps. But I had been told he would jump anything! There could be no better time to find out, and I didn't see how I could hurt him since the saplings would surely fall or break if we did hit them. So I headed him for the gap, giving him a hearty

boot as we approached. The gallant Victor took off and sailed like a swallow. I heard a shout from Mrs. Watt, busily forcing herself through the thorns.

"There goes the American!"

Just then a hail from the upper field told us that the wire-cutter maneuvers had been successful, and we galloped back, I again preferring my little barway to the twelve-foot bank and ditch. We still had to ford the river, but before long we came to a place that had sloping banks on both the near and the far sides and what might have been cart tracks leading to them—evidently the official ford. Fitzgibbons went first and got across safely, though somewhat wet. Peg Watt followed, and I was next. Victor stepped boldly in, hit a hole, plunged, and ducked his head under, but he kept his footing and came up under me. We then proceeded in a series of crow hops and presently scrambled safely out the other side. I had managed—barely—to keep my breeches dry, and the water had washed all the mud off my boots, so I was really more presentable than before. De Trafford came next, and we cantered up the slope of the field in a group, expecting that Rodes would be with us, the other two "Kentuckians" having disappeared on a line of their own. But imagine our surprise when on reaching the top of the rise, we were joined by a riderless horse! Looking back, we saw poor Rodes scrambling out of the river, water pouring from him in every direction. I helped to catch his horse while Major de Trafford and

Mike went back to help him. Mrs. Watt and I went on alone. Hounds, running hard, were nearing the limits of the country over which the Croom Harriers were permitted to hunt. We put on a burst of speed and hustled our horses over two more banks. Mrs. Watt looked back over her shoulder. "You're quite a Nimrod!" she called. "Men may come and men may go, but you go on forever!"

Now we found ourselves approaching a railroad embankment. Fitzgibbons appeared with the horn, and hounds, who were feathering on the far side, were called off. Together we turned and made our way back to a house which stood above the river and in which Rodes had taken refuge. "Major Webb will give us drinks and we'll try to dry Rodes out a bit," said the Master. We were greeted by Major Webb, owner of the house, and his sister-in-law, Miss Mills. (I was to come to know Miss Mills quite well, for it was she who volunteered to be our guide when Sydney and I later explored the Kerry country and found the beehive huts and the old, Bronze-Age fort called Dunbeg.)

We followed a trail of puddles up the front steps and into the house. Evidently Rodes had got here before us. Sure enough, he and de Trafford, glasses in hand, were standing in the dining room. Rodes was speaking. "The damned horse stepped in a hole and turned over with me, and there I was on the bottom of the river, with the horse on top of me." He made a swimming motion with his hands. "I tried to surface," he continued, "and all I got was flying horseshoes in my face. I damned near drowned!" Water ran out between the soles of his boots and the uppers as he stood there, and more dripped from his coattails.

"Get some newspapers!" commanded the resourceful Mrs. Watt. Miss Mills produced some.

"Now, don't be modest," said the Master of the Croom Harriers, busily stuffing heavy layers of newspapers down the pants of the luckless Rodes. When she had him firmly padded fore and aft, she stood back and surveyed her handiwork with pride. He rustled when he walked and moved with an odd, marionette-like gait. I wondered how he was to get on his horse, but at least the flow of water had been partially arrested. Another stirrup cup all around and we were ready to set off to look for Benny. Alas, for the first and only time, he was not where we hoped to find him and we had to hack four long miles, the water squelching from the boots of our semi-drowned companion.

Thus began and ended my introduction to the Irish banks and drains. After due consideration I talked myself into believing that their death-inviting appearance actually made them safe, for surely no horse in his right mind would voluntarily fall into one of them. Furthermore, looking at it from a logical angle, it really took no more effort on the part of the horse to jump a ditch fifteen feet deep than to jump one three feet deep. But on the part of the rider, however, it takes much faith in a deity that looks after fools, drunkards, and little children.

VI

The Golden Vale

When I returned to the Inn I found a welcome message awaiting me from Mr. Morley. He and the Irish Tourist Bureau had come through in fine style: a car would arrive at the Dunraven arms that night to be at my disposal for my stay. Now all I had to do was to learn to find my way around Ireland!

When Benny came around the next morning I asked him how to get to Cassustown Cross, where I was supposed to meet a guide who would show me the way to Rossestown Cross, the place of my next meet. Neither place was on the map, but the good Benny knew at once where they were.

"Is there really a cross at Cassustown Cross?" I asked, visualizing a wayside shrine.

"There is, Madam," said Benny. How was I to know that to the Irish "cross" was not a shrine but a crossroads!

After studying the directions provided by General Wakely, I set out to drive my newly acquired car. I found the first half hour nervewracking in the extreme, trying to remember to pull to the left, not to the right, when I saw a lorry in the middle of the road bearing down at me at full speed. A further road hazard was the cyclists' habit of swerving in pairs directly across my path and the tendency of every farmyard animal and fowl to cross to the other side of the road as soon as they heard me coming. Incidently, it is against the law in Ireland to run over a duck, but not to run over a chicken. This is not so illogical as it may seem; for, as everyone knows, when a duck starts to cross the road it always keeps right on going, and any reasonable person should be able to foretell its course and keep out of the way. But chickens are kittle cattle, and no one can foresee whether, having started, they mean to continue on the original line or reverse direction without warning. Goats also present a problem. On the theory that goats can be counted upon to disagree, they are always coupled together by the collars. This is fine until one meets a pair in the exact center of the road and one of the two decides to take refuge on the right side of the road while his mate favors the left.

A further delaying action was introduced by the friendly habit of the milk-cart drivers of stopping side by side to review the affairs of the day. Nor could I fathom why all the carts from Town A seemed to be carrying their milk to the creamery in Town B while those in the latter town preferred to do business with the creamery in Town A!

I had been instructed to take the Dublin road out of Limerick and to head for Thurles. And now I ran into a real snag. I found that Thurles might be pronounced to rhyme with "curls" or with "furless" or even with "tourless." Whichever way I tried to pronounce it I always found that the person from whom I was trying to get information invariably favored one of the alternate versions, and this made for considerable confusion.

The Irish signposts were a further source of befuddlement. In Ireland there are no route numbers as we have them here, nor are roads to the major towns marked. You cannot be sure that you are still on the Dublin road after a few miles, for the crossroads carry no such information. Instead they simply tell you the name of the next small town. In addition to this, the directional signs are utterly unreliable. The signposts are round pipes with tin signs only clamped on, and it is but the work of a moment for anyone with a pair of pliers to loosen the nuts and change the sign so that it points in an entirely erroneous direction. After an evening of gaiety, the village lads often amuse themselves by so doing, especially after such events as point-to-points; and there had been a point-to-point near Nenagh (rhymes with "Lena") only the day before. Several times I followed signs that had been twisted in this fashion and found myself on little winding country roads, to be told, on inquiry, that I must go the way the last signpost had definitely told me I must not. After a few such peregrinations I learned to inquire at every crossroads that looked suspicious—and thus, I am sure, established myself as an illiterate moron.

But I was not the only one to be misled by Irish signposts. Later on in my stay an Irish lady told me of an experience that she had had while travelling through an unknown part of the country. At a crossroads, the sign bearing the name of her destination pointed definitely to the right, whereas, although she had never been that way before, she was firmly convinced that she should go straight on. However, she turned right, as the sign indicated, only to find herself on a cowpath. Meeting a man on a bicycle, she asked for directions and was told that she should have continued on her original course. "But," said she, being

Irish and therefore liking to argue, "your sign said for me to come this way."

"Sure," said the passerby, "you must pay no heed to the sign. The lorries are forever knocking into it, the way it's set too close to the road, and so of course it gets turned wrong. About a year ago we decided 'twas no use turning it back just so the lorries could knock into it again, and it's pointed wrong ever since!"

In spite of these delays, I found myself, two hours later and fifty miles further from Adare, in the city of Thurles. Here again I had a choice of roads, but inquiry from the first car brought directions not only to Cassustown Cross but to Rossestown Cross as well, the site of the meet. I had said nothing about going to the meet, but my clothes told the story.

When I had followed the directions given me and reached what I thought must be Cassustown Cross, I looked for the expected shrine, but there was only a country crossroads, not even a signpost, and no one looking as though he had been sent out to direct a wandering American. There was a farmhouse, however, with a large, woolen-skirted, rubber-booted figure plowing through the muck carrying a pail and disappearing rapidly in the middle distance.

"Hi!" I called. "Where is Cassustown Cross?" The figure turned and made its way slowly back to me.

"Where?"

"Cassustown Cross," I repeated, trying to make the "o" in Cross sound like the "o" in "horrible," which is the way it is pronounced by the Irish.

"Sure'n it's here it is," she said.

"Oh." I looked about me. There was no messenger hiding behind the hedges. I might as well go on and find my way to the meet without further aid.

"Can you tell me where Rossestown Cross is?"

"It's the next cross down the road on your right, then," she said. Finally it dawned upon me what the Irish definition of "cross" was.

Sure enough, in a very few minutes I came to another crossroads, just as a car full of people in hunting clothes also drew up. General Wakely hopped out to bid me welcome. I was also introduced to Miss Breda Dwan, Joint Master of the meet, a lovely girl with the traditional Irish black hair, blue eyes, and creamy complexion. She wore the maroon-collared blue hunting coat which is the livery for the Golden Vale.

The Golden Vale Hunt took over the territory formerly hunted by the Thurles and Kilshane Foxhounds. It was originally organized as a harrier pack by Mr. Tim Hyde but became the Golden Vale Hunt-Foxhounds in 1951. Dr. D. Kinane was Huntsman until recently but his place had been taken over by a local farmer named Jack Quinn. Miss Dwan acted as Whipper-in.

The soil in the Golden Vale is the richest in Ireland. The farmers' houses seemed to be larger and more prosperous than those around Limerick, and I saw more ground under cultivation. The Vale is a rolling country with some rather steep hills, but not so rough as the country over which Peg Watt had taken me the day before. The fields were bigger, the ditches and banks not so big. The weather was the best I had had so far, brisk but sunny, with just a hint of a haze over everything. This hazyness of the atmosphere gives a strange quality to the landscape. Mountains that are really comparatively near seem on the rim of the world, and I was continually being surprised at finding myself riding past a house that I had seen only five minutes before and supposed to be ten miles distant.

After a few minutes there was a clatter of hoofs and the good Dr. Kennedy rode up, accompanied by a girl in an ordinary skirt riding astride on a big dark bay. The bay turned out to be Jack, the horse he had so kindly offered to lend me for the day. The girl hopped off, and I got my saddle out of the car and took it over to where Jack stood. I peered up at his withers. They seemed to tower over me, high above the tree line, and I wondered how I was ever to get my foot up into the stirrup, or if I would have to submit to the indignity of a "leg up." I have always said that on the day when I cannot mount my horse without assistance I would stop riding, but I hadn't counted on Jack. However, by standing him in a little hollow and letting the stirrup down as far as I dared (if I let it down to the end I should never be able to swing my right leg across his rump but would be reduced to spraddling on my tummy in the saddle and kick-

ing hopefully), I was just able to get my toe in and heave myself aboard. Of course the Irishmen all leap gracefully up from the ground, never troubling to use a stirrup, but then I'm not an Irishman.

Once up I fitted him very comfortably, but there was something about the set of Jack's neck and head that gave me an inkling of what lay before me. I said nothing, however, only asking if there were any particular thing which Jack did or did not like.

"Don't worry about the old fellow at all," said Dr. Kennedy. "I've hunted him twelve years myself and he's never been known to fall. Over the jumps you'll think you're in an armchair, a real armchair. There was a little lad hunted him last season and he had the time of his life on him. Of course . . ." he paused for a moment. "Of course, he does like to take a bit of a hold now and again, and he must keep up front, but he'll never lay his toe to a hound so you don't need to mind. Just let him alone."

Presently other members of the hunt arrived, including a van with Jack Quinn and his hounds. Since, in addition to my horse, both the Huntsman and Dr. Kennedy were named "Jack," I was somewhat confused throughout the day, especially when someone from the rear would shout, "Take it easy, Jack!"

There were not a great many in the Field. General Wakely was following in his car, and I inwardly hoped that my riding Jack had not prevented him from hunting. There was a groom riding so short that I didn't see how he maintained his seat at all, on a nervous Thoroughbred which, I decided, had had little previous opportunity to view hounds. Then there was another groom who was acting as escort to a twelve-year-old boy in a velvet hunt cap, riding a hot little thirteen-hand pony, which looked to be about three quarters hackney. There was a small little chap, immaculately gotten up on a beautiful chestnut Thoroughbred, whom I couldn't quite figure out. He had a rather delicate frame, almost that of a jockey, a fine face with high cheek bones, very closely cropped blondish hair with some gray in it, and a sprinkling of blond hairs on his upper lip. He rode well, with his feet well under him, and I saw his horse take an unexpectedly high jump over a hedge leading into a road without affecting his seat at all. We talked together for some time before I discovered that "he" was really a "she," with several grandchildren!

As we moved off down the lane, everyone expressed the opinion that because of the heavy rain the scenting might not be too good. I was also told that on Thursdays the hunting was never very good. The "Monday country," some distance away, was supposed to be much better. I was to hear this many times in Ireland and finally came to the conclusion that going hunting is like going to see someone's garden. One should always have come the week before, when things were really at their best, or else the following week or so, when the delphiniums were sure to be in bloom!

I quickly found that my premonitions concerning Jack were justified. He had the fastest natural gait of any horse out, and it was a trial to him to walk, trot, or canter slowly. It was even more of a trial to me to make him do it. Furthermore, as I found out later, Dr. Kennedy often whipped off of him, so he was accustomed to being well up in front or ahead of hounds. He had been ridden in point-to-points and he had been show jumped. In the off-season, summer, he was put to the plow. A truly versatile animal, but his racing and his work as Whip had given him a taste for speed, while his build and his plowing had taught him to bend his thick neck at the poll and lean against the bit. Before the day was over I would have cheerfully given my right eye for a pelham with a good tight curb-chain!

But over jumps Jack was all that they had claimed! Not the stiffest bank nor the widest ditch held any terrors for him. Several times he was called on to lead the way over a particularly nasty-looking spot at which some of the less massive and experienced mounts balked, and he certainly had the smoothest jump I had ever ridden. This was partly due to his size, for what required quite a spring on the part of the average-size animal was merely a slightly longer than normal step to Jack.

I finally evolved a system which prevented him from overrunning hounds and so ruining my reputation as a foxhunter. When we hacked along the roads, I took care to ride third, hoping that the two in front—the Master and some other member of the Field—would ride side by side. Of course, Jack Quinn would be up front of them, hounds at his heels. But whenever possible I placed Jack's great head just between the rumps of the two horses that rode in front of me. In this way he could have a good look at hounds and know for certain that they would not leave him behind; at the same time he would not be tempted to climb into the saddle with the rider of the horse ahead, which he seemed inclined to do if I placed him directly behind anyone.

When hounds were runnings and we were lined up at a jump, I held him back by keeping him turned away until I was sure that I had plenty of room. This prevented Jack, in his exuberance, from landing directly on top of the horse ahead. Once we were over the jump I was forced to let him set his own pace, which he immediately did, passing everyone else as though they were standing still. As I saw the next obstacle rearing up ahead of me, I would circle by pulling with all my strength until I had his great head in my lap. For though Jack was willing to set his own line and jump anything that might come his way, I did not feel that I knew the country well enough to allow him to do so. Some horses give most trouble at checks, being restless and unwilling to stand, but Jack was far too sensible and wise in the way of hunts to do this. As long as he could see the profile of a Whip in the distance, stand-ing at the edge of the covert; as long as he did not hear the magical "Tally-ho" and the note that told that Rey-nard and the hounds were on their way; just so long would Jack stand, firm and quiet as the Rock of Gibral-tar.

Hounds were first thrown into a big covert in a low, wet field, and the members of the Hunt took their positions on a plowed hillside above it. Away off ahead of me I saw snow-capped mountains, one of which had a curious formation. Just where the summit should have been there was a sharp, deep gap or crevasse, as though a giant spade had cut a slice out of it. My small friend on the tall chestnut Thoroughbred saw me look-ing at it.

"That's the 'Devil's Bit'," she told me. "Have you seen the Rock of Cashel?" (pronounced "Ca'shel").

I shook my head.

"You must! It's the home of the old Irish kings. According to the leg-end, the devil got mad and bit a piece out of that mountain over there. Not liking it, he spat it out, and that bit became the Rock of Cashel. Both the Rock and Devil's Bit are limestone, and there's no other limestone near Cashel."

Just then there was a whimper from the hounds working the covert below us, and I could ask her no more about the devil and his bit (bite), but I determined to see the famous Rock. Unfortunately there were too many foxes, and the pack was soon split three ways, each group of hounds going off with its own private quarry.

Jack Quinn was on the far side, and by the time he got back it was too late to get them together. Also, since he had been with this pack for only a short time, hounds did not really know him. We tried a number of other coverts, but all the foxes seemed to be of the opinion that the covert was the place to stay in such wet weather, and hounds were not able to get them out. We had a few short runs but nothing notable.

Little Tom, the twelve-year-old on the hackney, came to grief once, when we went over a nasty bank with a drain on the landing side. I thought I saw wire and called out to Dr. Kennedy, but he said there was none so I jumped it. I wondered why Jack jumped so high, and a moment later Tom and his pony followed. There *had* been some wire, and the pony caught in it, throwing poor Tom headlong into the ditch. I caught the pony and the lad came up, covered with mud from head to foot, with tears, which he tried to fight back, running down his cheeks. Earlier in the day he had been raked across the face with a thorn-bush, and what with the mud, blood, and tears, he was a sorry sight.

"Sure it's nothing at all to worry about, a bit of a spill like that," said the groom who was with him. "Isn't it always the best riders that gets the falls? Up with you now, lad, and don't let anyone tell you you haven't kept up with the hounds this day!"

"I'm fair drowned," said the poor little fellow as he climbed aboard again.

After the hunt Dr. Kennedy and I stopped off at Jack Quinn's house, an old, old farmhouse, bigger than any I had seen in Limerick. We went in through the kitchen, and the wonderful, familiar smell of it transported me back to my childhood. Once again I was in the kitchen of my grandmother's house, begging sugar cookies from the cook.

We sat ourselves down before a big turf fire and Mrs. Quinn plied us with sherry. I learned that her husband, in order to hunt, had to start the chores long before daylight. Dr. Kennedy told me that he, too, had made a number of calls before starting his eight-mile hack to the meet and that he would have evening calls awaiting him on arrival. Although he was a man of over fifty, the good doctor did not seem weary at the prospect. He told me that tuberculosis and other respiratory ailments were the main health problem in Ireland, but that if the people could be persuaded to open their windows at night and come out with the hounds there would be much less of this. Mrs. Quinn bewailed the fact that her sons were not following in the footsteps of their father but preferred mechanical vehicles to horses.

Presently Miss Dwan, who had gone with the hound-van to get her car, came to take me out to dinner, which she had already ordered at a hotel in Thurles. At dinner, which was very pleasant indeed, I was surprised to find myself served a good meal of soup, fish, meat, the usual three vegetables (two of them pota-

The Rock of Cashel

The steep, peaked roof is that of Cormac's Chapel. It has the only roof in the world supported entirely by arches of fitted stone. The tip of the round tower can be seen at right just over the top of the walls of the main church.

toes), and a sweet with no delay, although there could not have been more than three other people dining and no apparent prospect of others. When we had dined, Miss Dwan set me on the road home via the Rock of Cashel. On the way, she pointed out her own home, a lovely Georgian house set on the edge of a little river.

I got home safely, after catching a brief glimpse of Cashel in the early dusk. It was a huge mound surmounted by numerous stone buildings, and I made a mental note to take Sydney to see it when he got over.

On arriving at the Inn I found a very sad trio of "Kentucky Colonels." Poor Rodes had hit the ground four times, Bass had been lost all day and had had no decent runs at all, and Haggard had a badly cut cheek. To cap it all, whereas I, in the Golden Vale, had had beautiful weather, in Limerick it had rained hard. I asked about Haggard's cheek, supposing, of course, that a thorn bush had been to blame, but it appeared that the cause was not a natural hazard. Haggard had jostled an Irishman going through a gap, and the next thing he knew the man had ridden up beside him, hauled off and let him have it! Nothing could have astounded poor Haggard more, since he believed that he had barely touched the leg of the other man. He had made no complaint to the Master, who was not present, unfortunately, but on their return, the three "Colonels," after some discussion, had decided that the only dignified thing to do was to curtail their visit. So they planned to hunt with the Galway Blazers the next day, as they had arranged to do some time previously, give the dinner party that night to which they had already invited some twenty people, and then leave on Sunday for England. I was most distressed and tried to cheer them up a bit; telling Haggard that he had come to Ireland to gather new impressions and he was certainly getting his money's worth.

He rubbed his gashed cheek and allowed as how this was a pretty deep and unexpected impression.

The next morning the Earl of Dunraven stopped me on the street, where I was busily taking pictures of his castle, and asked me what I knew about the affair. He was very upset and said that he was going to write Haggard a note of apology and that everyone felt badly indeed about the whole matter. The Irish are proud of their friendliness and hospitality, and to have a countryman treat a guest in such a fashion was hard for them to take. I learned also that the man in question was noted for his boorishness and, further, that he was annoyed because the three Americans had not rented horses from him. Be that as it may, the froth was off the beer, and there was little one could do to mend a bad situation.

VII

A Dinner Party at the Dunraven Arms—Dancing in Limerick

The original number of guests invited to dinner at the Dunraven Arms by the three "Kentucky Colonels" was twenty. The list was given to Miss O'Hare, who, with her cohorts, had agreed to do the telephoning. Telephoning in Ireland is not like telephoning in the United States. Here one has only to twiddle a dial, listen for the ringing that indicates that the line is free, and in a moment the call will either be answered or not. In Ireland apparently each call must go through several exchanges. In the country parts one must allow a minimum of fifteen minutes to get any call through, and a half hour is safer. With Miss O'Hare's continuous efforts, most of the twenty guests had been reached by one o'clock, but the number of those who accepted fluctuated. At one time we were down to fifteen and things did not look bright. Then several others on the list asked if they might bring house guests. When dinner time finally came there were more than thirty of us.

Miss O'Hare, by pushing tables together, had arranged a horseshoe-shaped banquet table. I found myself seated between two gentlemen whom I had not previously met: Commander Fitzgerald, who owned a stud farm adjacent to the Fort Union Stud, and a Mr. Tillander. I was familiar with the name "Tillander," for there is an Olympic rider of that name. Inquiry brought the information that the gentleman on my left was the brother of the Olympic rider.

Commander Fitzgerald—another example of the fine-looking "sporting print" type — discussed horses and hunting with me and invited me to stop in for tea the following day. He had a lovely daughter sitting a few seats away, very busily talking with one of the "Kentucky Colonels." Mr.

Tillander and I soon got into a discussion of higher equitation. I learned that he was a collector of early harness and of early books and manuscripts on the horse. I wangled an invitation to come to see his collection the next afternoon, after my tea engagement with the Fitzgeralds.

After dinner we repaired to the big lounge for coffee; then four of the guests, including Peg Watt, Major de Trafford, and Major Waller, began a game of bridge in my private sitting room, next door to the lounge. A few minutes later I went into the sitting room to get my camera. I was immediately assailed by the following remarks and questions:

Major de Trafford: "Do you want to go to bed?"

Mrs. Watt: "Would you mind giving the fire a poke?"

Major Waller: "Can't you bring me a decent hand? I've had nothing above a two spot all evening!"

Three times I went back to the room, and each time I was asked the same three questions in the same order and by the same people. I could make out all but the first, until I realized that Major de Trafford was under the erroneous impression that they were using my bedroom, and not my study.

At twelve o'clock the party began to break up, but Mrs. Watt persuaded a number of us to go in to Limerick, where a dance was being held. Two of the "Kentucky Colonels" and Miss Fitzgerald went in a car with me. Mrs. Waller and Mr. and Mrs. Lee (the lady whose face had been stepped on by a horse) went with Mrs. Watt.

Miss O'Hare gave me the front-door key since, she said, I appeared to be the most responsible member of the party from the Inn. Probably my seven grandchildren had something to do with her opinion.

We arrived at a big hall, completely jammed with people dancing to the strains of an American tune, played by an excellent orchestra. All the Irish are good dancers, and how they love it! Like the hunt field, the dance floor was full of people of every age, description, and class. During my stay I went to several dancing parties, each different from the others. But in every case the music was excellent and everyone was having a wonderful time. Up on a big stage sat quite a large orchestra, composed of both men and women. At one point toward the middle of the evening a little man dressed in a well-worn tweed coat and a pair of flannel slacks decided to take over the leadership. He had long side whiskers and was, I should judge, in his seventies. He was feeling absolutely no pain and made a most graceful, though somewhat unorthodox, conductor. Most of the time he turned his back on the musicians and conducted the dancers instead, with the most wonderful curtsying and swooping motions. I would have enjoyed watching him all evening.

I found that I had no lack of partners, for, in addition to our own party, a number of men whom I didn't know joined us. Among others, I danced with a chap named Pat Scanlan, who later proved one of my most prolific sources of information, for he was the original Irishman whose tongue was "hung in the middle." He was a gay little chap in his early fifties who "travelled in tobacco," as the saying goes. He kept bachelor quarters in Limerick and, like Mrs. Maxwell, was usually being faced with some strategic crisis. At the moment he was worrying about the "lady sweep" who had agreed to come next morning and clean his chimneys, and whether the painters who were doing some interior decorating would be there early enough to let her in. In addition to himself, Pat's household consisted of two hounds of not untarnished lineage and an old horse who carried his master on the hunts in the winter and plowed for his keep in the summer. One or other of the hounds was always with Pat, waiting patiently in the car outside while Pat hunted, danced, or sold tobacco. He was the most kind-hearted person alive, but if he was willing to give you the shirt off his back, he expected you to be willing to give him yours in exchange if he needed it. He was always getting himself into impossible situations, but somehow managed to muddle his way out and bob up smiling. I soon discovered that he knew virtually everyone of interest in the whole of Ireland. And if he didn't know them personally, he knew who they were and all about them. His tales were often revealing, though always good humored, and if he ever found it necessary to mention a bad quality or action he usually excused it in the next breath with the words, "But he's got family troubles, poor chap!"

I have said that the Irish are loquacious. After hunting, dancing, and fighting, surely gossiping is their favorite pastime. I wish I dared tell half the stories that I heard while I was there, but if I did I would never be able to go back, and that I would not like.

When the band had played the Irish National Anthem, which ends each party, those in the know knocked at the door to a room next to the ballroom and, when it was opened, entered in a definitely clandestine manner. It was just like the old prohibition days in New York. Apparently there was something a bit illegal about the club's license to sell liquor, but it seemed to make as little difference to those with the proper credentials as did our Eighteenth Amendment in the twenties.

We went into a small, smoke-filled room with a bar running across one end. It was crammed full of people, many of whom I recognized. Peg Watt presented me to a short chap who, she said, was "Master of the Limerick Harriers," then introduced me to the "Mistress of the Master." The laugh that concluded the introduction indicated that it was not quite what it sounded. Both the Master and his "Mistress" expressed their disappointment at my not having come out with them, but I told them I would be sure to do so before leaving.

Presently the call "Time, gentlemen, please" was heard, but little attention was paid to it, and it was a full three quarters of an hour before the patient doorkeeper had swept us all out. Peg, who was the last one to go, insisted that such treatment was unwarrantable, that the night was yet young (4:30 A.M.), and insisted that we all repair to the "Horse and Hound" for a nightcap. The "Horse and Hound," which I remembered having passed on my way back from the Golden Vale, was dark and silent as a tomb. There was an illuminated sign which said "Veterinary Hospital" over a small door in the same building, and the redoubtable Mrs. Watt pushed the button several times, but no one came. I finally decided that we had come to the end of a good day and that it was time to call hounds off, so I blew the long "going home" signal on my horn (or, rather, my car's horn) and we left. At five o'clock I left the key on Miss O'Hare's desk and fumbled my way down the icy corridor. My room was equally icy, but the hot-water bottle in my bed still retained a semblance of warmth, and anyway, I was too sleepy to be kept awake by anything as trivial as cold.

VIII

Teddy Ryan and his Black and Tans

The Scarteen Foxhounds, otherwise known as the "Black and Tans," is one of the most outstanding packs in Ireland. The Joint Masters, Messrs. John J. and Thaddeus (commonly known as "Teddy") Ryan, are brothers. They come naturally by their aptitude as Masters, for the Ryans, father and son, have hunted the black-and-tan foxhounds of the Scarteen Hunt for about two hundred years. This breed is distinctive in that the hounds have no white on them. There is reputed to be more bloodhound in the strain than in the English fox-hound, which may account for their somewhat deeper voices and the beautiful carrying quality of their bell-like tones.

Teddy Ryan is a charming fellow. He is pure Irish, and if he were dressed in a gunny sack he could never be taken for anything other than a gentleman. He is younger than most of the Masters with whom I hunted, and if his hounds are noted for their voices, he, in turn, is noted for his ability on the hunting horn.

"He fairly makes it scream, that horn!" they say, and they speak with truth. The sound of Teddy's horn and the cry of his hounds will forever ring in my memory.

The Ryan brothers are undoubtedly among the most popular Masters in Ireland, partly because they have no strain of English blood in their ancestry, partly for their love and knowledge of hounds and hunting, but mostly because they are so very nice to young and old, rich and poor.

The Scarteen country has many ditches, varying in width from six to twelve feet, and universally deep. When a horse is unfortunate enough to slide into one of the Scarteen "drains," he is lucky if, by stretching his neck, he can see out over the edge.

The general advice in jumping these drains is not to look down. Excellent advice from a horsemanship angle it is, too, for, as everyone knows, as long as your eyes are up and your heels are down you will never part company with your horse. If, on the other hand, one does steal a peek while tottering on the brink, in addition to the joy of accomplishment which one experiences in successfully negotiating the drain, one has also that wonderful feeling of having come safely through a great peril. I would say that the size and depth of the Irish drains and the steepness of their banks have a great deal to do with the Irishman's belief in a personal deity.

The banks, incidentally, vary a good bit. There are some nice solid ones that look like the dykes of Holland. Having safely come upon the top of one of these, a horse could take a promenade down the center and pick his take-off instead of having to jump whatever lay before him, as he usually does on hooking his toes over the top of a razor-edged or a hairy bank. But there are plenty of the razor-edged and hairy banks, too, many of them made more treacherous by strands of wire laced through the ash and thorn shoots wherever there is a gap large enough to permit the passage of a horse and rider.

I had two escorts to this hunt—Pat Scanlan and Raymond de Trafford. I picked up Pat in Limerick, accompanied, as usual, by his little dog, Valiant. He said that he had no horse for the hunt but would follow in the car, hoping, if someone tired,

that he could get a run some time during the day. We went out the Tipperary road to fetch the Major at his house. He was very smart today, in topper and pink coat. His house was a beautiful white Georgian building set on a hilltop. It was all white plaster inside, with lovely arched doorways and a rich red carpet on the stairs, but it was colder than Greenland. Since Mrs. de Trafford was not at home, there were no cozy fires lit, but we had quick cups of coffee in front of an electric heater before taking off for the meet.

The weather was brisk, with beautiful clouds, and the sun shone brightly most of the time. In Adare there had been no sign of snow but outside Limerick there was a full three inches. All the gorse was powdered, and the thorn hedges had light coatings of ice that glistened and glimmered so that we seemed to drive between borders of diamonds.

The meet was in front of the pub outside Oola. Even Pat had to inquire his way once or twice, for we went off on little back roads to get to it. There were about forty in the Field, and, more young people than I had seen at the other hunts.

The Scarteen Hunt livery is black with a fawn collar, but there were a number of "pink" coats as well. I was introduced to one member of the field, a Dr. Harris, who wore tweed knickerbockers, bright green wool golf stockings, and oxfords. He explained that, since there was so much snow, it had not occurred to him that hounds would actually hunt, and he had come out only to have a look. Lord Harriman, whom I had met at the dinner party on Saturday night, was in "pink" as was Major de Trafford, and the coat plus his beautiful complexion, perfect profile, and English hunting seat made him look exactly like the old-time whiskey advertisements that used the slogan "First over the Bars." I was quite disappointed to find that he did not take off his topper and bow gracefully at the top of each bank.

I saw a miscellaneous group of women in Oxford gray, black, or navy coats, among them two young things from the States who I knew were staying at the very posh establishment highly recommended by the American Tourist Agencies as suitable for the "top social register." One of the proprietors of this inn, a Miss Cleeves, was in attendance on the young things and giving them advice. I lost track of them right after being introduced and, wishing to speak to them later, I was a little puzzled as to how to pick them out. I first listened for accents, but everyone, including all the Americans present, was being either very Irish or very British. Then I got the bright idea of looking at the position of their legs and was immediately able to identify them.

After leaving Oola we trotted along for fifteen minutes or so to a place called Mooresfort, a huge gray stucco house surrounded by magnificent trees and rhododendron bushes. Hounds were kept off in the rhododendrons, and the Field waited silently in the drive while a terrier was introduced into a drain by way of suggestion to the fox (who, of course, had mentioned the night before just where he was to be found) that it might be just as well if he got the hell out of there. Sure enough, in a few minutes the old fellow ran out and away into the shrubbery. Hounds picked up the line and streamed after him, their voices echoing the Master's horn, which screamed in approval, and the Field made its way through the devious paths as best it could.

I had previously asked Peg Watt if I might use her as pilot, knowing that no one knew better how to play Mary's Little Lamb to a fox than did Mrs. Watt. She led me away from the main group of riders. We pushed our way through some heavy underbrush and found ourselves on the edge of— the Grand Canyon! Peg's horse hesitated, as well he might. "G'wan there!" says Peg, with a flourish of her hunting thong. The horse gave a mighty leap, landed safely, leaped again, and disappeared from view.

"Hack on, there's no wire!" called a cheery voice from far below. Good advice it was, to be sure, but I was riding a rather unprepossessing-looking hireling named "Athlacca," of whose jumping abilities I knew absolutely nothing. So far, just hacking along the roadside, he had been a joy, with impeccable manners and a mouth like silk, but I would have appreciated being able to hop him over something reasonable by way of a trial before asking him to jump the crevasse that lay before me! However, it was clearly evident that I was not to get the chance, so I followed Peg's tactics, growled loudly, waved my crop and added a prayer for good measure. And Athlacca, with no further ado, followed exactly in the footsteps of his companion. As he soared through the air my heart soared with him, for I realized at once that here was a horse to be trusted, one that would conquer any obstacle that came his way. Nor was I misled; for during the hunt, which lasted from eleven-thirty until nearly six, we went over all types· of banks, ditches, walls, gorse hedges, gates, barways, and even barbed wire. Horses were refusing and falling to the right and to the left of me, before me and behind me, but the noble Athlacca, despite losing a shoe; despite a full hour's run at the very end of the day all up and down tremendously steep hills, with jumps every few hundred yards; despite mud to his hocks, snow balling up underfoot, and miles of hard, flinty road, down which we hacked for half an hour at a time at a fast, posting trot, and sometimes at a gallop; the noble Athlacca never refused, never hesitated, and never laid a toe wrong! Furthermore, I could have hunted him with fine cotton thread instead of leather reins, so light was his mouth and so obedient was he to leg and weight.

But to get back to the hunt. We crossed a rolling meadow, and the hard-packed balls of snow which were dislodged from the horses' hooves as they galloped flew in every direction, forcing us to duck and dodge to avoid them. The mud was deep under the slippery coating of snow. We crossed a wide, deep ditch and checked beyond on a knoll. Across a hedge of thorn and well below us hounds were circling. They lost the line and were called back to try again; then we returned over the same ditch. But the scent in the snow was hard to follow and again they were at fault. Twice more we did this and finally we were away across the fields at a fast gallop, hounds in full cry. It was only a short run, however; we jumped onto a bank and from it directly on a hard road, Athlacca landing so lightly that I felt the expected jolt was being absorbed by invisible springs. There we waited while the hounds, Whips, and Huntsman nosed out the line. A false start took us down the road to the left, but presently we circled back, and the fox went to ground in a ditch, where, since the day was young, he was allowed to remain.

The going was slow for a bit. Several foxes were started but, scent being as unpredictable as Irish weather, there were no long runs. I had seen de Trafford from time to time, but Pat Scanlan had been unable to get a horse and was following in the car with a tweed-clad woman named Mrs. Ryan. (In fact, nearly everyone today seemed to be named "Ryan," just as in the Golden Vale country everyone had been named "Jack.") Evidently the Master decided that scenting conditions might be better in a different sector, so after a long hack we stopped in a road at the top of a hill. Here we found the cars that had been following waiting to meet us and give us sustenance. When we were all mounted once more, the Master led us through a gap and onto the top of a hill.

Rarely has it been my good fortune to see such a view. Behind us was the ruin of an old castle that had guarded the hilltop for over a thousand years. In front of us sloped the hillside, covered with low gorse bushes just beginning to show their first yellow blossoms. Later the gorse would burn with a golden glow. The sun had come out again. I rose in my stirrups and, from this vantage point, looked around me. In every direction there was a wide expanse of countryside, checker-boarded with hedged banks. Small woodland patches glistened with snow in the bright sunshine. Tiny thatched cottages, huge square mansions, and the red roof of a cottage or barn now and again standing out against the white fields gave interest and color. Encircling me, at the very edge of the horizon, were sweeping, sheer, snow-capped mountains, the Galtees to one side and the Silvermines to the other.

"Magnificent country you have here," I said to a man on a big brown horse near me.

"It's all right, but there's too much wire!" he answered.

Before I could correct my statement by substituting the word "landscape" for "country," there was a "view-halloa" off to the right, and past us ran Reynard. Down the steep hillside he galloped, disappearing into the gorse, and we slithered down after him, following the narrow cattle tracks. But he was a wily fellow. Three or four times we climbed up and then slid down that clifflike precipice. He ended by eluding hounds entirely, and it was decided to lift them and be off to another covert.

At this point Pat appeared, saying that he needed some exercise, so I turned Athlacca over to him and set off with Mrs. Ryan to drive the six miles to Oola. We were to meet outside the town, near an old, white-washed farmhouse with the usual thatched roof and mucky courtyard. Mrs. Ryan and I waited and waited, but no Pat and no horses. After a bit Mrs. Watt arrived in her car, and soon afterward her man came along with her horse. Then a horse-box with six horses aboard appeared, but no Pat. At last he arrived riding de Trafford's horse and leading mine, with the announcement that the Major had quit for the day so that at last Pat had a mount.

Together we rode through the barnyard and along a rough trail on top of a bank, ducking thorn bushes to keep from being scraped off. Presently we came out into a field. Beyond this field was another and beyond that ran a railroad embankment. In the first field was a big metal "shore" (Irish for culvert). This had been blocked up after Reynard had come home, so it was to be presumed that he and possibly a companion were waiting for us. Pat, Peg Watt, another woman, and I hid behind a shed and waited while men in tweeds, black, or "pink" took turns with shovel and pick to clear the drain and introduce the terriers. After half an hour a mangy-looking fox ran out and galloped slowly away. He was given a long grace, but hounds quickly caught up with him and he ducked into a badger hole. Since he was obviously not fit, no attempt was made to bolt him and we returned to the original shore to try for his companion. At this point Peg Watt bade us an informal adieu, since she had to catch the train at Oola en route to Cheltenham, England, for the races. I told her to bring the three "Kentucky Colonels" back with her since we would miss them no end. She promised to do so. It is typical of the Irish that though a trip to England might mean a curtailment of a hunt it should not be allowed to interfere entirely with it.

A little more shovel work, a new introduction of terriers, and the second fox came tearing out and galloped across the next field. Ah, here was a fox after my own heart—speed, knowledge, skill, he had everything! With screams from the horn reverberating in the hills, we were off, just as Peg's train came tooting by. I had a panoramic view of Reynard, hounds a couple of hundred yards behind, racing parallel with the rocketing little green carriages while the engineer added his engine's whistle to the encouragement of the Master's horn.

Up hill and down dale our fox led us, through hairy hedges and over banks that towered above my horse's head. To date there had been few spills, but now they came thick and fast. I saw the chap who had given my nice young "Kentucky Colonel" a

black eye land in a ditch, and rejoiced, though I felt sorry for his horse, which was being mightily cursed and belabored in an effort to get him out. A gray horse, ridden by a girl, misjudged his leap and landed spraddle-wise on a muddy bank. Even the Master tangled with a strand of barbed wire and bought a bit of real estate, but he was remounted in an instant.

Shortly after that we came through a gap and were faced with an odd obstacle to find in the hunt field—a gate leading into a farmyard, but a gate consisting of an iron bedstead wired to the posts. Not a high jump, to be sure, but the kind most horses don't care for. I had utmost faith in Athlacca, however, and I also had a lead, for the man who owned my bold steed was just in front of me. Without hesitation he flew it and, since he said nothing to me that would indicate that Athlacca could not do the same, I took his silence for encouragement and followed him. Nor was my trust misplaced. I soon had the satisfaction of realizing that we two alone of the field had taken a short cut which enabled us to come up with hounds almost immediately. Shortly after that we found ourselves in a field that was a veritable bird cage of wire, with no alternative but to jump it. Taking Athlacca back, I brought him up at a good clip, telling him meanwhile to remember the bedstead. As we reached it I gave him my spur. He responded nobly and soared over wire and bank without mishap.

We maneuvered another high

Hunt staff and hounds hacking down a typical Irish "Bohireen"

bank and were out on a road—to my surprise, the same road where we had eaten our luncheon. Again we went through the gap and onto the brow of the hill, and again we checked. This time the view was even more lovely, for the low-lying clouds picked up the pink light of sunset. It was now nearly five o'clock and the shadows were long. A mile or more away on the white fields stood three figures, the sun behind them, their shadows stretching out before them. They were too far distant for me to be sure that they were really people, but if they were they were well rewarded for their cleverness and patience, for after fifteen minutes or so, hounds being at fault somewhere behind us, suddenly our noble and worthy fox appeared at the very foot of the hill, still running strongly. He crossed directly in front of the waiting figures and, ducking under fence after fence of wire, disappeared into the far distance. "View halloa's" echoed through the hills and valley. The horn screamed and screamed again as hounds were called up and put on the new line.

"He's the lad we're after, your Honor, for he's that muddy!" shouted a farm boy, blessed with the eagle vision of his breed. At breakneck speed we descended the hill that, from the top, had seemed unnegotiable. Then we were off through heavy mud, on a zig-zag course, for, whereas Mr. Fox and his companions the hounds were able to run straight, we, because of the wire, could not.

And now I realized that Athlacca was at last beginning to tire. It became necessary for me to save him as much as possible, so I contented myself with watching ahead to see where the staff and the few of us that still remained were going, letting him take the lung-bursting hills at a trot rather than a gallop. My tactics were wise, for some of the obstacles were high, and though the depth of the mud often made me feel that I was going *through* the fields rather than over them, Athlacca bore me bravely onward, not faltering once at the big banks and wide ditches. We finally halted at the top of another long hill, and the Master's horn told us that the day's sport was ended.

I'm sure our clever quarry watched as we walked our tired horses slowly down the hill and then went home to tell his children and grandchildren about how he had led the famous Black and Tans for a full hour at top speed until hounds, horses, and riders admitted his superiority.

IX

Tea at the de Traffords'—A Farmer's Ball in Tipperary

Major de Trafford shortly appeared in a car and announced that we were all to go to his house for tea. I, meanwhile, had asked Lord Harriman to take me back to Oola to pick up my car, putting my saddle into his car. But when the Major turned up I decided to accept his invitation and transfer my saddle to his car. What was my distress when Lord Harriman came trotting over to say that my saddle had disappeared and that he feared it had gone on with the horse-box.

"But we only just finished packing it into your car. How could that have happened?" I wailed.

"I'm sure I don't know," said the noble lord, "but I can't find it."

This was most distressing. A further search, however, revealed the saddle neatly tucked away in the "boot," and the kind man, still impeccable after all the mud we had been through, hauled it out and put it in with de Trafford on the back seat.

Our next problem was to locate Pat Scanlan, whom I had last seen climbing out of a ditch, de Trafford's chestnut horse, which had been seen climbing out of the ditch after Pat, and my car. Arriving at the farm near Oola where I had left the car, we found only an inquisitive donkey and two goats. Nor was there anyone about who could throw light on the missing Consul. I devoutly hoped that the insurance covered theft, but the Major assured me that he fully expected Pat, the horse, and the car all to appear together for tea at his house. Personally I couldn't see just how poor Pat was to drive the car and lead the chestnut too, but perhaps I underestimated the talents of the Irish. At all events there was little I could do about it.

We found several others ahead of us at the de Traffords. There was one quite tall woman with a most blasé attitude toward nearly everything. She had been among the few that were still with us for the last glorious run but seemed unwilling to admit that it was anything special and had not noticed the view from the hilltop! Presently all kinds of good things appeared on the table, the main *pièce de résistance* being shirred eggs. I ate large amounts of everything, hoping against hope that Pat would show up. Sure enough, when I was on my third cup of tea he appeared.

"Where have you been? What kept you so long?" we asked.

"It was those two poor things from Cleeve's place," he said. "I came across them standing on the side of the road with their saddles and their girths and no car and no horses and nobody to look after them, so I picked them up and took them down to a pub and gave them a drink and then I had to take them on to where their car was."

"But what about the Major's horse?" I asked.

"Oh, I took him into another pub and got the man to let me put him in a stall. I had just finished giving him a drink of water and a handful of grain when along came a boy. He looked wet and lost so I says to him, 'Will you have a drink, lad? I don't drink myself but I'll be glad to buy you one and then you can rub down this horse and blanket him for me.' And if it didn't turn out that he was the Major's lad and had come looking for the very horse I was just after giving the grain to! He should be along any moment now."

As usual, faced with a difficult situation, Pat had found a quick and ready solution and helped a couple of other people out of their dilemmas while so doing.

There was to be a Farmer's Ball given by the Scarteen Hunt at Tipperary that night. Nearly everyone seemed to be going, and Pat had offered to escort me. Since by this time it was nearly seven and I had to drive the twenty miles back to Adare, bathe, change into evening clothes, get a bite to eat (I might feel hungry later, though at the moment I was rather full of shirred eggs, tea, and jam), and get back to Limerick by ten, I had to hurry, so I left, after thanking the Major for his hospitality. I left in a bit too much of a hurry, as it turned out, for I forgot all about my saddle, still reposing in the car that had brought me back from the hunt! This was to cause no end of telephoning and arranging later.

At ten o'clock I was back in Limerick to pick up Pat. He had not yet arrived so I sat down in the lobby, feeling a bit conspicuous since I was the only one dressed in evening clothes. Presently he came in, all togged out in white tie and tails, accompanied by a reddish-haired, pink-complected young man whose name, I was told, was Frank. Frank, it seemed, had just arrived from Malaya, and Pat, who had run into him unexpectedly, thinking he might be lonely, had suggested he come with us. All evening he worried about Frank and whether he was getting around enough and finding plenty of pretty girls to keep him amused. Frank seemed to me entirely capable of looking after himself, shyness not being a characteristic of the Irish race, and the Irish dances being as informal as they are.

Tipperary is some little distance from Limerick and it was nearly midnight before we got to the dance. The ball was being held in a very large hall, and if I had thought the other two dances I had been to were crowded, this one made those seem deserted. I have never seen such a crowd nor such a variety of costumes. Teddy Ryan was there, whirling around rapidly and gracefully in the formal scarlet evening coat which the Scarteen wears at night. Lord Harriman was there, also in scarlet, and there was a large contingent of girls in ordinary sweaters and skirts or short dresses and men in tweeds. But the most amusing figure I saw was a little short chap dancing with a very tall young woman. The room was very hot, and I had taken off my evening sweater to dance in my short-sleeved silk evening blouse. I seldom remove the sweater, even on warm nights, but the hall was so filled with humanity that it had reached and passed blood heat, I am sure. Anyway, to my amusement I saw this little man dancing toward me wearing a pair of brown slacks and a long, heavy, khaki overcoat, obviously army issue. It was buttoned right up to his chin

and was so long that only the very ends of his trouser cuffs showed below it. For all I could tell he wore only these two garments, for he never removed the coat all evening. As he danced past me, he looked me straight in the eye, and I was most astonished to hear him say, in a low voice but very distinctly, "I'm a shy man, I'm noted for being shy. . . ." I was to meet him later and find that he was a member of the press. Evidently he wanted to pick me up and get a bit of copy, but he wanted to reassure me while doing so.

The charming Joint Master of the Scarteens did me the honor to dance with me, and we had our picture taken together (though Pat promised to see that I got a copy, one has not yet made its appearance). The orchestra was very versatile and played waltzes, fox-trots, congas, rhumbas, and even a tango. We also danced several Irish dances, which put me in mind of the old-fashioned "gallops" and "Schottisches" popular in my dancing-school days. Pat and Frank worked hard to see that I was well supplied with partners. Presently we saw a long line forming for dinner, which was being served upstairs on the balcony. Since Pat said he was starved, we joined the queue, which was exactly like a subway jam. Several times I found myself, one toe on the edge of a step, the other resting on nothing, my arms across the shoulders of whoever stood next to me, my weight borne by the crush of the crowd, hanging or semi-floating in the air. There I would remain until another shove from below pushed me on to the step. At last we reached the top, were admitted past the official who was standing at the head of the line, and shown places at a table. I couldn't eat a bite, (I never can at such times) but I took a full plate. What Pat alone couldn't eat he put in his pocket to take out to Valiant, who was waiting, as usual, in the car.

I don't know at what time the ball ended, but I do know that after waiting in line nearly an hour to get my wrap out of the cloakroom, driving Pat and Frank back to Limerick, and then going on to Adare, I turned the key in the lock at the Dunraven Arms long after six o'clock. I tiptoed down the long corridors and plunged into bed as quickly as ever I could.

I was supposed to hunt with the County Limerick Harriers at noon. Mrs. Lee having come forward with the offer of a horse, but when Kathleen came in at nine and threw back the draperies to show long, slanting rain being blown in heavy gusts against the windows, I asked her to have the secretary cancel the horse I had arranged to borrow, rolled over, and went to sleep again. It was three in the afternoon when next I woke and still raining. This was the only day during my whole trip when it poured hard all day, and I slept through it!

X

Mr. Tillander's Collection—A Late Snack with Mrs. Hedderman —Paddy Punch and Family—Dancing in Adare

On Sunday my friend Harry Kenny turned up, bringing his sister with him. He was a most delightful chap and I was dying to ask him whether I lived up to his expectations, but I didn't dare. We had luncheon at the Dunraven Arms, then went to Patrick's Well to see the Fort Etna Stud.

Patrick's Well is a very tiny and most picturesque village on the main road from Adare to Limerick. The entire hamlet consists of two rows of old, old plaster cottages leaning companionably against one another. Some are thatched and some are slate-roofed, but all are painted in such brilliant colors that one has the impression that a child has got loose with a paint-box. Many are still in use as stores, pubs, or private dwellings; others have been abandoned and are in various stages of disrepair. Behind these old cottages there is a most uninteresting row of new cottages, color-

less beyond belief, especially when contrasted with the rainbow hues of the old-timers. They are of a depressing gray, all just alike, but with big windows and high roofs as compared with the old buildings. I have no doubt they are heaven on earth as far as living conditions go for anyone accustomed to the original buildings.

The name "Patrick's Well" derives from a legend that St. Patrick blessed the village well and that it is holy. I was never able to find anyone who could point out the well or tell me any of the details. Had there been miracles performed? Was the magic quality of the water still active, and had the good Saint actually blessed it? Or should these numerous wells to which he is supposed to have given his benediction be classed with the many beds along the Eastern seaboard in which George Washington is reputed to have slept?

At the Fort Etna Stud I saw and photographed a Thoroughbred that was being raced in the point-to-points. He interested me because he had the typical Irish hunting clip, quite different from the hunting clip which we give our horses here in that only the hair under his belly and on his flanks had been taken off. The reason for this seems to be that, in hunting, a horse often has to stand at a check for fifteen or twenty minutes. Leaving the hair on his back protects him from rain and wind. In the American hunting clip everything is taken off except the hair on the legs and under the saddle, on the theory that, since a horse sweats mostly on the body, he dries out more easily without long hair and thus does not run such a risk of catching cold. In other words, he doesn't have to stand around in wet underwear, as it were. But I can see the Irish point of view.

The "Kentucky Colonels" took their departure and I was most sorry to see them go, as was everyone else. I got a good picture of them and Benny standing in front of their mountain of luggage, while the invaluable James watched from the door of the Inn.

I had a most pleasant tea with Commander Fitzgerald and his family but missed seeing his horses because I got there an hour late (my watch stopped). This was a great disappointment to me, and I also was sorry to have put the Fitzgeralds to the trouble of making preparations to show me around, only to have me come too late. Obviously I needed my husband

The three "Kentucky Colonels"

Taken outside the Dunraven Arms at Adare with the invaluable Benny (left) and the equally invaluable James (in doorway).

to keep tabs on my engagements!

From the Fitzgeralds' I went to Mr. Tillander's house, and here I had a real treat in store, for he had a most interesting and unusual collection of old bits, spurs, and stirrups, many of them medieval in period. They were not just ordinary articles of equipment but real works of art, made with loving care and by a master hand. They had silver chasings on the arms and branches, bas-reliefs, and all sorts of other ornamental work. (A few are shown on pages 97 and 98.) Many were hideously severe and I wondered how the horse was ever persuaded to accept and respond to them. But some were like our own "bitting" bits that are used in the mouths of young horses and have keys and other dangling pieces to induce them to play with the bit and relax the lower jaw.

In addition to these collector's items, I was shown a museum collection of early manuscripts and books. I was familiar with a few, but most

96

(a)

(b)

(c)

Courtesy of Mr. N. Tillander

Some old bits

(a) *German, sixteenth century. Blackened chiselled steel; weight, three and one-half pounds.*

(b) *Bronze snaffle, Gallo-Roman origin, second century. This is one of the earliest "double ring" snaffles.*

(c) *A curious type of bit, sixteenth century, used in France, England, Italy and Spain. The horse's chin is slipped through the iron ring which thus acts as a curb.*

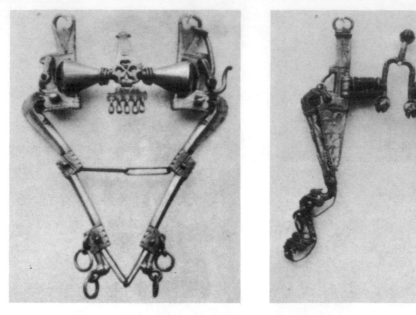

(d)   (e)

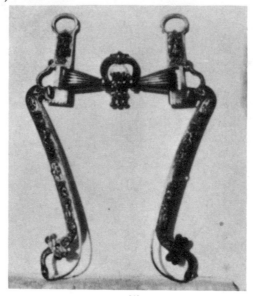

(f)

(d) *German, 1420. This is of polished steel and the tongue plate with its dangling keys is hinged. Similar ones are used today to teach the young horse to play with his bit.*

(e) *A very elaborate-type bit, probably designed especially for the owner. It is German and the date, 1490. The branches can be lengthened by means of screws.*

(f) *This is a truly lovely work of art. It is of the Italian Renaissance period. Intricate sculpture and gold plaques ornament the branches and depict birds, foliage, classical armor and other figures. It is probably of the school of Verrochio.*

were new to me. One of the most interesting was a bit-makers' pattern book with beautifully drawn designs in black and red pencil. The draughtsmanship was astounding—the lines were so perfect and delicate.

Another interesting book was one called *Markham's Maister-Peece,* published in London in 1651. The title page (see page 100) gives a careful enumeration of the contents and is bordered with pictures of horses in various attitudes. On the opposite page was the explanation in verse form:

The figure 1 a compleat Horseman showes,
That Rider Keeps and Cares and all perfection knowes.
The 2 Diet; 3 letting bloud
Best Balme of Balmes, for inward Griefs most good.
The 4 wounds, Gals and Sores doth firmly cure,
The 5 helps Nature's Marks; 6 doth procure
Help for Sinews, Griefs as Slips and Strains,
Knock or Convulsion, all are helpt again.
The 7 wholesome Drinke, the 8 doth take
Bloud from the Mouth that sudden Death doth slake.
The 9 showes the Horse-caudle or the Mash
Good as the best yet some Fools count it Trash.
The 10 shewes Fury in untamed Things
The onely Fountain whence Diseases springes.

The last two lines might almost have been the inspiration for Christian Science beliefs!

Mr. Tillander most kindly offered to get me photostats of some of the bits and of this frontispiece. One of the books he showed me was among the earliest ever written; in fact, he told me that there are only three other copies in existence, all in museums. When I asked him how he was able to lay his hands on such treasures, he told me that he had book dealers all over the world alerted and as soon as a likely item for his collection came on the market he was sure to hear of it. How I wished I had had access to these rare manuscripts when I was writing the historical sections of *Horsemastership!*

After dinner Pat Scanlan turned up to take me to see a friend of his in Croom, a Mrs. Hedderman. She was a most delightful person with a beautiful, quiet face. She is a widow with two grown children and a dear little granddaughter. She keeps one or two horses which she lets out occasionally. She had been one of the most fervent followers to hounds but when her husband died she lost interest in the hunt. Pat told me that everyone was so fond of her that they couldn't bear seeing her drop out of things and so were making every effort to get her back in the field. We sat in a tiny room, close to a turf fire, and Mrs. Hedderman plied us with tea and home-made bread and cake. I had just finished dinner so couldn't eat much but Pat has the Irish capacity for food and drink at all times and

The frontispiece of Markham's book on horsemanship

manfully did the honors for us both.

My hostess urged me to come to the tea she always had for all her friends after the point-to-point on March 18. I accepted with alacrity, for I knew Sydney would want the pleasure of meeting her. As I was leaving a sudden thought struck me—an old house, the warm feeling of hospitality, the informality. "Do you happen to know the Philip Van Wycks?" I asked. A joyful smile spread over Mrs. Hedderman's face. "They're the very nicest Americans I ever met!" she said, "They sent me a lovely Christmas card but forgot to put their address on it so I have never been able to write and thank them for it!" I had run Katy's and Philips' "Old Gal" to ground!

One of the reasons Pat had wanted me to go to Mrs. Hedderman's was to ask her to let me have a horse on the following Tuesday so that I could go out with Mrs. Watt again. Alas, she had already promised hers to some more fortunate person! But Pat was not to be defeated. "We'll just take a run over and see Paddy Punch. He'll be sure to have something," he said. Eleven o'clock on a Sunday night seemed rather an odd time to be making calls but Pat insisted that Paddy would be delighted.

So we drove several more miles through countless little country lanes while Pat told me about Paddy. He is in his eighties, one of the best-known and loved of the farmers in the locality. For years he has kept horses, training them himself. The present Queen of England, her sister,

and her parents were frequent visitors at Paddy's house, for they often rode his horses when they came to Ireland.

"He's a bit absent-minded nowadays, and if you see him nodding and dropping off to sleep suddenly, don't be surprised," said Pat. "You see, he got an awful bang on the head last year and he's never been quite the

Paddy Punch

At eighty-five he still goes to the meets and shows how the Irish farmer of his generation looks on a horse.

same since. There was a horse got in a ditch and it was one of the nervous ones and it was thrashing around so nobody would go near the animal, only Paddy. Everyone else was for sending for the veterinary to put the poor beast out of its misery, but Paddy comes along with a bit of rope and he gets it on him and he gets him out, only the beast gives him an awful clout in the head while he was doing it! Would you believe it, he was in the hospital for I don't know how long and the people that owned the animal only went to see him once! And then they only stuck their heads in the door! And after Paddy saved their horse for them and got such a terrible clout for it!"

Paddy's house was different from any I had seen before. It had a big, stone-floored kitchen with an enormous fireplace. A row of hams and some flitches of bacon were suspended overhead. The ceiling was quite high, the walls whitewashed, and the whole room spotless. We went through a hall into a parlor, where Paddy showed me pictures of his horses. Here there was another fire, but we soon returned to inglenook, which was cosy to a degree.

"How old is this house?" I asked.

"Sure, it's old, very old indeed!" was the answer.

Mrs. Punch and a young son of fourteen joined us in the inglenook. Paddy also had two grown boys who had finished school and college and were in professions. Evidently Paddy was an example of an Irishman who had worked hard enough to give his boys a good education and see them well started in life. Even though he might remain on the place himself they would not have to emigrate to make their way. I met the two older boys when we went out with the Limerick Harriers and again that night at the Irish Kagle, and I found them most charming. I doubt that there is a soul alive who has aught but good to say about Paddy and his family.

Paddy asked if I knew Jean Slaughter and was delighted to learn that I did. He said she had ridden one of his horses in a hunt and that people were still talking about how she had followed the Master over a river. It must have been the same river that Jean described so graphically to me the day we had luncheon at the Red Barn. We talked horses for nearly an hour, and I told him tales of little *Rocket*, who was bought out of pity and has since won many ribbons, including some firsts in the Garden.

Alas, Paddy was afraid that he had no horse for me for Tuesday, but he promised to let me know if anything turned up. Meanwhile he took me out and showed me his chestnut mare, which he promised to give me on St. Patrick's Day, when I planned to hunt with the Limerick Harriers. As we were leaving he took me by the elbow, led me around to the front of the house, and pointed out an enormous trimmed hedge, five feet high and at least as wide. He told me that one of his sons had jumped the chestnut mare over that hedge only a few days before. I told him I should consider myself most honored to ride her.

Since it was hardly midnight when we left Paddy, Pat suggested that we take in the village dance being given in Adare for the purpose of raising money to buy radios for the eight blind people who lived in the community. I had heard the Fitzgeralds talking about it at tea and the cause seemed a worthy one, so the Adare Village Hall was our next port of call.

Pat talked the doorman into letting us in for half price on the theory that the evening was more than half over. Like the dance in Limerick, this one was jammed, and we moved around slowly, pressed together like herrings in a kit. I saw the secretary from Dunraven there and one or two others whom I had noticed around the village. The orchestra was small but very spirited. They played many familiar American favorites of the twenties and thirties, such as "Smoke Gets in Your Eyes," war songs of World War I (naturally, "Tipperary" was the most popular), and Irish and Scotch melodies by the score. Everyone sang as they danced.

I was wearing a charcoal-gray skirt, yellow twin sweaters, and yellow bobby socks for warmth over my nylons. Apparently the Irish had never seen bobby socks before and they were fascinated. As we waltzed along, hundreds of eyes stared at my socks, with many a resulting collision. In fact, it might be said that our progress was accompanied by a steady stream of apologies.

But if the Irish were fascinated by my socks, I was equally fascinated by some of their coiffures, particularly on the men. One especially fetching hairdo adorned a long-legged Irishman dressed in mismatching tweeds. From the nape of his neck to an inch and a half above his ears he had been shaved with a razor. Above this shining white area his dark red hair curled in long, luxuriant waves. I couldn't help thinking of a tropical island—lush vegetation surrounded by naked beaches.

At one thirty the national anthem was sung and we went home, though I am sure had Pat been able to think of any place else of interest we would have continued on till daylight.

XI

Ballykisteen and Victor Studs—Tea with Tim Hyde

Raymond de Trafford had most kindly offered to take me to the Ballykisteen Stud, near Limerick Junction, to see the two famous stallions there, Denturius and Phoenix. Since his house was on the way, I planned to stop and pick him up; then we would go on to Ballykisteen together, and from there to the Victor Stud. (The Victor Stud is the private stud of George Harris, manager of the Ballykisteen Stud, and Mr. Harris had invited us to lunch.)

Following my usual indecision at the traffic light in Limerick, I finally got on the Tipperary Road and found my way from there to the de Traffords' without difficulty. Mrs. de Trafford, a most charming and attractive lady, whom I had not met before, greeted me at the door with the sad news that the Major was in bed with a stiff neck and would not be able to accompany me. I had been past Limerick Junction on my way to Cashel

from the Golden Vale, so I was sure I would have no trouble finding it. At the Junction I had noticed a huge fence of corrugated iron, ten or twelve feet high, which enclosed a race track. The Ballykisteen Stud was directly across the road from this fence, and Mr. Harris was right there to meet me.

The layout of the stud was very attractive, the buildings all of whitewashed stucco with dark wood doors and trim. I had been told that Ballykisteen was operated by a syndicate, and I asked Mr. Harris to explain just what that meant. He told me that the syndicate had been formed by a group of men for the purpose of buying two stallions, Denturius and Phoenix. Each took a number of shares worth seven hundred and fifty pounds each. A total of forty shares was issued, thus setting the value of the stallions at thirty thousand pounds, or a little

Ballykisteen from the air

under ninety thousand dollars. Each share entitled the owner to send a mare to the stallion for breeding. Each shareholder also had to contribute a designated amount of money toward the keep of the stallions. Outside mares were also permitted to be nominated (*i.e.*, sent for breeding), the fees being applied to the cost of maintaining the stable. Thus the stallions were jointly owned, but the get belonged to the owners of the mares.

The groom brought the Phoenix out first. I took some photographs of him and was fortunate enough to take one that met with Mr. Harris' approval. (A horseman is rarely satisfied with a photographer's conception of a good picture; the picture must show the animal in the best possible pose to display his good points.) The Phoenix was a magnificent seal-brown stallion with tremendous animation and style. No photographer until now had been able to catch him at his best, but Mr. Harris was very pleased with my picture and I promised to send him a copy.

Denturius was not so easily han-dled—in fact, the groom did not handle him at all. A temporary runway had been constructed leading from his stall door to the circular building which he used for exercising, much like the exercising shed I had seen at the Fort Union Stud. The groom opened the door, quick like a mouse, and ducked behind it while Denturius dashed into his play pen. It was too dark to take a picture of the horse inside but Mr. Harris gave me a fine one later. See page 42.

When I had seen my fill of the two stallions, the groom brought out some beautiful yearlings and some mares and foals for me to inspect. One, a brown yearling colt out of Lady Ursula by Denturius, was particularly outstanding and was expected to bring a fat sum at the yearling sales. After several trials I was able to get a good picture of her as well.

We then drove to the Victor Stud. On the way, Mr. Harris called my attention to a wayside shrine to St. Matthew, the patron saint of abstemiousness. He remarked that when

Two outstanding colts bred at Ballykisteen

(a) *Bay colt by Solar Slippe out of Bray Melody. Sold at Doncaster Sales, 1953, for ninety-two hundred guineas (about eighteen thousand, six hundred dollars).*

(b) *Lizanno, chestnut colt by Royal Charger out of Bray Melody.*

it was erected, with proper honors and celebrations, all the local pubs, though officially closed, did a really outstanding business. This, he was sure, must have scandalized the good Saint.

At the Victor Stud, I saw for the first time a house which was not of the Georgian or earlier era but which had been built by its owner. It was a lovely house with big sunny rooms and the most beautiful paintings of horses that I had yet seen.

Mr. Harris told me with great amusement of his experience with an American veterinarian who had come over to buy one of his mares and her new foal. The mare was the mother of a two-year-old that had just completed a highly successful year on the tracks. The foal was full brother or sister to this same two-year-old.

"What's your price?" asked the American.

"Twenty-five thousand pounds."

"I have a check here for twenty thousand pounds made out in your name," said the veterinarian, laying it on the table in front of Mr. Harris. "How about that?"

"Twenty-five thousand," said Mr. Harris. The American hesitated, then drew another check out of his pocket.

"This is the last check I have with me; it's for three thousand, and if you won't take it I'll go over to France. There's a mare there I've been looking at and I can get her instead."

"The price is twenty-five thousand," said Mr. Harris, "and not a penny less."

"You're a hard man to do business with," said the American, but he reached in his pockets and from one or another pulled enough miscellaneous travellers' checks to make up the difference.

"It was a terribly hard deal to close," said Mr. Harris to me. "He was tough, really tough."

"But you were tougher," I said.

"And after the deal was closed,"

went on Mr. Harris, "I remembered that the mare had a nomination to Tulyar, but of course that would normally be cancelled if she changed hands. But I called up the National Stud and they said it would be all right, but not to say anything about it. Then the next morning didn't I get calls from half the papers in Dublin saying they'd heard the mare and foal had been sold to an American and what about it!"

Mrs. Harris was most hospitable. We had a delicious luncheon and then I took off, as I had planned, to go to pay my respects to Tim Hyde. My directions for getting there were not too exact. "He lives outside Cashel. Just go into the town and ask anybody where he lives. It's only a few miles."

So I drove into Cashel. I was directed to take a road that went almost under the famous Rock, and after following this and asking once or twice more I found the place I was looking for.

Mr. Hyde greeted me most cordially from his wheel chair and wanted to know all I had been doing since I reached Ireland. He was sorry that he had been unable to let me have a horse the day I hunted in the Golden Vale. He, his charming son, and I talked horse for about half an hour. I found my way home with no trouble and packed my suitcase, for the next morning I was to leave early for Clogh Jordan to see a point-to-point and go on from there to Mrs. Maxwell's place in Birr.

XII

Jack and Esther Maxwell—An Irish Cocktail Party—On to Dublin

For several days messages had been coming in, either by phone, by post, or delivered personally, regarding various people I must be sure to find as soon as I got to the point-to-point at Clogh Jordan. Harry Kenny would be there and would be looking for me. He was anxious to show me around. Mr. Maxwell would probably be there and would also be looking for me. If I didn't see him I was to watch out for a Mrs. Perry, who was eager to meet me. How I was expected to locate these people I don't know, but it began to look as though, stranger though I was, my social obligations would leave me little time to watch the horses.

The weather was not very good, nor was it very bad, in spite of Kathleen's freely expressed opinions. As soon as I was dressed I gathered my hunting equipment and brought it down to the front hall to be stowed in the car immediately after breakfast.

"Be sure to have Pat put my saddle in," I said to the secretary in a carefree manner, and went into the dining room. When I came out I found no saddle. Further inquiry brought the information that Pat did not have my saddle. In fact, he had seen neither hair nor hide of it since my hunt with the Black and Tans. Horrors! It must still be in the trunk of the car of the dark-haired young woman who had driven me from Oola to Major de Trafford's! But what was her name and where would I find her?

I put in a call for Major de Trafford. In half an hour came the answer that he was out. Would I speak to Mrs. de Trafford? I would. I explained the situation to her and she promised to get in touch with her husband, find out who the lady was, and see what she could do. I waited another half hour; then Mrs. de Trafford called to say that she had located the lady but there were complications. It seemed there was a saddle left in her car, but one of her friends had identified it as hers. There was nothing to do but telephone the lady direct and describe my property. I called at once but was told that she was out hunting. That meant she wouldn't be in again until evening.

Now, here was a predicament indeed. The lady in question lived at Cashel. I planned to spend the night at Roscrea and was going on from there to Dublin in the morning, a drive of about seventy miles. To go back to Cashel from Roscrea and return would put sixty more miles on my trip! But there was no use making any plans at all until I had first ascertained whether she really had my saddle. I told the maid to whom I spoke that the saddle had a nameplate on the cantle reading "Gay Venture" (the name of the filly that usually wears it at home), and said I would call back later in the evening. The maid, who seemed most intelligent and interested, promised to relay the message, but I hung up with a heavy heart. How could I have been so careless! One might mislay a riding crop or spurs or even a bridle, but a saddle! Clearly, another time I would simply have to bring Sydney with me to keep me in order.

Clogh Jordan was beyond Thurles and not too far from Birr, which, in turn, was almost next door to Roscrea. As I began my usual inquiries, no longer trusting to the migrating sign-posts, I found myself running into the same sort of difficulties with pronunciation that had proved so confusing on my trip to the Golden Vale. The "Clogh" was easy—it was pronounced exactly like "clock"—but the "Jordan" was something else again. Sometimes the "o" was like the "o" in "horrible" and the word rhymed with "guard on." Sometimes the same vowel was like the first "o" in the word "Colonel," and we got "Jerdan." Whichever way I chose to say it was inevitably wrong and completely incomprehensible to my informant.

I was somewhat late in starting due to all the delays, and the point-to-point was scheduled to start at one-thirty. But by hurrying I was able to make it and drew up exactly on the dot in front of a pub in the tiny village of Clogh Jordan to ask directions to the course.

Here disappointment awaited me, for the point-to-point had been called off.

"Sure, didn't you see it in the papers, Madam? 'Tis the cars they're worried about. The horses would get over the course, God bless them, but the cars in the parking lot would be sunk to the axles and we'd be digging them out 'til St. Patrick's Day."

This was indeed a blow. One of my articles for *Life* was to be on point-to-points. A photographer was coming to take pictures of the one I planned to attend on the eighteenth, the day before I flew home, but I hated to plan a picture sequence without ever having been to an Irish point-to-point. However, there was nothing to be done, so I went on.

The Maxwells lived just between Birr and Roscrea, and I had been told to get directions to their house from the local doctor in Birr. Anyone in the town, I had been told, would be glad to point out his house. I knew that I was not expected until later and that the busy Mrs. Maxwell was planning to go out to a cocktail party, but perhaps I would find someone at home.

In Birr, I had little trouble finding Dr. Ritchie's house, thanks to a passerby. As I drove toward the driveway I saw a car about to come out of it. It might be a patient, of course, but then it might be the doctor himself. I took no chances but rudely drove halfway across the drive so that the poor man had no choice but to stop. It was Dr. Ritchie. He obligingly invited me in to meet his wife. We went through a hallway into a small room at the back. On the floor was one of the most beautiful and buxom babies I had ever seen. She lay there contentedly on her back on a blanket and looked around. She was about ten months old and had enormously plump pink cheeks and curly blondish hair. She would have been the perfect model for baby-food advertisements, and had I been Dr. Ritchie I should have kept her on permanent display as an example of what the child of a pediatrician should look like.

Dr. Ritchie's wife told me that Mrs. Maxwell, having already learned that the point-to-point had been called off, was expecting me to go to the cocktail party with her.

"How do I get to her house?" I asked. The doctor and his wife looked soberly at each other.

"It's hard to find, very hard," said he, and she nodded her head in solemn agreement.

"It's a way off in the country."

"And over terrible roads!"

"You'll be lucky to make your way there at all!"

"Oh, well, all I can do is get lost, and I'm used to that," I said. "If you'll just be so good as to draw me a map."

So Dr. Ritchie got a bit of paper and a pencil and we sat down at a table, where he proceeded to give me my instructions. First he drew a line leading diagonally across the paper toward the right-hand corner.

"This is how you start," he said. "I'll put you on the road so you'll be all right at this end." He continued drawing the line, then drew another going off to the right. "A couple of miles out of town you come to this road here, do you mind it?" I said "Yes." "It's not very much of a road, but it's there, right there," and he pointed again with a pencil. "Yes," I said, "I see it." "Well," said the doctor, "you ignore it and go on." So I ignored it and we went on.

"Now," he said, "just a little further beyond you come to another road coming in on your left, like this—" and with care he drew another road with a cottage.

"Do you see that one?"

"Yes, I see it, it's on my left."

"Right," said the doctor. "Well, you ignore it, too." So I ignored that one too. The pencil continued going to the northwest.

"Now here you have a bad road, a very bad road indeed. There's bog on both sides, so mind you don't drive off it." I said I would so mind.

"And after a long way you come to a cross. You can't miss it, there's a chapel and a little churchyard on the left." He drew them, "And some cottages on the right." He drew these. "And a bit of green. Do you see?" I said I did. "Well, you ignore it. Just go straight through, and after you've gone for another couple of miles ask the first person you see where Jack Maxwell's house is and he'll tell you."

I looked at the map. My road was a direct line with never a waver or a turnoff. I thanked him kindly, promised to ignore everything, said goodbye to his wife and the baby, and got into my car to follow the doctor.

Needless to say, I had no trouble. The Maxwell's house was the easiest to find of any that I looked for in all my stay. The road that had been described as so terrible was narrow, to be sure, and it did not have a hard surface, but it was in good condition. When I had gone the prescribed distance, I saw a man standing beside the edge of the road with a bicycle, exactly as though he had come out on purpose and had been waiting there to direct me. He pointed out the gateway not a hundred yards ahead. A long, narrow drive wound its way between plowed fields. Some cattle and two horses watched me until I had gone through an iron gate and stopped in front of an old Georgian house with one of the most beautiful beeches that I have ever seen in front of it.

Mr. and Mrs. Maxwell both came to the door to greet me. They were of medium height, and every inch of them exuded cordiality. Jack Maxwell, a broad-shouldered man with a shock of black hair, was in corduroys, a flannel shirt, and gum boots. He had evidently been working when he heard the car. Esther Maxwell had the serene face and beautiful bone structure that I had come to identify with the Irish gentry. With cries of welcome they brought me in, got my bag from the Consul, and asked about the Abernethys. Three small children came forward, one a little girl of two, Allison, the second a seven-year-old named Lucinda, and the third Dr. Ritchie's son, a boy of five or six. This was the only place I visited in Ireland where the children were on display, and it made me feel at home.

Jack Maxwell had inherited the house and property, along with a bundle of debts, from his father. His grandfather had had eight daughters, and when he finally had a son—the ninth child—his joy knew no bounds. I don't know how the daughters fared, but the old chap had built this house for his son, exactly a hundred years ago. It had the same big rooms and high ceilings, the same spacious hall, broad stairway, and beautiful mouldings of the other houses of the period. When Jack inherited it it was in a bad state of disrepair and had no modern conveniences. For the first seven years of their married life Esther had cooked over a turf fire and had to go outside for her water. They now had a bath and electricity downstairs and an "Esso" stove, which I judged to be similar to the Swedish "Aga" stove.

Along with the house Jack had inherited two hundred and eighty acres of land, only five or ten acres of which were then under cultivation, one horse, one cow, and one donkey. But Jack, unlike many of his countrymen, was ambitious, and through hard work he has paid off his debts, increased his herd seventy head, and now has two hundred and ten acres of tillage. But the road has not been and still is not easy. Under one of the large fields which he recently plowed up, Jack discovered a buried forest, the trees, possibly two thousands years old, still well preserved. These were several feet under the surface and will all have to be removed—a truly herculean task for one man with not too much in the way of help or modern machinery. But Jack, with his broad shoulders, is tackling the job without question. He plans, this year, to put everything into wheat, hoping to make enough money to finance the modernizing and decoration of his house so that eventually he can add to his farming the profession of running a country inn, where paying guests can come to stay and enjoy the hunting. If this project ever comes to completion the guests will be lucky, for nowhere will they find a more charming host and hostess.

Esther Maxwell was a perfect fund of information. I asked her questions on every conceivable subject and she answered all of them. She was interested both in Ireland's past and in her future. She said that her husband's Irish blood was pure, but hers was slightly tainted: two hundred years before she had had an English ancestress. She took a tremendous interest in the welfare of the villagers and told me something of the dire conditions under which many of them live.

I asked her about the "national" schools, which correspond to our public schools, She told me that they were not patronized by the gentry, not because they did not want their children to associate with the farmer boys and girls but because many of the teachers were both brutal and incapable. She confirmed what I had read elsewhere, that the biggest problem facing the women in Ireland was the fact that it was usually impossible for them to marry under the age of forty, due to poverty, unemployment, and lack of ambition on the part of the men. This leads to a high rate of illegitimacy and infanticide.

It was Esther who told me about the law regarding chickens and ducks and the legality of running over the former but not the latter. She also had a very amusing tale concerning the themselves with little or no cash and the payment of debts. Many Irish families, formerly well to do, find themselves with little or no cash and are often forced to go heavily into debt. When they get in too deep the bailiff pays them an unannounced call and has the right to confiscate anything he may find on the property, but nothing that is not actually on the property when he arrives. The favorite and most salable belongings are, of course, livestock, so the minute a rumor gets started to the effect that the bailiff is on his way, the owners hustle out and drive all the livestock onto a neighbor's land. Since the neighbor may soon be in the same predicament, he is usually glad to play host to the visiting herd. And how is the man of law to prove that a given herd, even though it may bear the initials of the people he knows in his heart to be its owners, has not been given or sold five minutes before to the owners of the adjoining property?

One day, so the tale went, word came to a certain family that their creditors had lost patience and the bailiff was on his way. When the bailiff arrived, stall and pasture and paddock were empty and bare. Furious and frustrated, the bailiff took a walk around the property to make sure for himself that there was nothing available. Naturally, he left his car standing in front of the house. All the members of the clan went with him, some running on ahead to make certain that none of the cattle had, by misadventure, strayed back to its native homeland. While this was going on, who should drive up but the income-tax collector, bound on the same errand and governed by the same rules. Seeing the bailiff's car standing most invitingly in front of the house, he naturally supposed that the owners of the house, instead of paying their taxes like honest citizens, had bought themselves a new car. "The dirty, murdering so-and-so's,"

said the tax-collector to himself, and, jumping into the car, drove off without making further inquiries, allowing his assistant to take his own car back.

When the bailiff returned from his guided tour, not only was he without loot in the form of confiscated animals, he was without car as well, nor was there any indication as to just what had happened to it! By the time the matter had been untangled the bailiff's car had been converted into cash, the land-owners had received credit for having paid their taxes, and everyone except the bailiff was very happy.

"Probably," concluded Mrs. Maxwell, "the poor man is still trying to get his car back, with very little help from the parties involved."

When I had remarked on the democratic spirit I had observed in the hunt field, Mrs. Maxwell told me another story.

"I remember one hunt," she said, "in which hounds ran through a field in which a farm girl was plowing. When she saw them coming she quickly unhitched her horse, took off the harness, knotted up the reins, jumped on bareback in her long woolen skirt and gum boots, and followed along. It was a long, fast run over rough country with some big ditches and doubles, but the girl and her mount kept manfully on. Three quarters of an hour later the fox went to ground, and the only ones left in the field who had not come to grief were the Master, the Whip, and the farm girl.

"How in the world did you manage to stay on bareback over all those banks?" asked the Master.

" 'Sure'n why wouldn't I stay on, your Honor, riding shkin to shkin!" was the answer.

The cocktail party was great fun, held in the first new house I had entered in Ireland. The house was well built and well planned and attractively decorated, though my own inclination would have been to paint or whitewash the outside instead of leaving it the depressing gray of the natural stucco.

We went through a nice hall into a living room full of people, all chattering about horses. Such a contrast to my usual experience in America, where horses are the last subject of general conversation! And whereas in England and often at home one is expected to take care of oneself at a gathering of this sort, introductions being few and far between, the Irish have a highly developed sense of responsibility toward guests and made sure that I was never left alone. I was introduced to a young girl who hoped to come to the States to get a job teaching riding and to the mother of another young lady, unable to come because of illness, who had artistic leanings. I was asked where I had hunted, what I thought of Ireland, and how about Joe McCarthy. I was told that I must definitely go out with the Ormund Hounds and that someone could certainly find me a horse.

Then I was led over and introduced to a tall woman wearing a white wool shorty. She had blonde hair hanging in ringlets on each side of her face, a very high complexion, and she wore a monocle. She was in the middle of a hot argument with a stocky, animated little man, who, I learned, was a "Moony of the Doon." They were discussing a certain chestnut mare which the man had been riding.

"If I had a hundred and forty pounds I'd buy her tomorrow," declared Mr. Moony.

"And if I had forty I'd buy three like her and have a pound or two left over," said the lady in the monocle. "What good is she, I ask you? You'd never be able to show her, with that rump on those hocks!"

"What good is she! Why, she's the best performer in the field I've ever ridden. If I owned her I'd show her in two point-by-points and she'd be ready for the Grand National!"

"Performer! I never saw her perform, at least not the way I would want a horse of mine to perform!"

"A lot you know about it! You're never far enough up in the field to see what she's doing!" said Mr. Moony of the Doon indignantly.

"Well, all I know is that the last time I saw you on her we came to a bit of a lane with a high bank on either side and everybody else had the good sense to jump into it, turn, go down a ways where there was a decent takeoff, and jump out again. But what did you do? You jumped in and out again like a flea! Neither you nor the mare had any control!"

"Show me another mare that would have done the same!" said Mr.

Moony, but the lady of the monocle was far from convinced and at intervals throughout the afternoon I heard the argument being continued.

On my return to the Maxwells' house I once more put in a call to see if I could find my saddle. This time I talked to the husband of the dark-haired gal.

"We have your saddle, all right," he told me, taking at least some of my worry away, "and now the question is how to get it to you." After some discussion it was decided to send it wrapped in a gunny sack by train to Dublin, where I could pick it up at the railroad station the following night. So that was settled.

We spent the evening talking horse, and Mr. Maxwell told me about a little bay pony that he had trained and that he would like to have me ride. I said I would be back with Sydney a week from the following Saturday, after hunting with the Galway Blazers, and that I should love to try her then. It was also arranged that when we came back, Mrs. Maxwell would take us sightseeing.

Nine thirty next morning found me on my way to Dublin. I had no trouble, since the route took me only on main roads, but was held up for a half hour in one little hamlet where a cattle fair was going on. Like an animate brown sea, lowing bullocks surged forward and back across the sidewalks and down the center of the streets. Of course, all the villagers were out to see the fun. In addition to the bullock there were a few tinkers with the usual procession of "colored"

horses, ponies, donkeys, goats, etc. in attendance. There was one man driving a black and white plow horse that limped so badly from what was obviously founder that one wondered how he moved at all. Tied to the cart was another cripple with a bog spavin on his hock as big as a fair-sized watermelon, and then, running free, was a very breedy-looking young pony, thirteen hands or so in height. The pony was so completely different in quality from the first two animals that I had the uneasy feeling that probably only a short time ago he had been frolicking in an adjacent pasture and that the tinker had simply invited him to go along.

It took me nearly a half hour to get through the throng of people and beasts. About twenty miles outside Dublin I came to the famous Curragh, an old, old parade ground and race course. The track, about a quarter of a mile away, can be seen from the road. Except for the track, the Curragh is simply a huge, grassy plain intersected with paths and sectioned off with shrubs and sheep hurdles. Over this plain wander small herds of sheep, each branded in red or blue. Some of these brands are small, but others are large and have run to boot so one has the impression of herds of completely red or completely blue animals grazing on the green grass.

After passing through the Curragh I met another drove of sheep being led along the road to their pasture. They seemed rather reluctant, and it took two shepherds and a dog to keep them moving. A quarter of a

On the road to Dublin

A typical Irish scene with thatched cottages, a church and a herd of bullocks. Passing the latter is sometimes a problem.

mile further on I met one sheep all by itself with the same marking as those I had just passed, but this one was trotting along in the opposite direction—evidently on its way home to get something it forgot! I hoped it got there, but knowing the tinkers to be out I somehow doubted it!

I also passed a truck of pigs, and never in my life have I seen such complacent, contented animals. The Irish pigs are all the same breed; it is against the law to breed any other type but white pigs. When you see them around the farmyards they are mud-colored, but when you see them on the way to market they are bur-nished and shining and a bright pink. (I wonder whether there are pig-shampoo parlors in Ireland or whether each farmer does his own.) The owner of this particular bunch must have got up very early, for there were at least forty pigs in the big, open-slatted lorry, each spanking clean. They were reclining in comfortable positions, some lying full length, some sitting half upright giving the general impression of dilettantes leaning on their elbows. All were obviously enjoying the ride. It was as though they were saying, one and all, "Now, this is something like it, this is the kind of entertainment we deserve. Drive a little slower, James, so that we can get a good look at the scenery!"

Several days later I saw another pig on his way to the fair, but he took it with quite a different attitude. He was alone in a box cart with fairly low sides, and the farmer, afraid that he would try to jump out, had invented a new method for the restraint of pigs. Standing in the cart with the reins in his two hands, he had straddled the animal just behind the neck, and, with this scissors grip on him, was galloping down the highway, the pig protesting to his gods with a wide variation of tonal range and, I am sure, a wealth of piggy expletives.

At approximately twelve thirty I found myself on the outskirts of Dublin. The traffic was heavier now, but it was not until I reached the Liffey and drove along its banks to O'Connell Street that I realized the full horrors of driving in Dublin. Nowhere in the world have I seen such confusion! The main avenues are wide, but the side streets are narrow and go off from each other at all angles. Except on one or two crossroads there are no guards, and most streets are not clearly marked. Lorries, cars, horse-driven vehicles of all kinds, and, above all, the ubiquitous bicycles swerve in and out and around each other from all directions. There appear to be no rules on parking, so cars park on both sides of the streets facing in both directions. This means that cars coming from the north, for example, often swing directly across at an angle to park on the opposite side of the street, still facing in their original direction.

To add to the difficulties, a number of the streets are one-way. Being a stranger, I continually found myself, on my way to a certain street, completely defeated by these one-way streets. Since there are also dead-end streets, and since some of the streets are winding, once started on a different line it is hard to find one's way back to the original course. I finally solved the problem by the following most effective technique. Finding myself having to turn in the opposite direction from the one I wanted, with signs ahead prohibiting my turning again, I would stop at the nearest guard, look as confused and dumb as possible, and ask my way.

"Sure, you're going just the opposite, Madam," would be the anticipated reply. I knew that fact only too well!

"Oh, dear," I would say, "I must be all turned around, and I'm already late for an appointment."

"Don't worry, Madam, just wait now 'til I stop the traffic and we'll soon put you right." And, blowing on a whistle, the guard would hold up a mighty arm, stop all traffic, motion for me to circle around him and send me on my way with a cheerful smile. It worked perfectly every time!

I was not able to poke around Dublin enough to get to know it, but I saw some beautiful bits. O'Connell Street, with Nelson's Pillar and several other statues, one of them being O'Connell himself, is so wide that the whole center is given over to parking It is even wider, I think, than Park Avenue. Near the Liffey, O'Connell

Street becomes the main Dublin shopping center, though not the only one. Here I found the Irish Tourist Bureau.

Crossing the Liffey over one of the many bridges and bearing left, one comes to Trinity College, and a half block further on, a right-hand turn leads to the Royal Hibernian, the hotel I had chosen. There was a scaffolding in front of the main entrance but I was able to distinguish the sign. A porter came out for my bags and ushered me into the lobby. At the desk I found various messages awaiting me, including one from a Mr. Montgomery, of whom I had never heard. A telephone call to the designated number brought the information that he was with the Irish *Times* and was the *Life* representative. He asked whether I had heard from *Life* regarding the arrival of a photographer named Larry Burrows, who was supposed to meet me to take pictures of the National Aga Kahn Stud. I said I had not heard from them but had planned to take pictures of these studs and of the stag hunt the next day. However, considering that I had arrived in Dublin so nice and early, perhaps he could find me a photographer so that we could go down and take pictures of the studs that afternoon, leaving the whole of the next day for the stag hunt. Mr. Montgomery, being both agreeable and obliging, allowed as how he would at once get to work to find me a free-lance photographer and would call back.

The tiniest lift boy I have ever seen took me up to the second floor, where my room was. The hotel employed several of these boys and none of them looked older than eight or nine, although I was assured that they had to be fourteen to qualify for the job. Never have I seen more able young fellows; they never forgot their manners for a moment, anticipated all wants, and I'm sure were sprouting cherubic wings under their uniforms!

My room was large and spacious. It would have made three ordinary hotel rooms. The bath attached was equally large, with the usual gigantic tub. There was central heating throughout the hotel, and though the temperature that was maintained was perhaps a few degrees colder than one finds in a hotel here, I had long ago become accustomed to it and was not tempted to light the little electric heater provided. The furniture was very handsome and quite old. In fact, the whole place seemed to breathe such an air of luxury that I thought I had better inquire at the desk to make sure that this was not something special and that a lone woman could not find cheaper quarters in some other part of the hotel. But I was assured, on inquiry, that a single room would cost no less than my present splendid quarters—about six dollars a day, including breakfast—so I stayed where I was.

XIII

The Ballymanny Stud of the Aga Khan—The National Stud— Dinner with the Laidlaws

At one thirty Mr. Barry, the freelance photographer provided by Mr. Montgomery, turned up. He was one of the nicest and most obliging chaps I have ever met; nothing was too much trouble, nothing discouraged him, and he was as full of stories and anecdotes as a colt is full of bucks. He it was who told me the tale of the Empress Elizabeth of Austria and the President of Maynooth.

Each year the Empress of Austria came to Ireland to hunt. (She was a very famous horsewoman, as all those interested in history know, and, in fact, really lived for horses.) It seems that one day she met with a minor hunting accident just outside the walls of the seminary of Maynooth, near Dublin. Not knowing who she was but naturally wanting to help, the President had her brought in and her wounds bathed, comforted her, fed her tea, and set her on her way. She did not reveal her identity at the time, but when she got back to her own country she commissioned the court jeweller to make up a suitable trophy for presentation to the seminary by way of a thank-you note. The court jeweller got out his geography and history books and, on learning that Ireland was part of the British Empire, made a very beautiful little statue of King George and the Dragon. In view of the Irish attitude toward the British, nothing could have been more tactless.

The President of Maynooth was in something of a quandary. He hardly liked to insult the throne of Austria by not publicizing and displaying the beautiful gift, nor did he want to risk the criticism and unpopularity that would be his if he did so. Somehow, through underground channels it was conveyed to the Empress that, beautiful as the trophy was, it was not quite *comme il faut*. On her next visit to Ireland Elizabeth went back to Maynooth and brought the matter up with his Reverence. The outcome of the conference was that Maynooth was to keep the statuette, but not to display it or even tell anyone except an occasional V.I.P. about it; meanwhile the Empress would send another gift. The second gift was much more appropriate and is one of the treasures of the seminary. It consisted of a complete set of vestments for the Archbishop made from gold threads drawn from the Empress's coronation robes.

Mr. Barry told me that he had come across the tale by chance. He was at Maynooth taking some pictures at the same time that some visiting royalty was there, and the President of the seminary told them both the story and showed them the silver statuette.

We went first to the Aga Khan's Stud, Ballymanny, which adjoins the Curragh that I had passed on my way up only a few hours before. There we were met by Major Hall, who was formerly with the National Stud. Since there is no stallion standing there, Ballymanny is really a stud farm, one of five studs and stud-farms belonging to the Aga Khan. In the five there are ninety-five brood mares, some of which belong to his son, Prince Aly Khan. When we arrived, the men were just bringing the mares and foals as well as the yearlings in from the fields, just in time for us to get some good pictures. The stud farm is in a beautiful location and, as one would expect, perfectly kept. Mr.

Barry was busy as a bird dog, snapping pictures, asking questions, and making copious notes.

We then went on a mile or two to the National Stud. Here the buildings are all of gray stone and so not as colorful as the white or yellow stucco structures of other studs I had seen. Mr. D. W. Hyde, who had just taken over his duties there, met us and showed us around. First, of course, came Tulyar, the prize stallion purchased from the Aga Khan for 750,000 pounds. Tulyar seemed quite accustomed to public adulation. He was apparently easy to handle and posed most obligingly for us. It will be interesting to see whether his get merit the large sum of money that he cost the government. I heard that there had been a good deal of criticism concerning the advisability of spending so much on a horse when there was so much poverty among the people, but quite possibly the money he brings in in stud fees (his fee is six hundred pounds) and the purses his get win will more than make up the initial cost.

The head stud groom, Tom Lynch, who has been with the National Stud for forty-nine years, brought out Happy Laughter's dam and her new foal for us to admire and photograph. Then we went to inspect the famous Japanese garden. I found this fascinating, although it would have meant nothing had it not been for the head gardener and guide, Patrick Doyle, who showed us around. He had been on the place for many years also, and it was apparent that his

Courtesy of Fogra Failte

The Aga Khan's Stud at Ballymanny, Curragh, County Kildare

Grooms lead the yearlings in from the field. Behind is a beautiful panorama of Irish countryside with a snow-peaked mountain in the distance.

Courtesy of Fogra Failte

Major Hall

The manager of the Aga Khan's Stud at Ballymanny, with photographs of famous Aga Khan stock. This collection of horses would be valued at well over the million-pound mark.

Evening parade of mares and foals at the National Stud

Tulyar

The sale of this stallion by the Aga Khan to the Irish National Stud for seven hundred and fifty thousand dollars was the cause of much dissension, many feeling that so much money should not be put out on one horse when many people needed help. The government's answer was that if Tulyar lived up to the promise of his pedigree and his racing record, the money was well spent.

Tom Lynch, Head Stud Groom at the National Stud, holding Bray Melody, outstanding brood mare of Ireland

Lynch has been with the National Stud for forty-nine years. Bray Melody is the dam of Happy Laughter (winner of the Thousand Guineas Classic in England in 1953), and of the two colts shown on page 107. She has been bought by an American and is waiting at the National Stud to be bred to Tulyar. With her is her new foal by Arctic Prince, a Derby winner.

Mixing Tulyar's evening mash

His feed is the same as the others at the National Stud except that it is augmented by a pint of Guiness Stout. The groom also gets a daily pint.

125

Mr. David Hyde

The manager of the National Stud points out horseshoes on the wall of the exercising hall. These show the annual winnings since 1900 of all horses bred here.

Yearling fillies at the National Stud

Patrick Doyle

The gardener and guide for the Japanese gardens at the National Stud points out some trees that are between four and six hundred years old.

Joe Cardiff, aged twenty-four

He has been with the National Stud for six years. These little windows make it possible for the groom to watch, without disturbing her, a mare about to foal.

Fleur Bleu examining her new baby

127

whole being was wrapped in his work and his responsibility. He had learned his lines and studied the dramatic effects which went with them as carefully as any actor and got them off perfectly. He had a curious, almost cockney, accent. Perhaps he started out a cockney and then acquired a brogue on top of it.

"This is the story of man from the crydle to the gryve," he told us, and went on to say that the garden had been originally conceived by a man who had lived for years in Japan. In 1904 he had imported an army of workmen from Japan, and they had labored seven years to build it.

We started at a curiously formed cave, which represented the Birth of Man. By a narrow path, we entered a larger, even darker cave, representing Man's Ignorance. Coming out of that, we climbed a narrow, winding path up a small hill, the Hill of Knowledge. "Having achieved the summit," said our guide, "man has several choices: he can go on to the Peak of Ambition; he can take the easy path through life; or he can just go downhill to nothing. He chooses the Peak of Ambition. Along the way he meets a woman. Their paths diverge and then come together again. Finally they cross a broken footpath of stones set in a stream, and again man has a choice of marrying and continuing toward the Peak of Ambition or of going an easier way. He chooses ambition again," said my guide, "and behind you is the Marriage Table." Sure enough, here was a tree pruned so that its surface was round and flat.

Man and his wife now continue on their way toward the Peak of Ambition, looking longingly at the Well of Wisdom, which they cannot yet reach, and having a quarrel or two on the way. Finally the Peak of Ambition is achieved. From there the path is ever-descending as man grows older. He attains the Well of Wisdom, stops in the Rest House, sees his wife ensconced in the Maternal Chair and his line of descendents safely established (this last scene was represented by a tree most interestingly pruned and trained to show man, his wife, and his progeny), and finally leaves through the Gates of Oblivion.

Among other things, our guide showed us some trees about three feet high that were several years old, some rocks that had been beautifully carved with tiny mountains, houses, etc., and other rocks in whose tiny crevasses grew trees not more than eight or ten inches high, and eighteen or nineteen years old. It is said that nothing in life can remain static—everything either progresses or recedes—but these little trees seemed truly to have arrested time. Nearby were wild trees of the same species, several feet high. The small size of those in the rocks was caused by the minute amounts of earth from which their roots took nourishment. They had not grown or changed in appearance in years, yet they looked healthy and showed no signs of dying.

On the way out I noticed a tiny pagoda apparently growing out of the water of a pond. Our guide told us that one of the workmen had annoyed the man whose project this garden was by always boasting of his ability to do anything better than anyone else. So he was told, by way of an impossible problem, to try his hand at building a Japanese pagoda on a tiny cone of land jutting up in the lake. The man did so, completing the task in one day, and his departing words were, "There's your damn pagoda! It's up to you to thatch it!"

On the way back we stopped at the station to pick up my wandering saddle. It was almost seven o'clock, and there was only one rather sad-looking baggage master in attendance.

"I am looking for a saddle done up in a burlap bag, addressed to Mrs. Sydney B. Self, and put on the train from Cashel this morning," I said. The man looked at me blankly. I tried again.

"In a gunny sack—a saddle, addressed, etc.—"

He poked around and finally pulled out a small cardboard box about eight inches square.

"No," I said, "a saddle, the kind you ride on. It must be here." He brought out a book and looked carefully down one column after another. Meanwhile I noticed a pile of boxes at the rear with what was obviously a saddle in a bag sitting on top.

"No," said he, "it didn't come in."

"Are you sure?" I said. "What's in that bag over there?"

"That couldn't be it," he said, looking vaguely in the direction in which I was pointing. "Those things just came in this afternoon."

"Would the train they came on stop at Cashel?"

"It would."

"Well, do you mind looking on the tag on that gunny sack on top, which obviously conceals a saddle, and see if my name is on it?"

After a short hesitation he moved, with great reluctance, to the object indicated, looked at it from several angles, finally took it down, brought it over to me, checked again in the book, asked my name and address, and, obviously with suspicion, handed it over. My saddle had come home to roost once more.

I had been invited out to dinner that night by family connections— David Laidlaw, who lived outside Dublin, was a cousin of Philip Hayes, my daughter Gincy's husband. David's father was in India and he and his young wife were living in the lodge, while his two aunts, one an invalid, lived together in the big house. Since David's other aunt was leaving for Scotland the next morning, the timing was rather awkward, but they invited me out for dinner and at eight o'clock David turned up to fetch me. We drove through a park, said to be the largest in the world that is completely enclosed. Barry had told me of a roundup of deer there—some outlyers that had escaped from the Ward Union Hounds and others which had been allowed to wander there for years. Now they had become a nuisance and it was decided to thin them out. A great number of horsemen were collected and a form of corral built, into which the deer were to be herded. But, alas, Irishmen are not American cowboys. All went well until they had the deer just ready to push into the chute that led into the corral; when the men tried to drive them suddenly, the deer panicked and, instead of going ahead, turned and charged the riders, knocking some down and vaulting over others, and escaped into the park. The upshot was that the horsemen were never able to capture them alive but had to shoot them.

The Laidlaw house was one of the lovely Georgian ones with paintings of their most cherished horses on the walls. The dinner was delicious, and I was sorry indeed that Miss Betty was not going to be in Dublin so that I could have had the pleasure of a longer acquaintance. On the way back David Laidlaw and I got into a discussion of the Marshall Plan. He remarked that in his opinion it was inadvisable in that outside aid simply delayed the arrival of the time when the governments and peoples of the various countries realized that they must learn to survive under their own power. He added that if he were an American he would feel very indignant at having to pay high taxes in order to support people who in many cases were simply lazy; that he, David Laidlaw, had been impressed, while visiting the States, by how hard the ordinary American businessman worked as compared to the ordinary European; and that he felt the whole situation most unfair. Of course, he did not take into consideration the value of the Marshall Plan as a means of preventing the infiltration of Communism. But Communism, since it is not a real threat in Ireland, is usually looked upon as a "bogie-man" and not as an actual fact.

XIV

The Ward Union Staghounds—A Chat with Stanislaus Lynch

At ten o'clock Barry and a pal of his turned up, towing an impressive array of equipment. We drove through Dublin and about ten miles into the country to the kennels of the Ward Union Hounds. This was to be my first experience with the famous stag hounds. I had been told that the ditches over which we would charge were the biggest and deepest in Ireland.

"Heaven help you if you get in one of *them*," my informants had said. " 'Twill be Easter before we get you dug out!"

Staghunting, to my mind, has all the advantages of fox hunting plus the fact that the quarry runs no danger of being hurt. A dozen or so stag and deer are kept in captivity at the kennel. During the season, one of these is loaded into a van (box) at each weekly meet and carried to the scene of action, where he is released.

On finding himself loose, he hesitates for a moment, looks around, then gives a mighty leap and is off. A stag can clear an eight-foot barrier with ease, and his flight is one of the most graceful and beautiful motions in the world. Stags run very fast and very straight, seldom circling, and depend on their speed rather than cover for escape.

Staghounds are larger and faster than fox hounds, but they are not nearly so fast as the stag. As soon as quarry and hounds are well away, the Field follows, and woe betide the unfortunate who gets a refusal or is held up for any reason, for unless he is very lucky he will not see hounds again that day. After an hour or so the stag may begin to feel that he has had enough exercise. He then runs into one of the many streams or drains and waits quietly for everyone to find him—a sort of hide-and-seek idea.

Stag, in their outdoor run

They look anxious when their pictures are taken.

Hounds and Field come up, the Huntsman hops off and catches Mr. Stag, the van is called, and the hero of the piece is reloaded and goes back to his stable. What could be nicer— a run in the country on a good day, then free transportation back to the hotel, where ample food and comfortable shelter awaits.

But sometimes, try as they will, hounds cannot keep up, or the stag goes through property forbidden to the hounds. In this case he escapes, so beginning in January or February, the hounds and riders follow not a carted stag but one of the so-called outlyers. Here the procedure is a little different. First the Huntsman ascertains where the stag has taken cover and sets people to watch to see that he is still there. These coverts are much larger with more and bigger trees than those I saw around the Limerick country. The meet is then held at the covert side, and hounds are put in just as in fox hunting. If

and when the stag is found, the procedure is the same—the Whips give him grace, get hounds on the line, then give the signal for all to follow.

The Ward Union Kennels is at a very old stagecoach inn. This inn, in Ashbourne, is where coaches entering or leaving Dublin used to change horses. Standing behind the inn, where the drive sweeps around in a crescent with the old cobblestones underfoot, it is not hard to picture those colorful days and hear again the shouts, the rattle of the hoofs, the jangling harness, see the steam rising from the tired horses and the torches of the link-boys as they came out to light the passengers. The courtyard and buildings have not changed since that time, nor have the faces; only the clothes are different.

The country now hunted by the Ward Union was first hunted, in 1828, by two packs of foxhounds, the Dubber and Hillyhood. In 1830 these packs were amalgamated and kept by a Mr. Gerrard as the Wards. Fallow deer and later red deer, the breed now hunted, were obtained, and in 1840 Lord Howth brought Mr. Broadley's staghounds from Leamington and hunted them with a subscription until 1842. These hounds were then sold to the Dublin Garrison and called the Garrison Hounds. When the Crimean War broke out, the Garrison Hounds and the Ward Hounds were amalgamated under the mastership of Mr. Peter Alley and called the Ward Union. The present Master is Mr. G. V. Malcomson and the Huntsman, T. Fitzsimons.

Courtesy of Fogra Failte

The Kennels of the Ward Union Stag Hounds at Ashbourne, County Meath

The huntsman, Tom Fitzsimons, gives his hounds their final instructions before going in to put on his pink coat. This is the back of the main house in which Tom and his family live. It used to be an old stagecoach inn where horses were changed for the final lap into Dublin.

It was Fitzsimons who met us at the door of the old inn, where he and his family now live. He led us through the house, into the back courtyard, and thence to where the stag and deer were housed. The animals had both indoor and outdoor apartments, and Barry and his friends busied themselves with pictures for about half an hour. Fitzsimons and his Whip, McCann, then brought the hounds out and again pictures were taken as they swarmed around him and up over the old pump in the center of the yard.

Then it was time for the Huntsman to go and put on his scarlet coat, so we went next door to a little pub for a snack. In a half hour's time we heard the sound of the horn and the whimper of hounds. Out into the street we went and coaxed Fitzsimons, now in his gay finery, to accept a stirrup cup from the attractive daughter of the pub keeper while more pictures were taken. Hounds were to be walked three or four miles to the meet, so we

133

Tom Fitzsimons

A stirrup cup is handed up to him by June Flannery at Ashbourne before he moves off to the meet at Ratoath, three miles away.

piled into our car and drove off to rejoin at the appointed place.

This was the usual village crossroads with a pub. Just around the corner was an old church with a pretty churchyard, the grass growing green between the stones. One by one the horse vans and trailers arrived. Mr. Malcomson, the Master, was among the first and greeted me most cordially. Presently a big van with six horses stopped and I was informed that my horse was aboard. I brought out my saddle and the lady groom took it but remarked that they would use their own girth. This proved to be a nylon one of the type that consists of a number of cords fastened to-

The Ward Union Cross Roads Meet at Ratoath Village, County Meath

Early arrivals were Mr. Eric Craigie and Mr. Patrick Hendron. Note that the signs are in both Gaelic and English, one of the government's ways of fostering Gaelic speech.

134

Fitzsimons and hounds (waiting in the background)

Meanwhile, the Master, Mr. George Malcolmson (center right in velvet cap), prepares to move off.

gether at intervals. I have seen them in cotton many times, for they are often used on horses that tend to get girth sores, but never before in nylon.

My horse, whose name was Fergus, was quite tall, a bay, with a rather large head, light quarters, good shoulders, and a kind look. I inwardly prayed that he knew his ditches and could keep up.

Presently we heard hounds and riding around the corner. I saw them just coming to the little churchyard, the red coats and black velvet caps showing brilliantly against the gray stone of the wall.

When we moved off I realized that we had quite a large Field, between seventy and eighty people. Many of them came up and spoke to me and a number of them called Fergus by name and assured me that he was a pearl. This was very good music to my ears.

We hacked a short distance along the road and then across two fields. In front of us was a large covert with several sizable trees. We were all bidden to hide ourselves over in one corner while Huntsman, Master, and Whip went to call on the stag. There was light, intermittent rain and a sharp wind. I looked around me. Most of the horses were all or part Thoroughbred and some were most disinclined to stand still. I got into conversation with a gentleman on a gray.

"I'm afraid we're rather rude here," he said. "People *will* crowd at the jumps, and unless you can stay in the first flight you're apt to find yourself bogged down and unable to jump at all. It's been pretty mucky, too, because of the rain."

I felt that "mucky" was an understatement. Fergus was over his fetlocks in mud, even where the going looked firm. I wondered how he was going to manipulate the coming ditches.

"I hear your ditches are rather large," I said.

"Yes, twelve to eighteen feet, most of them," he said, cheerfully. "That's width, of course. They can be any depth! You'll find the horses here have rather a different technique. But you've got a good mount, you don't need to worry."

I hoped he was right. A restive

Hounds putting to covert to find an outlying stag

chestnut Thoroughbred idled up and let fly, catching the gray on the shin. I took careful note of him and his rider to be sure that I didn't follow too close on his heels. The Field Master now decided to investigate what was going on in the covert. Dismounting, he turned his horse over to a little boy of about seven who happened to be standing by (evidently it was taken for granted that any child in Ireland knew how to handle a nervous horse) and, bidding him walk the animal, burrowed his way through the brush.

A few minutes after this came a wave of excitement. Everyone swung around, and a hundred yards away, over the high wall sprang the stag. He landed galloping. Another hundred yards behind him came the hounds, followed by the staff. All of us got underway as quickly as possible, and I was glad that I had been standing nearer to the point of departure than three quarters of the field. Fergus was willing and swift. Ahead of me but fast disappearing were the deer, hounds, and staff; all around me were galloping horses, the riders standing

Courtesy of Fogra Fuille

The chase

The stag (a tiny dot in the left background) breaks covert and is pursued hotly by hounds (middle distance) and the field.

in their stirrups; behind, the little boy held on as best he could to the Field Master's horse, which, naturally enough, was determined not to miss the fun.

And then we came to the first ditch. Peg Watt's admonitions rang in my ears: "Never look down!" But I couldn't resist a peek when my turn came to jump. I found myself balanced on the muddy edge of a bottomless pit. Three feet below me was a little shelf less than two feet square. To my amazement, Fergus gathered his feet under him and slid down to

this little shelf; then, with a mighty spring, he sailed in an arc, landing perceptibly later on another little shelf, of the same dimensions and equally muddy, on the far side of the pit. Another spring, shoes pulling out of the mud with a squelching, sucking noise, brought us to the top again, and we were off. I had successfully maneuvered my first Ward Union ditch—or, rather, Fergus had; I had nothing to do with it.

For sixteen miles we ran with never a check, except for the moment of waiting for a turn at the ditches.

I tried to keep out front as I had been warned to do, for I could see that there would be little left of those shelves after sixty riders had crossed. I was lucky and always managed somehow, though many times I wondered how Fergus ever spanned those huge chasms.

At the end of an hour we finally pulled up. There were not so many in the Field now, and some looked pretty jaded, but Fergus was not even breathing heavily! We could hear hounds but could not see them. Then there was silence. I was directly behind the Master. Presently one of the countrymen who seem to spring up out of the earth at such times appeared and said that the stag had gone off to our left, where wire prevented our following. We went down a lane and onto one of the main roads. Traffic was not thick, but there were cars and lorries going fast in both directions. Down the hard road at a gallop went the Master, one Whip, and the remainder of the Field. How could the horses stand it, and what would happen if one of those big lorries decided not to pull over? But we got to the next lane in safety and again were off.

Presently we were told to wait while the officials reconnoitered, and then I had the good fortune to see one of the most beautiful sights in my experience. A hundred yards away, on the other side of a poplar-bordered stream, ran a farm road. Almost opposite me was a high barway, which looked to be over six feet, of natural saplings. As we stood there, the stag came loping at an easy, rhythmic gait along the road, took off fifteen or twenty feet from the barrier, floated like a feather in a long arc, landed lightly and easily and continued his canter, disappearing presently in the distance. There was a moment of quietness, then along the same track came the hounds and the hunt staff. They were forced to stop at the barrier until a rail was removed. On our side, we galloped parallel until we found a place to jump over the river, then followed.

We had several more runs but none so fast, long, or exciting as that first one. However, I was well up with hounds when the deer entered country over which the Master preferred not to hunt. Hounds were called off, and we started for home. I was glad to find myself in this position; for once I was able to go up to the Master and thank him for a fine day. We rode along together for several miles and he told me a number of things which I, occupied with staying on and up front, had missed. It seems that several of the Field were in disgrace for riding over freshly planted land.

"They said they were sorry, of course," said the Master, "but I sent them all in to apologize to the farmer themselves. And most of them should have known better." At this point one of the culprits, an older man in a topper, rode up.

"I'm terribly sorry, Master," he said. "I know it was very careless of me, but I guess we fixed it up with the man."

"Maybe you did," said the Master,

"but remember that though he won't forbid us his land now, the next time some fool does the same thing he will, and there'll be nothing any of us can do about it. Nor can I blame him."

It appears that there had been a good deal of other grief in the way of horses in ditches which I had not seen, but no one was hurt and all the horses were rescued somehow or other. Again I felt that there is nothing in the world that can compare with the stamina, courage, and willingness of the Irish hireling.

On my return to the Royal Hibernian I inquired at the desk as to whether there had been a call for me, for Mr. Stanislaus Lynch had promised to give me a ring. Nothing had been heard from him, so I went up and took a quick bath, then came down to sit in the lobby, have a most delicious tea, and wait for the call. I pointed out my position to the telephone operator and told her to be sure to let me know when my call came through.

The Royal Hibernian tea is just what the doctor ordered after a strenuous hunt. An enormous major-domo in white tie and tails takes the order. "Plain or afternoon?" he says. This, translated, means, "Just tea, or tea with fixings?" I chose the latter. A tray containing the tea things and a plate of buns was brought up and placed on a table before me, then a boy in a tuxedo rolled up a wagon with two shelves piled with all kinds of goodies. All this munificence cost two and six, or less than fifty cents.

Five o'clock came, five thirty, and six, but no call from Mr. Lynch. What could have happened to the man! Then, at six twenty, the P.A. system called my name. At last! I went to the phone booth, expecting to hear Mr. Lynch's cheerful Irish voice, but instead, a voice with a heavy unidentifiable accent greeted me. It was Major Miville, calling from London. Major Miville is the brother-in-law of Mrs. de Trafford. She had assured me that my tour of stud farms would not be complete unless I visited Major Miville's, outside Dublin. The stud farm, called Ballykeane, was reputedly one of the most beautiful in Ireland. She herself had to come up to Dublin on an errand and had agreed to meet me on Sunday morning to drive me out, since she was sure that I could never find my way alone. Now this was Major Miville calling from London to confirm the invitation and to suggest that I spend the night at his house in Dublin. Later I learned that he had come all the way over from England just on my account! He is Swiss and speaks English, or, rather, the Irish version of English, with a heavy French accent. No wonder I had a bit of trouble understanding him, especially since the connection was anything but good!

When my call was terminated the telephone operator asked me if I had got the other call that had come in at five twenty from Mr. Lynch. I looked a bit startled. "I have been sitting right here in the lobby waiting for that call since five," I said.

"Now isn't that too bad," said the operator. "Sure, we paged you, but it must be the loud speaker isn't working. It does that sometimes, but we've no way of knowing when it's on and when it isn't because we can't hear it from here. And Mr. Lynch said you were to call him right back!"

Well, there was nothing to be done but call Mr. Lynch then, but when I got his house he himself had gone out. So I sat down again to wait! I tell this story as a warning against anyone's depending on getting calls in Ireland. Not only must you tell where you are waiting; it is well to ask every few minutes whether anything has come in, or else bribe one of the little page boys to stand at your elbow and be your contact with the switchboard. Eventually I reached Mr. Lynch.

"I said to myself when you didn't call, 'they're still digging the poor lady out of the ditch!' " he said. He then agreed to come over about eight so that we could have a chat.

Mr. Lynch turned out to be just as nice as I had supposed he would be.

He is a writer, doing articles for magazines and papers all over the world on various aspects of horse activities, and has also published several books of poetry. He gave me the name of his illustrator and promised to arrange a meeting between us when I came back to Dublin with Sydney. He also advised me to stay over on Monday and hunt with the Meath rather than try to get a hunt with the Ormund. I had rather planned on the latter, since the Ormund was not too far from Dromoland, where I expected to spend Monday night, but I took Mr. Lynch's advice and called the man who had provided me with the gallant Fergus to make arrangements for Monday.

I had hoped to find time while in Dublin to go to the famous Abbey Theatre, but it was now too late for that. Tomorrow night I would be spending with the Mivilles, and the following night, I hoped, would find me a hundred and twenty miles away.

XV

Ballykeane and the Mivilles

Mrs. de Trafford arrived at ten thirty to drive me out to Ballykeane. I had already been on the telephone for over an hour. To begin with, I had called Dromoland to check on my reservations for the following night. After I had been assured that they were being held and had reminded them that I would be getting in very late, the secretary said, rather casually, "By the way, did you get that long cablegram that came to you from *Time,* Inc., last Thursday? We forwarded it to the Dunraven Arms for you." Of course I hadn't. Fortunately she had a copy. I had given *Time* a detailed explanation of why I had wanted their photographer for this weekend. The gist of their cablegram was that they were sending a man over from London to take pictures of the National Stud on Monday. But I had already taken these pictures and was planning to hunt with the Meath on Monday. There could be no point in having the National Stud photographed again; I would far rather have their man come down to Adare a day early and take Lord Dunraven's stud the day before he took the point-to-point. I had had difficulty from the beginning in convincing the editors that just because the National Stud was owned by the government it was not necessarily the most important and colorful stud in Ireland. Now that I had visited several studs, I felt even more strongly than before that I could not give a true picture of the Irish horse industry unless I had pictures of and material concerning several stud establishments, each prominent for a different reason.

The thing to do was to contact Mr. Montgomery. I tried several times, trailing him from one place to another, but failed. I was still trying when Mrs. de Trafford arrived.

"Can we call him from Bally-keane?" I asked.

"Yes, but we had better check to be sure that the telephone service is on all day Sunday," she said. "It is an exchange that doesn't function at certain hours." So we asked the operator, who looked it up and told us that we could call until seven. With this in mind, I left a message at Mr. Montgomery's that I would call between twelve and two. Alas, for the inaccuracy of the Irish! Numbers certainly confuse them. On arriving at Ballykeane we discovered that we couldn't call *before* seven, and poor Mrs. de Trafford had to drive me another several miles to a different town.

The drive out to Ballykeane was lovely. We kept catching glimpses of unusually formed peaks and of the sea. On both sides of the road were great plantations of rhododendrons, which must be magnificent in the spring.

In one little town I noticed an oddly shaped "caravan," or gypsy trailer, perched on blocks. "A most unusual old woman lives there," Mrs. de Trafford told me. "I picked her up and gave her a lift one day. She looks like one of the ordinary tinkers, but I was surprised to find that she is a woman of culture, intelligence and education. She just *likes* to live in a caravan! She has lived there the greater part of her life, and though her children and other relatives are perfectly willing to take her in or even to set her up in a proper house, she will have none of it! They think it's quite a scandal, I assure you."

Ballykeane is near Killbride, and glad I was to have a guide, for it would not have been easy to find the first time. Later I came out alone with Sydney and had no difficulty, partly because I asked directions frequently and partly because Major Miville is one of the few gentlemen in Ireland who has signposts pointing the way to his place. This was essential, for the last two or three miles was along isolated little country lanes, with frequent crossroads.

We wound down a hill and made a sharp turn. Then, against the green of the hill, the lovely pink Georgian house came into view. Of all the houses I saw in Ireland I think this one will live longest in my memory. The front of the place was guarded by a huge monkey puzzle tree. (Ever since I had first read Kipling's amusing story, "The Monkey Puzzler," I had wanted to see one of these trees.)

Courtesy of Major Eric Miville
Photograph by Mrs. Raymond de Trafford

Ballykeane House

A very beautiful example of Georgian architecture. It is of pale pink plaster with an Adam doorway and a huge monkey puzzle tree beside it.

It would indeed puzzle a monkey to climb one, for the leaves are sabre-shaped and saw-tooth-edged, the branches grow very close together, and the foliage is very luxuriant. The sharp leaves are two or three feet long and about four inches wide, and are very thick and inflexible. The Mivilles use them as guards between the copper fire railings and the fire, to keep their French bulldogs from lying there!

The doorway at Ballykeane is unusually beautiful, as can be seen in the picture on page 142. Like the ceilings and walls throughout the building, the doorway has lovely floral designs of sculptured plaster. When Major Miville bought the house the plaster was in bad condition; much of it was missing, other parts were in fragments. With infinite patience he restored these frescoes and the old mantlepieces, many of which were also missing. The old house was brought back to its original glory. When I visited the house, the job was not yet finished. Mrs. Miville's room was being redecorated and remodeled, with two tiers of doors in French blue and white, one above the other, forming a recess for the bed. All the furniture is old and of lovely design. The rooms are large and almost square, with high ceilings. There are two living rooms, one an informal one hung with colorful banners brought by the Major from Africa when he was a member of the Foreign Legion.

In this room also were many photographs of Major Miville when he was active as a show jumper. One

Courtesy of Major Eric Miville
Photograph by Mrs. Raymond de Trafford

Looking through the doorway at Ballykeane

particularly striking shot showed him going over a very big triple-bar, the spread over six feet and the height of the highest element certainly five. The horse is shown in the air, its body level, well above the height of the jump; yet the hind legs have already cleared the obstacle. The trajectory of that horse's flight, considering that the jump was untouched and that, having cleared it, the animal had still not started to descend, is phenomenal. On another table was a photograph of Major Miville in his days as a member of the French Foreign Legion. I had been told that he, in his white uniform, was considered the most romantic unattached male in a society consisting largely of unattached males in alluring uniforms of one kind or another, and I can well believe it.

For to the glamour of the uniform was added the glory and honor of an almost unbelievable military career.

Major Miville, a Swiss, enlisted in the Finnish army when that little country was besieged by Russia. When the Finns capitulated he fled by ship to the United States. Since he had no papers and not one penny, he was detained at Ellis Island. Fortunately he was able to get word to Bernard Baruch, whose daughter he had previously met, and Baruch immediately arranged his release and relieved his temporary financial dilemma. Miville's one idea was to get back into the army, any army, and go on fighting. The English wouldn't have him because they had not called up all of their own young men. The French army was in the process of capitulation. The United States had not yet entered the war. There remained the French Foreign Legion. Somehow Miville got himself to Africa and enlisted. He then fought in one theatre after the other, going through Africa, Europe, and Asia. At the end of the war his regiment of 3400 men had been reduced to 46. If there was a bullet with Major Miville's name on it, it never found him.

For some years after the war he bought troopers' horses for the French army. In so doing he spent a great deal of time in Ireland, combing the country for suitable mounts. When injuries sustained in jumping competitions made it inadvisable for him to continue riding he bought Ballykeane, rebuilding the original stone structures, which were in a semi-ruined condition, and making them into stables. These buildings date back to the early seventeenth century. They are beautiful in their simplicity of line, and I wish I could have seen them in the rose season, for the walls are covered with climbers.

Ballykeane is a stud farm, not a stud, for there is no stallion kept there. Major Miville sends his yearlings to Doncaster. He had one beautiful chestnut two-year-old that was injured in transportation and consequently missed the sales, but she is recovering and he expects her to come through without a blemish.

The most notable colt that Major Miville has bred of recent years is Turn To, the gelding that was shipped to America, won the Garden State Stakes at Camden, New Jersey, and was, when I was in Ireland, the favorite for the Kentucky Derby. Unfortunately, a few weeks before the race he bowed a tendon and has had to be retired to stud.

Since the horse market is unpredictable, Major Miville also raises sheep, which he finds very profitable. Certainly his whole establishment seems beautifully kept and organized. Although he spends a great deal of his time in England or on the Continent, Major Miville is obviously not the typical absentee owner who buys a place, finances it, and leaves the running of it to a hired manager.

Mrs. Miville, Mrs. de Trafford's sister, is another Irish beauty, with the characteristically Irish lovely skin, dark hair, and delicate bone structure which so delights the eye. With ap-

Courtesy of Major Eric Miville
Photograph by Mrs. Raymond de Trafford

Ballykeane Stables

These buildings date back to about 1640. They are of stone and are covered with climbing roses. Major Miville found them in bad repair and reconstructed them from the original materials, following the original lines.

parently everything that life can offer —a devoted and romantic husband, a show place, perfectly trained servants and personal beauty as well—Mrs. Miville showed not the slightest signs of being spoiled or complacent. I cannot imagine an American in a similar situation (if there actually is one) welcoming a stranger in as charming and unself-conscious a manner as Mrs. Miville presented to me. Everything was done to make me feel comfortable and at home, and when I heard that they had both come all the way over from London just so that they could be there to show me around I was ashamed to have put them to so much trouble.

It was three o'clock before I was finally able to reach Mr. Montgomery again and learn from him that Burrows, the *Life* photographer, had been put off and that I could hunt with the Meath.

Very early on Monday morning, Major Miville, who was going back to London, Mrs. de Trafford, and I drove back to Dublin. On our arrival I found that I had acquired a flat overnight. The car was parked in a lot adjacent to the Royal Hibernian. Thinking myself fortunate that the flat had not occurred on the road, I gave my key to the porter and asked him to have it fixed while I was hunting.

This day was going to be a tough one: I certainly could not get back from hunting before six; I had then to change, have dinner, and drive the many weary miles that lay between Dublin and Dromoland, finding my way for the first time late at night. I hoped to reach Dromoland before midnight, for I had to meet Sydney at Shannon at three A.M. I told this to the porter, who promised that he would see to the car, and at ten thirty my friend Barry, the photographer, arrived to take me to the hunt. The Irish Tourist Bureau had thought it would be a good idea to get some pictures of this both for my purposes and for theirs. I was always delighted to have Barry along, for he knew everyone and told so many anecdotes.

XVI

Hunting with the Meath

The livery of the Meath Foxhounds is red with a dark blue collar, evening-dress sky blue. The kennels are at Nugentstown, Kells, outside Dublin. The pack consists of forty couples and has a joint Mastership, Lieutenant Colonel Cameron and Mr. J. P. McAuley sharing the honors. The kennel Huntsman and first Whip is D. Dunne, and the second Whip is D. Durney. The country is more rolling and hilly than that over which I hunted with the Ward Union. I was unable to find out anything about the history of the Meath but it is certainly one of the oldest packs of Ireland.

Hounds were meeting outside Rainsford House, which made this the first "lawn meet" I had attended. Rainsford House is owned by a delightful gentleman of ninety-seven named Captain R. H. Fowler (his picture is on page 148). When I stop to think that at his advanced age

Captain Fowler not only has full possession of his faculties but also still drives a car, shoots, and gave up active hunting only a few years ago, I am again impressed by the stamina and active longevity of those remarkable people the Irish.

True to their traditional courtesy, when Colonel Cameron, who was first on the scene, found that I wanted to take some pictures of hounds he had the Huntsman bring them up to Rainsford House itself so that we might have the mansion as a background, and then most obligingly posed for us.

Although this day with the Meath was not outstanding from a hunting point of view—we got no really long runs and ran only a few foxes—it was very outstanding from the point of view of variety of members of the field. To begin with, there was Captain Fowler's nephew, Briga-

Captain Fowler, aged ninety-seven, outside Rainsford House

dier B. J. Fowler, who rode a scrubby little pony not over thirteen-two, though he himself was tall. They came to grief once, as the picture on page 150 shows, and the pony got a wetting, though his rider seems to be dry enough. Although he was wearing a rather odd assortment of clothes, I was told that normally Brigadier Fowler was turned out formally, so it was apparent that, like Dr. Harris, the man in the green golf-stockings with whom I hunted with the Scarteen Hunt, Brigadier Fowler's decision to hunt that day had been a hasty one. This type of incident shows most clearly how truly the Irish love hunting as a sport. No American I know would have the temerity to appear under such circumstances.

Courtesy of Fogra Failte

Lieutenant Colonel Cameron, Joint Master of the Meath Hounds, outside Rainsford House

Waiting for the hounds to be thrown into covert

The Brigadier's wife was also out, as was their little girl, who rode a pony, accompanied by a friend on another pony. These little ponies are grass fed, never stabled or clipped. They are clever and willing and, I think, greatly to be preferred for children to the hot-blooded variety such as the little one Tom rode in the Golden Vale Hunt. In addition to this little girl there was an older daughter of the Fowlers who was schooling a very hot Thoroughbred in a thoroughly workmanlike manner, and a young man who told me that he himself had hunted the same pony on which his young sister now rode.

One of the members rode an Appaloosa horse. This is a most unusual breed to see in Ireland, so unusual that the Irish themselves knew nothing about it and supposed it to be a freak. Appaloosa horses have become quite common in the United States. They are distinguished by their peculiar markings, which take the form of large, circular splotches in black or chocolate brown on a white or mottled gray background. For this reason they are sometimes called "raindrop" horses. They are a breed that was cherished by the American Indians for their speed and stamina. Along with the mustang, they were

149

A rider

Having come to grief on the far side, he negotiates a hairy bank on foot. The seemingly cloven hoof of his shaggy mount is an optical illusion caused by the proximity of a rock.

introduced by the Spanish under Cortez. One sees pictures of them in very early paintings, including those of Lippizan horses. The Appaloosa horses also are one of the few breeds with pink skin. I think it was the Huntsman who rode the Appaloosa, and everyone was very much interested when I told them the history of the breed.

One of the most colorful figures in the Field was Dr. Dunn, a sporting priest who has given up material gain so that he may indulge in his favorite sport. Dr. Dunn has a teaching posi-tion, as I understood it, at a seminary. He had refused offers of a parish of his own many times, for he did not want to leave the vicinity of the Meath Hounds nor take on duties which might curtail his freedom to follow them. He told me that he often hunted four days a week, sometimes five, and that it was his ambition, as yet unachieved, to hunt six. He was a man certainly nearing if not past, sixty, with a benign expression and a twinkle in his eye. He wore a pair of black hunting boots, meticulously polished and patched and repatched

Small fry on a typical shaggy pony

until one wondered if any of the original leather was left. His corduroy breeches, originally black, had acquired a beautiful patina of age. His coat was cut like none I have ever seen outside the drawings of Cruikshank, his clerical collar and black vest proclaimed his profession and looked startlingly new in contrast to the rest of his garments, and his high silk hat had been raked by all the thorns in Ireland.

He rode a brown or dark bay mare named, I think, Molly, who I am sure was thoroughly educated in the art of plowing as well as in that of hunting. He told me that he had two more like her at home, both mares, and I was told by others that he had named them for ladies of his acquaintance.

Dr. Dunn and I had quite a chat on the merits of a countryman of mine who had hunted with the Meath and with whom the good Doctor had become very friendly.

"He was a very terror in the Field," he told me. "He took his own line and nobody could keep up to him. I never saw such a bold man. We became good friends but the only thing was he insisted on keeping me up every night until three o'clock arguing about Communism. 'Don't be trying to get me excited about Communism,' I told him. 'We've no such problem here in Ireland and I'm too taken up with the ones we have to worry about somebody else's.' But he kept at me, and before his visit was over he had me near wore out from lack of sleep. Other than that he was a fine fellow and I doubt if I'll ever see another like him in the Hunt Field."

I asked him how he managed to get in so much hunting. "I just tell my young people not to come to see me before six o'clock on hunting days," he said. "And if they do they just sit and cool their heels 'til I get back. There's one going to be doing that tonight, I'm sure, but if we're in luck the fox will run back toward where I'm to meet the boy that's to take my horse and I won't be too late."

Quite early in the hunt, I had an opportunity to savor Dr. Dunn's wit as well as his good humor. The little Fowler girl, on her nineteen-year-old mount, had essayed a jump that was a bit big and come a cropper.

Only her feelings were bruised, but since this was just her second hunt, she was a bit upset. She was sitting rather glumly beside the other little girl, who was looking smug at having taken the same fence successfully, when Dr. Dunn rode to them.

"Have you two young ladies been out with the Ward Union?" I heard him ask. Now, the Ward Union, with its big ditches and the speed of the chase that the stag and staghounds provide, demands more in the way of fine horseflesh and experienced riding than any other hunt in Ireland. Both the little girls looked a little surprised at the question. And then the older admitted shyly that they had not yet had that privilege.

"Well," said the good Doctor, "I don't know your parents, but I'm sure you're most unfortunate in having them"—implying, of course, that any intelligent parents would have had such prodigies out with the Wards long since.

The Irish are very proud and fond of their sporting priests. Father MacCarthy, whom I met in Limerick, was another example. He was at the dinner that the "Kentucky Colonels" gave and I also saw him at the point-to-point. I never saw him in the hunting field, but he was no less enthusiastic about the sport than Dr. Dunn. He confirmed a story that had been told me concerning the great good luck he had had in picking up hounds again after a funeral.

"Irish funerals come at a bad time," said Father MacCarthy. "They are all held at one o'clock, and natu-rally this usually interferes with hunting. But on this day I had really good luck. I went to the Meet at eleven and hunted for an hour and a half, then I turned my horse over to the boy and told him to take him along to a covert that I knew they were going to draw, not too far from the church. It all depended on how the fox broke, of course. After the funeral was over I drove down and picked up my horse. I hadn't any more than got my feet in the stirrups when right past me went the fox, the hounds boiling along on his tail, and I fell in behind. I tell you I had them all to myself, and were the others jealous!"

What a delightful race! Not rain nor hail nor sudden death shall interfere with the all-important sport of hunting the fox!

Another member of the Field who was most helpful in pointing out various things of interest was a long, lean, youngish Irishman in brown corduroys, a bright flannel shirt, and gay galluses. When first I saw him he was sprinting over the fields on foot. Then I saw him driving along the road in a car. He tried to be helpful to the photographers but they were entirely unable to keep up with him. Later in the day I saw him mounted on three different horses. Evidently, like Pat Scanlan, he sometimes went to hunts with no mount but had the good luck to take over for someone else.

It was he who pointed out a castle in the distance which had belonged to the Duke of Wellington. From where I first saw it, it looked habita-

Beautiful views in County Meath countryside

ble, but some time later we passed behind it and I saw that the front was just a shell. All around it on every knoll were curious, pointed concrete structures. They were quite high, spirelike buildings which spread out at the base into covered areas with open archways. I could not imagine what their purpose was, but my friend of the galluses explained that the Duke was inordinately fond of picnics and loved having his friends drive up from Dublin to enjoy these little parties with him. Now, obviously, the best place for a picnic is some sheltered spot, preferably with a view. Of spots with views there were plenty,

but shelter was another matter. So the Duke solved the problem by building these "gazabos," putting one on each hilltop that was desirable and within easy riding distance of the castle. There, regardless of weather, he and his friends could enjoy their meals *al fresco*—surely a wise precaution in view of the surprising suddenness of the rain storms in Ireland.

If we did not have many runs, we certainly had many foot followers and spectators on this Monday afternoon. I gathered that hounds did not often hunt this territory due to the sparseness of foxes, so all the farmers were out. They made picturesque groups silhouetted against the sky on the sharp little knolls.

Our last fox was found in a field of kale and run to ground after a short mile or so. Vans and horse-boxes were waiting on the roadside nearby so I thanked the Master, collected my escorts, and we wended our way back to Dublin. They had taken many pictures but had not got any very good action shots.

I am completely convinced that the only way to get good action pictures of fox-hunting is to wear a camera around your neck and snap them as you go over the jumps!

XVII

Dromoland—The Arrival of Sydney

I arrived back at the hotel shortly before seven to find that nothing had been done about my flat tire. The porter said he had not taken the keys. They must have been given to the other man, he said, and he had gone off duty without reporting it.

"But I have to drive down to Dromoland tonight."

"Sure, just sit yourself down, Madam, and have a bite to eat and we'll have it done right away," said the porter. So I went to my room, finished packing, had a bath, and came down again. I could see my car out of the window, still standing sadly on three wheels, the other tire flat as ever. I reminded the porter, who assured me that all was being taken care of, and went in and had dinner. Three quarters of an hour later I returned to see the car on a jack. This was at least progress, but it was nearly half past eight before the tire had

been repaired and I finally set out for Dromoland.

I was somewhat weary to start with, and after the first fifty miles of trying to dodge bicycles and watch road signs at the same time I was even wearier. I know nothing more nerve-wracking than driving in Ireland at night. The bicycle riders must have the most implicit faith either in a protective deity or in the skill of the motorists, for they amble gaily back and forth across the road, forgetting that the minute reflecting disks which some of them wear on their rear fenders are useless when a car or lorry, headlights on full, approaches from the opposite direction.

Although hunting does not seem to engender an appetite in me, it develops an unquenchable thirst. So I stopped at every other town, searched for some place which looked as though the inhabitants might give me a glass of water, and went in to beg one. This is not so easy as it sounds, for the Irish are not a water-drinking nation. I had trouble finding likely places at which to assuage my inordinate thirst, especially as it grew later and midnight came and then one o'clock. What with thirst and fatigue, I was delighted when the lights of the Shannon airport finally showed up. Now I had only to find my way for the remaining fourteen miles, which were new to me. It was now after one thirty. I reached Newmarket-on-Fergus, a tiny hamlet where not a light showed, and went on. Finally, on my right I saw the demesne walls which I hoped belonged to Dromoland. Then came huge iron gates, firmly fastened with an enormous padlock that looked like something Walt Disney might have conceived. There was a tiny lodge beyond the gates and, thank fortune, a dim light. I honked my horn loudly, the sound coming back to me from the lonely hills. After a long wait the door opened a crack and a woman appeared.

"Dromoland?" I asked.

"Yes, Madam, just follow the drive," she said, unlocking the gates and swinging them wide.

"I'll be coming out again shortly, so you'd better not lock up again—that is, if you want any sleep," I said. The woman looked dubious. Somehow, with the light traffic, I didn't feel she'd run too great a risk if she left the gates open, but I had an idea that as soon as I was out of sight they'd be locked again.

"Just follow the drive," she had said. I did so for what seemed miles, with hares and rabbits hopping out in front of the car every fifty feet. And still no sight of the castle. Then I came to a fork. There was no sign as to which way I was to go, and both roads seemed about equally well travelled. I chose the right. After a bit I could see looming in front of me, a vast pile of rock bigger than the Louvre, and as black and silent as a sepulchre. I wandered on, through archways, past plazas and steps. At last I could go no further; there was a low wall in front of me and what was obviously a parking area on my right. I got out of the car and looked up. The sky overhead was velvet black pierced with millions of stars and against them was silhouetted the huge towered and ramparted stone pile that was Dromoland. High up at a tiny window at the very top of a round tower was a light, the only one in all that great mass. Yet I had telephoned and said that I would be in very late. In the ordinary house one might find an unlatched door, an open window, or some other way of legal or illegal entry. If this failed one might even throw a pebble at a likely window and hope to get attention that way. But how does one storm a medieval castle, built to repel hordes of invaders, whose only sign of life is a light several stories in the air?

I climbed the steps and fumbled around the enormous oaken doorway. To the right I found a dangling knob which might or might not be a bell pull. It had about as much feeling of attachment as a broken wrist and

Dromoland Castle, near Shannon, owned by the Earl of Inchiquin

waggled feebly when I gave it two hopeful yanks. I could determine no immediate reaction so, giving one more pull for good measure, I retired to the car in case the knob released mastiffs instead of bringing succor to a lonely tired woman seeking sanctuary. Of course I could always curl up on the back seat. But what about Sydney, due in at Shannon in a couple of hours? Somehow I didn't feel he'd take kindly to this kind of reception. After long, long minutes I saw a light in one of the lower windows, and then another. And then, oh then, there was a clanking of iron and the great door opened! A bewrappered, sleepy figure greeted me.

"It is Mrs. Self?"

"It is," I said in my best Irish.

"We had given you up."

We were soon joined by a maid, who had got quickly into a gray cotton uniform. By this time I had the bags out and was looking around the great entry hall. On all sides were pictures and portraits of men and women of another era. They looked down on me in their bygone finery as though to ask how anything as drably dressed as I could have gained entry. And the place was cold! It was the first time I had really felt cold in Ireland. (It developed later that Lord Inchiquin had been having trouble with his central heating.) I explained about having to go out again almost immediately and the housekeeper-secretary who had let me in said she would call the airport and find out what time the plane was actually expected. This she did and came back with the news that it was not due until four o'clock. I didn't know how literally to take this, since my own plane had not been due until four forty-five and I had arrived at three.

I was now led up a beautiful stairway, down a long gallery where more lords and ladies stared down at me, around several corners, and was finally ushered into a huge bedroom. There was no fire going but the maid disappeared in search of kindling.

Meanwhile I was taken into an adjoining suite of small rooms, one of which was a bathroom, and given a demonstration of how the "geyser" over the tub worked. My kind guide then left me after I had assured her that there was nothing more she could do for me. The maid came back, got my fire going, and disappeared again to fill my hot-water bottle.

By the time she had done this and I had taken a few things out of the suitcase it was two thirty, obviously too late to go to bed and too early to go to Shannon, and too cold to sit around and read! I decided the best thing was to have another hot bath. Here I met with two problems: first, I could find no bathtowels, and second, I wasn't sure I could remember the intricate system of knob turnings which I had been assured would produce hot water in an instant. Since a bath without towels would be worse than useless I went on a prowl for these first. Have you ever found your way around a medieval castle at two thirty in the morning with no knowledge of what other lodgers there may be or of the lighting system? It is quite an experience. Fortunately, there was apparently no one at all in my end of the building and no ghosts either. The third or fourth door I opened proved to be a bedroom equipped with bath towels and I stole two. They were lovely and big and soft and well worth the stealing. Then I worked on the geyser. With the well-known trial-and-error system I finally got it to work and, sure enough, in an instant boiling water poured down

from overhead. When I tried to turn it off I found this quite a different problem. When I screwed the knob as tightly as I could, the water stopped, but an ominous groaning continued. At intervals, while I lay and luxuriated, there would be a sudden spurt of water. The geyser was not located over my head, which was fortunate, but over my knees, and after the first attack of boiling water I kept my knees out of the way. After a long soak I went back to my room, leaving the geyser still grumbling and the intermittent showers still descending.

At quarter of four I crept down the long passageways and out again to my car. I had been told that the shortest way back to the lodge was not the way I had come but straight ahead in the direction in which my car was pointing. I don't believe my informant could have looked very carefully at the way my car was pointing, for it was heading directly for the low stone wall. The drive appeared to continue to my left, which seemed a logical route. I got in and started the motor, drove forward a few feet, turning to the left, and then some inner sense or perhaps my personal guardian angel stopped me. It might be well to do a little reconnoitering. I got out of my car and walked forward—to find that I had been about to drive down a steep flight of stone steps! If Sydney would not have appreciated having to spend his first night in the back seat of a car, he would like even less to get off the plane and be told that his cherished wife, having come scatheless through numerous hunts and avoided the pitfalls of the Irish bathtub, had ended up by driving down a twelve-foot precipice and was now in the hospital. Somehow I felt that the Irish Tourist Bureau would take a dim view of my wrecking their car, also.

More reconnoitering led me to a nice, gently sloping driveway on my right. This I took and presently found myself at the lodge gates. I had done the caretaker an injustice. This time the gates were open and I did not have to stop.

At Shannon I had to wait another half hour but at last the plane came in and through the plate-glass window I saw my dear husband, along with the other passengers, making his way toward the customs and immigration officials. How welcome was his smiling face! But not nearly so welcome as mine was to him, for I discovered that my last letter telling about the arrangements and promising to meet him had miscarried or been delayed and he had no idea where in Ireland I was or who would meet him!

The room at Dromoland was slightly warmer when we got back but Sydney was not yet inured to the climate and had not had the forethought to bring any long-johns, so he felt chilly. I had told the secretary-housekeeper that we would not be down before nine and had ordered breakfast for that time but since neither of us had got to bed until five we did not actually get downstairs until nearly ten. In the big dining room we found a long sideboard with a tremendous electric warming plate running the length of it. On this plate our breakfast was patiently waiting, still hot, as was the coffee. It is the custom at Dromoland for all the guests to sit at one long refectory table. Our places had been set for us at one end of this table, and while we ate we admired the beautiful silverware on display. Presently Lord Inchiquin joined us, explaining that he was busy trying to get someone to fix his heating system but would be free to show us around the place after we had finished breakfast.

I wish we could have come to Dromoland at a different time of the year, for one could see that the formal gardens would be lovely in spring. They were beautifully laid out and kept, but, of course, now nothing was blooming. I took some pictures of the castle and one of a formal garden with Lord Inchiquin disappearing rapidly out the gate to meet his heating man. A little later we were shown the family portraits. The Earl's family name is O'Brian and he is "The O'Brian." His family records go back to the old King Brian Boroimhe, who was killed at the Battle of Clontarf in the year 1014 A.D. King Brian himself goes back to King Milesius of Spain, whose three sons, Heber, Ir, and Heremon, became Kings of Ireland about 1500 B.C. Not much is known of the sons of Ir. The sons of Heremon, the youngest of Milesius' children, were founders of many of the famous Irish families, such as the O'Neils, the O'Connors, the O'Reillys, and the O'Malleys. From Heber descended two main lines, the MacCarthys and the O'Brians, and of these the

O'Brians are the only family that has carried the male line all the way down. How sad it is to think that the present Earl of Inchiquin has no son so the long direct line will be closed at his death.

Brian Boroimhe was said to be a wise ruler, a very religious man, and a terrific fighter. In one battle he is supposed to have split an adversary through his coat of brass from the top of his head to his rump with his battle ax. And this when he was sixty-three years of age! Brian ruled with a just hand. Because of his personal character and ability, both as a ruler and as a fighter, the Danes were conquered completely, and for a hundred and fifty years Ireland had peace. It is also noteworthy that the surname was Brian's idea. Until this time there had been much difficulty in tracing genealogy, for the descendents of, we'll say, four different sons might all bear the same name. It was Brian who added the "O'," meaning "son of," so that Brian O'Brian, for example, was not just a Brian but Brian-son-of-Brian. "Mac" has the same significance in Irish names.

Many are the interesting relics at Dromoland, but we were there for too short a time to study them thoroughly. We did see one most magnificent and gigantic refectory table, beautifully carved, that came from a wrecked ship of the Spanish Armada.

After luncheon we drove back to Adare. Miss O'Hare greeted me warmly, and I promptly began calling to find a horse to carry me on the hunt with the Duhallow the next day.

Meanwhile I must plan something for Sydney. Fortunately Mr. Tillander showed up, and he and Sydney immediately made a date for Sydney to go to see all Mr. Tillander's beautiful things. He was in the process of dismantling his house, having sold it at auction a few days before.

We heard of another auction, one which wrung our hearts with pity. This was a forced sale of a house belonging to an older man who came into the Dunraven Arms to have a drink. For many years the man had worked as manager on one of the big estates and saved his money. When the time came for retirement he and his wife decided that they would take their capital and buy blooded grayhounds, for these dogs bring several hundred dollars apiece and breeding them is one of the big sporting businesses in Ireland. All went well for a while, then the kennel was hit by a new disease for which no cure had been found. In one week they lost fifty dogs and had nothing with which to replenish their stock. The only thing to do was to realize what they could from their beautiful old things which had been in the family for many generations and try to make this last for the years that were left to them. But there was no complaining or self-pity. The old gentleman told us that he was not going to be at his house the following day or the day of the auction; rather he would go out and follow the hounds. "If you reach the bottom you can go no lower," he said, "so perhaps now I can begin to climb again."

The next morning it developed that the de Traffords also were going to the man's house to look things over and they took Sydney along. He told me subsequently that he had rarely seen such beautiful things and that it was all he could do to restrain himself from bidding on various items, including a very beautiful mirror. He did bid for and succeed in buying an old punch ladle in delicate, thin silver. We have no punch bowl, though we sometimes borrow one for a big party, but the ladle is beautiful, and each time I look at it I think of those dear people who were facing such desolation, and hope that they are making out well and are happy.

XVIII

The Duhallow Foxhounds—Off to Kerry—The Beehive Huts and Fort Dunbeg—Dingle—Over the Hills and Far Away—Killarney —Dinner and Bridge at the Watts'

After a good deal of telephoning, I finally located what I was assured was an excellent horse. When I arrived at the meet and was presented to him I had the feeling that I had seen him before. When I had galloped him across a couple of fields, pulling his head into my lap to stop him, I was more certain of it, and after the first jump I was positive. This was the gray that my friend Bass (one of the "Kentucky Colonels") had had so much trouble with on that famous hunt with Peg Watt and the Croom Harriers. He had all the disadvantages of Jack, Dr. Kennedy's paragon, and none of Jack's virtues. In a few minutes I knew that if I were going to get into trouble in Ireland it would be today, not a comforting thought when ditches and banks loom ahead and one does not know the country, for the Duhallow territory, like the Scarteen, offers a wide variety of jumps.

The first few banks were negotiated without trouble, although I had the feeling several times that we got on and over them by luck alone. I remembered seeing Bass slide backward into a bank and determined to ride farther forward than usual.

The third bank was a nasty one —the razor-edge type, with no turf and very slippery sides made more so by roots which were visible. My horse planted his front feet and sat down behind. I yelled at him, keeping well forward, and then, seeing that he would not be able to regain himself, turned him and took him back. Fortunately there was no ditch. Someone behind said that he had got caught in one of the roots, but I knew better; he just hadn't tried hard enough!

We went along pretty well for another bit, and then, in jumping off a bank over a ditch, he misjudged and plowed along for a moment on his nose. I was lucky, however, and managed to stay on, and he soon recovered himself.

"Three times is out," said I to myself. And three times it was. A few minutes later we again had a double. He made the bank and cleared the second ditch. Thinking I was safe, I relaxed my vigilance, whereupon the wretched animal pecked again, went down on one knee, and I was off—just plain carelessness on my part. I hung on to the reins and was on again in a second, but furious that I had let the beast fool me that way. Whether he had determined at the outset to put me off just once for his own satisfaction I don't know, but the fact remains that both he and I were more careful from then on and we had no more grief.

The Duhallow is one of the best and oldest hunts in Ireland, but, since I cannot find its history in the *Hunting Who's Who,* I cannot give the details of its history. We did not have a very exciting day. As usual, everyone said that the hunts on Tuesdays were over the poorest country and that I should come out with them on Fridays. I had a good time, nonetheless, and the people were most courteous and friendly. I learned later that I could have had Mrs. Lee's lovely chestnut cob for the hunt instead of the clumsy gray, but then I would not have learned the lesson that with a brute like the gray to be over the jump is not necessarily to be done with it.

When I got back to the Inn I found that Sydney had returned from his very pleasant day with the de Traffords and Mr. Tillander. He told me about the lovely things that were to be auctioned off next day and I am sure, had I given him the least encouragement, he would have called the auctioneer to put in a bid on the mirror and other *objets d'art* that had caught his eye. I sympathized with him but drew his attention to the difficulty of shipping large objects and, more important, to our rapidly dwindling supply of travellers' checks. So, with reluctance, he abandoned the idea.

The next day was to see the initiation of our trip, with Miss Mills as guide, through the Kerry and Clare county, to see the beehive dwellings and other things of interest there. Miss Mills was to meet us at ten and when I came downstairs at nine I found that for the second time the Consul had developed a flat tire overnight! How very considerate of the Consul—first in front of the Hibernian and then in front of the Dunraven Arms. In both cases I could get immediate help. How much worse it would have been had the flat occurred at midnight or later the previous night when I drove to Dromoland!

The garage in Adare sent a man up and while we were at breakfast he repaired the damage. Miss Mills arrived in her car on the dot (evidently the women of Ireland have a much better time sense than the men), and by ten thirty we were off.

Our way led through Tralee, a lovely little town with a very wide main street, then on south through beautiful farming country. The weather was not good this first day and got worse as we went on but it did not actually rain until we were well down on the peninsular of Slieve. The Slieve mountains were on our left but we could not see them too clearly because of the mist. On our right was the Bay of Tralee, the water looking cold and gray. Then we crossed over to the other coast and headed for Dingle, where we were to leave our bags and continue on.

Because Dingle is a very hilly town, some of the streets are nearly vertical and very narrow. The Inn, which is a very old one, is on one of these streets, and the gateway leading into the yard is extremely narrow. I begged the Consul to suck in its breath as we squeezed through.

For many years, the Inn at Dingle and the one at Tralee were kept by people named Benner, and they are still known as Benner's Inns, although the present proprietors of the Inn at Dingle are a couple named McDonald. Mrs. McDonald had spent a number of years in New England, where they had had a hotel, so we were "home folks" to her. Like all the people in the south of Ireland, she had a most endearing way of speaking. One is never called "Madam," as in other parts of the country, but "love" or "dear." Somehow it sounds right coming in the soft Irish voices, though there is nothing I loathe more in the States than to have a salesgirl address me as "dearie."

The Inn itself was interesting and had evidently been quite a place at one time. In the dining room was an enormous sideboard, which must have not only been made for that particular room (it fitted in the space exactly) but also assembled in the room, for it could not possibly have been brought through the doorway. It was of mahogany with a roll top and intricately carved columns. I saw a mention of it in the guide books later.

We had two bedrooms with a little sitting room between us. Looking up at the ceilings we could see elaborate plaster decorations, and from them we concluded that the original rooms had been much more spacious, for now partitions had been built that cut across these lovely plaster designs.

Outside we could see the remains of what had once been a well-cared-for garden, but the weather was too cold and damp for us to explore it, although Sydney did look hastily through it. Across the street was a church that was supposed to have some interesting tombstones and relics of the invasion of the Spanish Armada, but again we did not explore.

After we had left our things we went on to Slea Head, following the shore road all the way. The weather by now was wild; great gusts of wind threatened to blow us off the road and over the steep cliffs and there were occasional torrents of rain. But the weather was very much in keeping with the scenery, and had I been painting this bleak countryside I would have portrayed it with just such a grim sky as we had that day. On

Sybil Head, Dingle

our right the hillsides rose steep and bare, with little bunches of hardy mountain sheep here and there. As in New England, the land was so stony that it had been necessary to clear it before it could be cultivated. The resulting heaps of stone were used for walls, some of them separating two fields, others running hither and yon with no apparent purpose. The cottages looked poor and there were but a few of them. On our left the road paralleled a cliff which in many places dropped right away to the sea. Here the waves dashed against the stone headlands with a mighty roar. The road was under construction and at one point we had to wait while a truck unloaded a pile of rocks and a steam roller smoothed them out for us.

Presently Miss Mills asked me to stop. There was no marker or sign, but there was a little farm cottage on our right. "This is the place, I think," she said, and we all got out.

She led us behind the farm, through the stable yard and up a steep hillside. No other human soul was in sight. Finally, after climbing several walls and clambering up slippery stony paths for a couple of hundred yards, we reached our goal—two of the ancient beehive dwellings in almost perfect state of preservation!

These fantastic buildings are so old that no one can actually determine their age, but they must date back to the Bronze Age. They get their name from their conical shape. They are perhaps six or seven feet in diameter at the base. Some are perfectly round; others have three squared-off corners, with the doorway forming the fourth. They are made of different-sized stones piled on one another and so perfectly fitted and balanced that, without mortar of any kind, they have remained intact some thousands of years. Think of the engineering skill that was needed—remember, the roofs meet overhead but have no supporting columns or rafters, just the rough stones, which are so laid that they support one another.

The only ventilation is through the chinks between the stones; the only opening is the door, which is very small and narrow. No one knows how many persons took shelter in these dwellings, but it must have got pretty smoky, one would think. However, standing inside and listening to the roaring wind and the rain outside, we could appreciate how great an advancement these crude dwellings must have been over the shelter of stones or rocks alone.

All around us were heaps of stones which were probably less well-constructed beehives. I read later in a guide book that there are more than five hundred of these buildings, in one condition or another, in this locality. Yet many of the Irish have never heard of them and the government does nothing to preserve them or to mark the road so that a stranger can find them. We did see the remains of a marker at the site which simply said that the buildings were under the protection of the Irish government. But it must have been there for many, many years; it was so defaced that the words were almost indistinguishable.

A few miles further on Miss Mills stopped us again. We got out of the car and made our way through two wet fields and over three walls and found ourselves at the ruins of the Fort of Dunbeg. This is one of the oldest and most interesting ruins in Ireland. It stands exactly on the edge of a cliff overlooking the ocean. As a matter of fact, it is believed that originally the fort was much larger but that the ocean has worn some of it away.

Here is a really remarkable construction. What looked like long banks over a hundred feet in length turned out to be the remains of long walled fortifications. Many of these appeared to have tunnels running along inside them. The main construction was beyond these, a fairly large apartment with a central hallway and rooms off to the right and left. The hallway had two methods of entrance and egress, the ordinary one and also a path through a tunnel, which probably connected with the fortifications. This also formed a "souteraine"—a removable stone designed so that when an enemy charged in he would fall into the tunnel below.

The rooms on the right and left were small and rounded in construction like the beehives. The one on the left faced out and was supposed to be where the sentry kept watch. When we were there it was occupied by a sheep, who had superseded the human sentry, but was keeping watch just the same. The apartment on the right was enclosed and opened into the hallway. It had the remains of a skeleton in it, but I think it was probably only that of a lamb.

The construction of the walls and roof was really fantastic when one considers the lack of tools. Some of the stones used were several feet wide, long, and thick. How the builders ever got them raised into position and how they figured out the stresses that would keep them there is a mystery.

Had it not been for Miss Mills we would never have found Dunbeg, for it cannot be seen from the road and, again, there is no marker to point the way.

We continued down Slea Head, and presently the Blaskets loomed up through the mists. Just before we got there our guide pointed out a wharf where the local variety of canoe is launched. These boats, called "curraghs," are made of wooden frames covered with tarred canvas. They are considerably larger than Indian canoes but have the same lightness and lack of draft. I did not see one in the water but was told that the natives were very skillful in handling them. I did see one of them turned upside down on the runway to keep the water out, and from a distance it looked like nothing so much as a large, slimy black slug.

The Blasket Islands used to be populated, but the inhabitants were very poor and hard put to it to scratch out a living. When the population of the largest of the Islands finally got down to thirty, including one child, the government decided to move these hardy remnants to the mainland and built a row of cottages for them. Here they have been ensconced and, like most peoples who have been treated in this way, have been complaining ever since.

Some little distance on, Miss Mills pointed out the famous Gallerus Oratory. This is a building of the same period as the beehives but oblong in shape and with a gabled roof. It is set way back in a field which at this point was running with water. We took our guide's word for it that the Gallerus had nothing that we had not already seen at the beehives and Dunbeg. Not very much farther on we left the coastal road and took a tiny country road inland. After some asking and looking we finally found our destination, the ruins of a very, very early church, Hilmalkedan by name. Here we saw a stone with the alphabet in Ogham (the early Celtic form of writing, composed of slanting parallel lines running above, below, or through a horizontal line). Here also we saw the famous needle stones —large stones like posts, about five feet high and a foot or so in thickness. They got their name from round holes pierced in the top very much like a needle's eye. No one knows exactly what these stones were intended for, but they are always found near sacred places. (In this connec-

Ross Castle near Killarney; a typical feature of the Irish landscape

tion it should be remembered that whereas the stones are pre-Christian, the churches were usually built on sites that had been used for pagan religious purposes.) Some historians believe that these stones are the origin of the wedding-ring ceremony: whenever a serious matter was to be consummated, both parties were required to put their fingers through the hole in the needle stone to seal the contract.

In addition to old graves and gravestones there were also new ones in the Hilmalkedan churchyard. The old Irish crosses are lovely, filigree in

form and with beautiful carvings on them. This church was well preserved, considering its age, and we could get a very good idea of what it was like originally. At the back near the altar was a tiny, very low doorway. This was called the "backache" door, for, by squeezing through it, the sufferer was supposed to get relief from that ailment.

After leaving Hilmalkedan we cut back to Dingle and had our dinner. The next day we were off bright and early, for we had a long drive ahead. We started back along Dingle Bay through Inch, where I saw one of the most beautiful beaches I have ever looked upon. The rollers were curling their way in a long, slow procession and seemed to be several miles in length. The sandy beach was deep and apparently the slope was very gradual. It would have been an ideal beach for children or for those who love to ride the waves on surfboards. A tiny inn was nestled down almost on the road, and Miss Mills told us that in summer it was always filled. But now there was not another human in sight.

We stopped not long afterward in a little hamlet, for I wanted to lay in a supply of peppermints. A darling old man waited on us. "Is it the hard mints you want, love, or the peppermints?" I said it was the former.

"Here they are then, love, and here's a penny for yourself," he said, taking a penny out of the till and handing it to me before he made change. This is an old Irish custom and is still carried on, especially when horses or animals are bought and sold.

We continued on along Castlemain Harbor. The day had cleared and though it was not sparkling with sunshine it was not rainy. At Castlemain we turned sharp right again and went back along the same harbor but on the other side. We went through Killorglin, where Puck's Fair is held each year, and Miss Mills pointed out the square where the platform is built for the goat who is chosen to reign for a week as King. Shortly after, we left the coast and cut directly across the peninsular.

And now we came into the real mountain country. Off to our left were the MacGillycudy Mountains. (The Irish pronounce it "Mac Licuddy.") Other peaks loomed up to our right and directly ahead. Miss Mills said that she was taking us on a little-known road over the Ballybeama Pass. As we went on I hoped that it was not only little known but preferably entirely unknown, for how we would ever have passed another vehicle was beyond me. The road was hardly the width of the car. The turns were sharp and often hairpin in shape. Steep ledges of rock rose on one side of us and precipices dropped away on the other. It was extremely difficult to get by even the occasional frightened sheep that found itself in our path, for there was so little extra room that the poor animal would often have to run yards before it could find a place to scramble out of the way.

These little mountain sheep are quite different from the valley sheep I saw around Limerick. The Limerick sheep were rotund and slow-moving, with heavy, thick, curly coats, tightly frizzled. The mountain sheep were agile and ran about on jet-black, toothpick-like legs. They had black faces, curly horns, and long silky wool, almost like cashmere. Sydney dug back into his childhood memories and produced the following:

"Oh the mountain sheep are sweeter
But the valley sheep are fatter
So we organized a posse
And we captured all the latter."

The Tim Healy Pass

Miss Mills assured us that the mountain sheep are indeed sweeter.

The views on every side of us were breathtaking. The pass is very high, so high that at times my Consul rebelled and I had great difficulty getting it to take the steeper slopes at anything but the lowest gear. At first I was inclined to blame the last batch of gasoline, but finally we came to the conclusion that it was just the altitude.

The rock and ledge formations on these hills were most interesting. Many of them are topped with great bogs from which the cottagers cut their turf. (It seemed odd to us that the bogs should be up so high; one would think that the moisture which makes them would have drained off.) Many tiny rivulets made their way down the gorges, sometimes with falls of many feet. All in all this pass was fascinating.

We had just come down the pass and reached a somewhat wider road when we met a car on its way up. Since we had been driving over the pass for nearly two hours: it was certainly a kind fate that so arranged our schedules that the two cars did not meet on top!

Some distance after we left the

171

Semitropical vegetation in County Kerry near Glengariff

high roads we came to the little village of Kenmare, where we had been
told we might find some tweeds. Sure
enough, there was a tiny shack, about
the size of a fifth-rate hot-dog stand in
the United States, by the side of the
road, and a sign over the door told
us that tweeds were to be had inside,
along with various other articles.
Since our route back to Dunhaven led
through Kenmare, we decided to stop
on our way back.

From Kenmare we took the Tim
Healy Pass over to Glengariff, the center of that part of Ireland which is
semi-tropical, at the head of Bantry
Bay. There was some difference in
temperature and a great deal of difference in vegetation. Palm trees were
very common and fuschia hedges, now
a dead brown but later to be a mass
of purple and crimson, were everywhere. How I wished I could see the
fuschia in its glory! Many of the
hedges were seven or eight feet high
and several feet in thickness.

The road over the pass is narrow
and winding but better marked and
in better condition than the Ballybeama Pass. The curves are marked
by whitewashed oil drums, for the
mists make this a dangerous thorough-

fare. On this day we were fortunate in having clear weather, and the views were stupendous. (On page 174 is one such view looking past one of the shrines which are the goals of pilgrims at certain times of the year.)

After going through Glengariff, we took a different way home over another pass, which took us, by a very winding road, back to Kenmare, where we stopped at the roadside shack and bought several lengths of really beautiful tweeds. The making of these tweeds is one of the largest of the cottage industries. The farmer raises his sheep, shears them, cards, spins, and dyes the thread, using dyes made from herbs and berries, and finally weaves the cloth on a hand loom. No two pieces are exactly alike, and there are interesting variations of color and weave within each piece. The tweed wears almost forever. I got a piece of russet material, in which could be distinguished lovely pinks and oranges as well as an occasional blue-gray, for a suit for myself and a sport jacket for Sydney. Then I got a check in browns and reds for a riding jacket for Chips and a purply blue for a suit for Gincy. The prices ran ten shillings, or about $1.40, a yard.

Leaving Kenmare, we headed back away from the sea to Killarney. So much has been written and said about Killarney that I shall not describe the lakes other than to say that they are most beautiful. But this is one place in Ireland which has been commercialized, and I was glad that I was there at a time when it was not overrun with tourists.

From Killarney we went back to Adare by way of Abbeyfield and New Castle, arriving home at about seven. It had been a long day's drive, but so beautiful! The only other drive I have ever taken which gave me the feeling of really viewing a country from the peaks is the one which runs along the summits of the Blue Ridge Mountains in Virginia. I have driven along the *Autostrada* from Genoa to Florence, where the sun drops into the Mediterranean on your right and peak after peak of the Italian Alps rises before you on each side. This drive has the same hairpin curves and the same little towns set on the road as the passes over the Irish mountains. But though it is beautiful, one never sees such a wide expanse of valleys as in some of the views from the Ballybeama and the Healy Passes.

We were invited to dinner at the Watts, Peg having returned from England, and since I had never been there, I knew it would be a little hard to find. We got what directions we could from Miss Mills, and, after a bath to wash the grime of the trip off, we set out.

It was still light when we started, though it got dark soon after we had left. Our way led through Croom and Bruff to Knocklong. By watching the road signs and making inquiries whenever possible, we arrived safely at about nine o'clock. This would be considered late for an informal dinner here, but in Ireland it is quite normal. Everyone was still engaged in before-dinner refreshments. Sydney immediately sensed by the general at-

Upper Lake, Killarney

Courtesy of Fogra Failte

mosphere that he was somewhat behind the others, so set to work to catch up. I think the Irish were rather glad to find that my husband was more congenial than I when it came to drinking, and I was glad to let him work for both of us.

I cannot now remember the names of the other guests at the Watts. I know Peg's sister, whom I had met before at the de Trafford's, was there, together with her daughter. Then there was a nice chap who apologized for still being in formal hunting attire. Major Watt, who was delightful and whom I had not previously met, was in tweeds. Peg was her usual jovial self in a woolen dressing gown, and there was one other guest, I think female.

When it had been decided that Sydney had caught up sufficiently on the drinks we went in to dinner. Since it was Lent and Friday and the Watts are Catholics we had only fish courses, which were delicious. The main hall was a large room, and the dining room, with its long refectory table, was also large, but the little room where we had had cocktails and to which we returned to play bridge was small and cosy. At one o'clock, after a delightful but unprofitable evening of bridge (Sydney seemed to hold good cards but I held hardly a card higher than a ten spot all evening!), I felt we must go. The others would have liked to stay and play all evening, but I was not sure we would be able to find our way home too easily, and I was right. At one point I accepted the statement of a signpost and turned off the main road and onto a dirt one. Evidently this was one of those signs that had been twisted, for we wandered for miles, stopping to ask our way whenever we saw a light. Eventually we got to Croom, though Sydney was quite resigned by that time to spending the night wandering down Irish lanes and knocking on the doors of whitewashed cottages. I think it must have been about three when we finally reached the Dunraven Arms, let ourselves in, and then, switching lights off and on in relays, crept quietly down the long cold corridors to our room. And we had to get up promptly the next morning, for we were driving forty miles to hunt with the Galway Blazers.

XIX

The Galway Blazers

Once more I was having saddle trouble, but this time it was not my fault. At the end of the Duhallow hunt my groom, who had been following in a car, took my horse to hack it the eight miles back to the van, but since he had forgot to bring his saddle along, and the gray was not too well padded over the spine, I had not the heart to make him hack the distance bareback. I had therefore lent him my saddle, with strict injunctions that it was to be delivered to the Dunraven Arms by Friday at the latest. I had not been able, since our return from Kerry, to find out whether this had been done. So the first thing the next morning I started making inquiries, wondering just what I should do if it were not there. But for once the Irish—I suppose because hunting was involved—had shown a splendid sense of responsibility, and my saddle was ready to pack into the Consul.

The weather was ideal; a clear sky, brilliant sunshine and just a few little cotton balls of clouds on the horizon to add interest. There wasn't much wind, but it was not so warm that the horses would suffer.

We picked up Pat Scanlan and his dog, Valiant, in Limerick, then started out the Ennis road. The meet was about forty miles away, near a town named Loughrea. I had thought that the fixture card said eleven-thirty, but when we got to the appointed spot at eleven-thirty we were told that hounds had already moved off. My horse was waiting for me, and Mr. Daley, the owner, offered to ride her on to the first covert, about three miles down the road, so that I might go on ahead in the car and find out which way the fox broke. So we climbed back into the Consul and drove off. Presently we caught up with the riders and followed them to the covert, keeping the lake for which the town is named on our right. The covert was on a hillside, and the cars were all stopped on the edge of the road. The Master held the hounds in a little meadow to our right while the Field rode through another large field, up a sharp incline, and stationed themselves out of the way on the crest of a hill. When all were in place the Master and the Whip cast hounds and they entered the gorse eagerly. It was a beautiful sight—the horses in the muted tones of chestnut and bay with here and there a gray, the riders in bright scarlet or black, all silhouetted against the green of the hillside or the blue of the sky, and the lake shimmering in the sunlight below.

Galway country is open and hilly with little covert. There are frequent small promontories from which one can get a good view of hounds, but not the magnificent long views of the Scarteen country. The Galway country is noted for its stone walls, and these were quite different from any I had previously seen. The stones are of medium size, a light gray in color, some rounded and some jagged. They are built into high walls running from three feet six inches to five feet in height and are never more than one stone's thickness in width. This construction gives the walls a delicate, lacelike appearance. There are no barways in the fields. When a farmer wants to put his stock into a given meadow he simply knocks a gap in the wall by leaning his shoulder against it and pushing, puts the ani-mals through, and builds it up again. All the fields are small, averaging little over an acre or two, and the walls run like crazy-quilt patterns in every direction and come at one like a procession of soldiers.

This is apparently the only section in Ireland where the horses actually fly their fences, for it would obviously be impossible for even the most agile of hunters to change legs on top of one of these slim barricades, and the Galway horses know it. But what about a visiting fireman from Limerick, for example? How amazed such a horse would be on his first attempt at "banking" one of the Galway walls, and what a terrific crash of showering rocks would result! Some of the walls were so high that the animals obviously had to be of the type that could hoist themselves well off the ground in order to clear them. I saw more Thoroughbreds in Galway than anywhere else, except when I went out with the Ward Union.

This was also one of the few hunts where women members as well as men wore the scarlet. Usually only a woman Master has the privilege, but the Whip, who was wife of the Master, and one of the best and most daring riders I have ever seen, wore hunting "pink," as did several other women members of the Field. The Master, Mr. Lancelot Smith, was also Huntsman. He was a popular Master and handled his hounds with great authority, but was noted for his rather sharp tongue.

The pack has been in existence for over a hundred and fifty years.

The country hunted covers a territory of about thirty miles, all but a small section of which is stone walls with little wire and no banks or ditches. There is limestone under the turf, so the going is lighter than in other parts of Ireland. A fast horse is needed, for with so little covert checks do not come often. The horse must be clever as well, for the country is so hilly that he has often to take off a foot or two lower than the base of the wall. Sometimes he may discover while in mid-air that the ground falls away from under him, with a drop of three or more feet. I had been told by the "Kentucky Colonels" that there would be many jumps, so I had decided to use the old herdsman's method of counting them. In my right-hand pocket I put a handful of mints, transferring one mint to my left-hand pocket after every ten jumps. By the end of the day I had nine mints in the left-hand pocket, so I had taken at least ninety jumps.

There were approximately forty people in the Field. I was interested to notice one lady who rode side-saddle in a conventional astride habit and who, in hacking from covert to covert, attached an extra stirrup to the off side of her saddle and swung her leg over so that she could post more comfortably.

Another very interesting-looking figure was a lady riding a big bay horse. She wore a topper, a cutaway coat, the conventional white stock and vest, and white leather hunting breeches. These last in America are usually worn only by men. But the thing that added color to her appearance, as well as being most becoming, was her hair, which was a lovely cerulean blue!

There were two young girls, obviously sisters, who must have been saving up their pocket money to buy hunting outfits. Their derbies, coats, vests, stocks, and breeches were all beautifully cut and fitted, but, instead of boots, they both wore golf stockings and oxfords. Perhaps it was just that their boots were very wet from a previous day's hunting. At all events, whatever the reason, I admired them highly, for it takes sturdy legs to hunt over the Galway fences without the support of boots. When I heard that they had hacked eight or ten miles to get to the meet and might have to hack twelve back, my admiration knew no bounds.

I soon picked out my pilot for the day, a most attractive girl with the beautiful hands of the good horseman. She wore a blue coat, rode a breedy-looking horse, and obviously knew the country well.

Mr. Daley arrived on the bay mare just as the fox broke cover, ran down the hillside, crossed the road, and was away through the green fields to the left. I mounted and joined the other riders and we had a good gallop. I was pleased to find that the mare had a good mouth and flew her fences without hesitation, though she was a little inclined to drag the top stone over with her if the obstacle was higher than three-six.

It was very exhilarating to be hunting fast over fences and to be able to view the hounds so well. The going was light, as had been promised, and the horses eager. The riding seemed to be more "educated" than any I had seen, with the possible exception of the Ward Union Hunt. As usual, everyone was most friendly. Many of the Field knew the horse I was riding and assured me that she was very capable. I had only one refusal and that was when I tried to make her go first over a quite low stone wall. Probably, having had so little trouble with her up until then, I didn't urge her along sufficiently, or perhaps she was just not used to leading but, unlike old Jack of the Golden Vale, preferred to have someone show her the way. So when she stopped I brought her back and let someone else go ahead. She only had one bad fault: she simply would not stand quietly at the checks unless I let her graze. I loathe this habit in a horse, but rather than make a nuisance of myself with her restlessness I let her eat away whenever we stopped.

We drew one very fine cover at the top of a big hill. It was thick and completely surrounded by a very high wall. By this time we had been joined by a number of foot followers. For some time we waited parallel to the wall while hounds nosed out their fox. Then there was a "view halloa" from below and we started at a gallop. Unfortunately, one of the hill toppers on foot had headed Reynard and he slipped back into the cover. A few minutes later I looked up to see a wise furry face peering at me over the wall twenty feet away. An instant

later it was gone. Then came a whimper from a hound and a few minutes after that we saw the fox break cover below us, cross two fields, turn to the left, follow down two more fields until he was at the foot of the ridge, and then, turning sharply left again, he ran like a streak along below us. Hounds were only a few hundred yards behind, their beautiful music echoing back at us. Right on their heels was Mrs. Smith, who had been the one to blow them away. The rest of us waited to see where the chase would lead us, then turned and raced down the hill and over one wall and then another. This was a long point, and the fox was sturdy and brave and stiff-necked.

Presently we found ourselves on the top of a hill. The ground was level but boggy, and a black drain about feet wide ran across it. Two horses had crossed before we got there. Then four, two grays, a bay, and a chestnut, all started for the drain abreast. The riders were not riding forward, and although the horses landed well, when they brought their hind legs down, the weight of the riders was too much. The banks of the drain crumbled under them, and in a split second there was a brouhaha of struggling horses and riders and a splashing of black water and blacker peat. All got out safely, though one poor chap had a nasty jar when his horse, in rising, caught him on the end of the chin with his knee. Meanwhile hounds were running further and further away. We all looked at the drain and turned away, except for one man who cleverly dismounted, took the end of his reins and ran forward, hopped lightly over the water, followed equally lightly by his horse, remounted and was away. At that moment I noticed what looked like a beaten track leading off to my right. I followed it and found a safe crossing, and once more we were on a steady gallop. Twice more we found ourselves in this same boggy field, but, thanks to our previous experience, we had no further trouble.

Shortly after this the Master decided to lift hounds and take us on several miles to a new territory. I looked vainly on the road for Sydney and Pat, for I knew Pat wanted to get at least a hack out of his day, but they were not to be found. And now we were in some really hilly country with tiny fields and high walls. Many times I went at a place wondering whether or not we would make it, for not only would the wall be towering above me but the take-off would have a pitch like a high-peaked roof. Again, in mid-air over an ordinary-sized wall, I would find myself looking down into nothing, and we would land way below the take-off side. How my mare was able to judge all of this and adjust her balance I don't know, but she did. All I had to do was keep my weight forward and let her mouth alone.

Presently we came to a real whopper. My pilot took it in fine style, and, with a prayer, I followed. Only the Master and the Whip were ahead. Not only was the jump big on the take-off side, but there was a ter-rific pitch on the landing side too. But the dear bay mare landed cleverly, and we flew up a gorse-covered hill-side, picking our way among the cattletracks.

"A nice private hunt," says I to myself. At that moment I heard a horse coming up behind and a shout. I looked around. It was the big horse of the lady with the blue hair and he was riderless. There was but one thing to do. I gazed forlornly at the disap-pearings backs of my fellow riders, jumped off, and caught the bay. I led the horse back, and there, under the huge wall which I had just taken, sat the poor lady, obviously dazed, with a great splash of mud on one cheek. She said she had landed under the animal and she thought he had stepped on her head. Presently she began to recover, and two girls rode up to say that a groom had been summoned to ride in with her and that they would stay and see that she was all right. So after getting her mounted again, I galloped back to the gorse-covered hill. The field had evidently checked right at the top and were just moving off again so I had lost nothing after all.

We hunted until almost six and then found ourselves about six miles from Loughrea. I followed a group that was going my way out onto the main road. Very soon, to my delight, Pat, Sydney, and Mr. Daley appeared. Mr. Daley took my horse, and Pat, Sydney, and I drove back to Loughrea, where we had a sumptuous tea at the hotel. The homemade bread was fresh out of the oven and hot, and the jam and marmalade tasted like nectar. All in all it was a most satisfactory day.

After a while Mr. Daley joined us at tea. I had to wait for him to get my saddle anyway. "How did you like it?" I asked him. "It's a wonderful saddle," he said. "A person would have to be a bad rider indeed to fall out of that one!" and I agreed.

The plan was for Sydney and me to drive on to Birr to the Maxwell's for the night and then see some of the interesting places around there next day with Esther Maxwell as guide. But what about Pat and Valiant?

"Sure, don't bother about me at all. Just drop me at Roscrea. There's a railroad there and I'll be sure to get a train."

"But, Pat, are you sure there's a train this time of night?"

"Oh, there'll be a train, and if there's no train there'll be a bus, and if there's no bus someone will be coming along and give me a lift."

So we drove through the darkness the twenty-odd miles to Roscrea. A pitch-black station boded little good and after looking everywhere for a guard we finally learned that the train had left some hours before. What about a bus? Oh, there was never a bus at this time of night!

"Well, let's go to a pub and wash up," said Pat, so we went to a little hotel where I called the Maxwells to explain the delay. Pat finally insisted on our dropping him and his dog at a street corner, vowing that he would easily find his way back to Limerick some fifty miles away and begging us not to give it another thought. We felt badly about leaving him but we need not have worried. We learned later that no sooner were we out of sight than the driver of a passing car put on the brakes and shouted, "Is it you, Pat? Sure, we knew it by the dog!" and he was driven all the way home.

XX

Sightseeing with Esther Maxwell—Doon Castle and the Sheela-magig—The Clonfinlough Stone—Clonmacnoise—Cashel—Mr. Fraser, Tailor Extraordinary

Sydney and the Maxwells took to each other immediately, just as I had known they would. We had a nice chat, then went to bed. We got up at eight thirty the next morning, and I rode Jack's darling little bay filly, Lucinda. She is fourteen-two, Arabian and Thoroughbred combination, and with a lot of quality. She has a lovely mouth and plenty of spirit with no bad faults or vices. We hopped a ditch or so and then flew a sizable one with a thorn hedge on the other side. I took it from both directions and she soared like a bird. If only the transportation costs were not so great I would have brought her home with me. She would have been ideal for showing and hunting over here.

Esther Maxwell took us first to Doon Castle. We could see where the original fortifications had been, the outline of the courtyard into which all animals were herded during sieges,

etc. The main walls of the castle itself are in excellent repair. The wooden floors are pretty well gone, as is the roof, but the supports on the walls where they had originally rested are there. A narrow stairway leads up one side and onto a little gallery. The old cement is as firm as ever. It is made of limestone and bullock's blood, and many of these unfortunate beasts were sacrificed to build these castles. Certainly the combination was strong to have stood up without cracking or flaking off after all these centuries!

The castle had two especially interesting features. One was a series of square, chutelike, slanting holes which we were told were among the earliest forms of what the Irish politely call "lavat'ries." The other was the Sheela-magig, which I am spelling phonetically. (I learned the Irish spelling, but to Americans it would bear no relation to the pronunciation of the word.) A Sheelamagig is a pagan symbol of fertility, and is usually found at holy pagan places. Since the Christian churches inherited these spots and preferred to wean the people gradually to the new beliefs, they adopted such primitive fetishes as the Sheelamagig and the needle stones and incorporated them in their own churches and buildings.

The Sheelamagigs vary somewhat in appearance but generally speaking they are hideously ugly hermaphroditic figures with leering masculine heads and faces, feminine upper bodies, and legs that either twine around each other or are crossed behind the heads in contortionist fashion. The Sheelamagig at Doon Castle was of the former variety. It was set high on the wall at a corner and though the rest of that wall was covered with a heavy growth of ivy there was none on the Sheelamagig. On inquiry I learned that ivy never grows over Sheelamagigs. Mrs. Moony, our guide, said she suspected the gardeners of assisting nature in this respect, but I could see no signs of the ivy's having been trimmed by human hands and can only suppose that the gods are still protecting their property.

After seeing Doon we went to luncheon with some charming people named Perry. Their young teen-age daughter, a lovely girl, with beautifully natural manners, took me out and showed me the pride of her heart, her new hunter, and also the pony chunk that had won her many ribbons and carried her without fault in the hunt-field for several seasons previously. The two horses were stabled together, separated by a partition more than four feet high. Although the stalls were not big, it seems that whenever the larger horse was taken out, the pony had to be restrained or he would jump the partition from a standstill.

After luncheon Esther took us to a churchyard many miles away. The church was not old and it was not in a village. We climbed a couple of walls, fought our way through some thorn hedges, and found ourselves in an open field. Here we were shown one of the earliest prehistoric stones —probably neolithic—in existence. Called the Clonfinlough (Meadow of the White Lake) Stone, it is a piece of arinacious limestone about three feet square with what appears to be a pictorial representation of a battle carved in it. Bowmen are represented by straight "stick" figures with circles indicating the bow and the arm that is drawing it. Foot soldiers without bows are also shown. If these drawings go back to the influence of King Milesius, whose three sons became kings of Ireland, it puts their date at about 2,000 B.C., but of course they could be older. Pictures of this stone are to be found in many books on the antiquities of Ireland; and if care is not taken, these books will be all that remain of it, for the winter storms are rapidly eroding the carvings.

From here we drove to the seven chapels of Clonmacnoise. This is also a very early ruin with many interesting features including another Sheelamagig, a tiny one with the legs crossed behind the head. The Sheelamagig—a fertility symbol, remember—is located in, of all places, a spot right over the nuns' chapel! The chapels, which have beautiful carvings over the doorways, are of different periods. The whole group is located on a branch of the Shannon, a truly beautiful spot. We had not enough time to study them thoroughly, and I know Esther Maxwell was scandalized at the haste with which we ran through them. But perhaps some time we can go back and look them over more carefully.

We were sorry to say goodbye to the Maxwells and promised to come back next year. Jack, in turn, promised to let me ride little Lucinda in a hunt, provided she has not been sold. I truly hope they are able to put across their project of turning their house into a place where paying guests may enjoy their hospitality and learn through their knowledge of both the people and the history of Ireland.

We arrived in Dublin with no mishaps, although we lost our way once. Sydney was delighted with the Royal Hibernian. I immediately called Miss Whitmore, who had agreed to do the jacket for this book, and we arranged to meet the following afternoon. Then Sydney and I went in and had a delicious dinner. I do not know whether my tummy was just not accustomed to such fancy food, for I had been eating very little, but that night I developed a very severe case of indigestion. The next morning I was still feeling rocky and had to stay

in bed while Sydney went exploring. He saw the Book of Kells, St. Stephen's Green, the old book stalls, and all the things I had put off seeing on my previous visit because I wanted to see them with him.

By luncheon time I was somewhat recovered and chanced a bowl of clear soup, but I am afraid Miss Whitmore found me dull company when she arrived at three thirty. We did get the details of the jacket decided upon and I told her how sorry I was not to be able to come out to her place and see her horses, which she shows in Dublin.

That evening we drove out to the Mivilles' for dinner, since I wanted Sydney to see Ballykeane. Although we were urged to stay the night, we had to leave soon after dinner, for we wanted to get an early start the next day, when we planned to see the Rock of Cashel and then go down to Hospital to be measured for suits of the lovely Kerry tweeds we had bought.

Monday was bleak and gray, with periodic storms of driving rain and high winds that seemed to blow from all points of the compass. Sydney had a chance to see the famous Curragh and all its brightly colored sheep, but I wished we could have spared the time to go again to the National Stud and see the Japanese Gardens.

When we reached Cashel, at about two o'clock, the rain had stopped, but never in my life have I felt such wind. The warden left his snug cottage to climb the steep slope and undo the great doors for us. He pointed out the old castle of the Kings of Munster, and made me promise to use this term and not "Kings of Ireland" in speaking of them. The date on this part of the ruin was about 900 A.D. One piece of the wall had fallen out and lay intact in a great chunk, as it had lain for the past hundred and fifty years.

From here the warden took us into the main chapel, a most beautiful piece of architecture, with fluted columns and lovely carvings. In one section was a tablet with carved figures of the twelve apostles. The warden rattled off their names and pointed out the identifying articles which many of them carried. I spotted a loose tablet over in one corner which turned out to be another Sheelamagig, a very large and especially ugly one, with the legs twisted like a barber's pole. I think the warden was a little annoyed at our finding it. He said that it had ben dug up quite recently and evidently didn't think that it should be allowed in his lovely church. When I asked him about the origin of the Sheelamagigs he said they were were spirits of the winds. I think he didn't want to shock my feminine ears; had Sydney been there alone, he probably would have had a different explanation.

There was no roof on this main part of the church, and the warden explained that, although it had been made of stone, the roof had been burned by the Earl of Kildare, who used as his excuse the fact that he thought the Archbishop was in it. How one successfully burns an all-stone dwelling I do not know, but perhaps fire was more potent in those days. Certainly it had not destroyed the beautiful archways. Mrs. Maxwell had had a different and more interesting idea of what had become of the roof to the Rock of Cashel. She said that there had been a very fat Archbishop who got tired of walking up the steep slope, so he built another chapel down below. As a matter of fact, we saw this one too, as we were leaving, but it was not nearly so interesting. Anyway, even though they had a nice new chapel, more conveniently located, the stubborn parishoners persisted in worshipping in their original chapel, so the Archbishop removed the roof and thus rendered it uninhabitable in bad weather.

Cormac's Chapel, the *pièce de résistance* which we were shown at the last, is the little one with the steeply pitched roof pictured on page 76. The roof of this chapel is unique in that it is supported by a series of stone arches; there are no wooden beams or trusses, and I understood the warden to say that the stones of the trusses are simply fitted together with no cement.

Cashel also had a round tower in an almost perfect state of preservation. The warden was a little annoyed when we told him that we had stopped to look at another one on the way down that was quite a bit taller. Although the other was taller, he insisted, it hadn't a patch on his, for it had no top.

These round towers are among the most interesting sights in Ireland.

They are prehistoric and no one knows their exact purpose. But how a people with the few tools that were available in those days could have constructed these absolutely symmetrical, smooth towers—some as high as a hundred and twenty feet—is incredible. The towers are so strong that when one fell recently it was not demolished but lay like the barrel of a cannon on one side.

We left the warden and his high winds and continued on our way to Hospital, a little town outside Limerick. There we met the jovial William Fraser, who has a tiny tailor shop there, consisting of three small rooms on the ground floor and a room below. There is no window display or anything to tell you that this is one of the best-known and most successful tailors of sports clothes for both men and women in the whole of Ireland. But on his shelves are more bolts of material than you would find at a big New York tailor's. He keeps six men busy, works until midnight himself, and turns out six or seven suits a day. He showed us his order book, with names and measurements of people from all over the world in it. Mrs. de Trafford had told me that she refused to go to him for clothes because any slight change in her size would be broadcast to the countryside. And when Lady Dunraven heard that we had been to him and had seen his order book, she asked whether I had noticed various little abbreviations in it. I said I had.

"I'm afraid I don't know you well enough to tell you what those mean," she said, "but I can assure you they are very descriptive." I was sure they were.

Mr. Fraser lovingly took our measurements, telling us all the while about the lady with the sixty-four-inch hips whom he had such trouble measuring, for of course he wanted to be tactful and could not let her see that his tape measure was not long enough to span them. In fact, he kept up a continuous chatter, and I am sure there would have been no secrets unrevealed had we only been able to stay a little longer. He was distressed to hear that we were leaving Thursday night (this was Monday) but promised to have our jackets ready for a fitting at seven o'clock on Thursday, before we left. We were both entranced by his woolens and went overboard in buying. I ordered a charcoal-gray flannel "costume," as it is called there, as well as the tweed, and Sydney ordered a business suit and some odd slacks as well as his tweed jacket —this in addition to a riding coat for Chips and a suit for Gincy.

We got back to Adare in time for dinner and found a message from Pat to the effect that Paddy Punch was still prepared to mount me the following day for my last hunt in Ireland and that we could then go on to the races in Limerick. Since it was St. Patrick's Day, he suggested that I allow plenty of time for getting through Limerick. He planned to meet us at the pub, where the fixture was. So I set out my hunting things for the last time and went to bed, regretful that I had only a few days left.

XXI

St. Patrick's Day—The Limerick Harriers—Races at Limerick

St. Patrick's Day was fair with light winds. Kathleen presented us with a large bunch of shamrock which she had picked. I had never seen this plant except in little pots in the States and have now concluded that what was sold to me as shamrock on St. Patrick's Day at home may have been a fourth cousin twice removed from the native stock but certainly could claim no nearer relationship than that. This shamrock had tiny leaves and a great profusion of stems.

At ten thirty we set out for Limerick, on our way to the meet of the Limerick Harriers, which was being held just outside the city at one of the usual crossroad pubs. Of course, all pubs were supposed to be closed all day out of respect for the good Saint, but we found this to be, like the premature report of Mark Twain's death, "somewhat exaggerated." The only difference seemed to be that whereas ordinarily you did not have to knock at the door of a pub, on this day you did, but you were promptly and courteously admitted.

When we reached Limerick we found most of the main street blocked off for the parade. The streets were all crowded, and every man, woman, and child sported a shamrock in his or her buttonhole. I am quite sure that had anyone appeared without the emblem he would have been promptly incarcerated for lack of respect, and I was more than glad of Kathleen's thoughtfulness.

Even without the help of the crossroads and traffic light, from which I was accustomed to begin my calculations when I went through Limerick, we were able to find our way to the appointed spot without difficulty. We were the first ones there, but presently others appeared, including the good Paddy Punch. He was in a car driven by a friend, and his sons were bringing the horses, including the chestnut mare. Paddy had not hunted since his bad accident, when the horse had "given him the awful wallop on the side of the head," but when he saw me taking pictures he could not resist climbing aboard a horse to pose. I took two and gave him one; the other is on page 000. It gives a good idea of how the Irish country people sit on a horse.

Soon hounds arrived in charge of the Master, Mr. Russel. Evidently Mr. Russel did not have as great faith in his pack as had some of the other Masters, for hounds were promptly ushered into a narrow enclosure and a gate was firmly closed on them. The staff could now take time to go into the pub, collect caps, adjust saddles, etc., without having to worry about the pack.

Pat Scanlan now rode up, having hacked from Limerick. This was to be the end of the winter's work for his horse, which was to be sent the following day to a farm, where she would earn her summer's board by plowing and otherwise rendering herself useful.

Presently the rest of the Punch contingent arrived. One lad rode a likely looking gray which, he told me, was having his second view of hounds. The horse went well throughout the day, and I should like the chance of hunting him myself some time. The other boy was on a bay. It seems that the bay had always been gentle and easily rated until Paddy's son got tired of staying at the tail end of the Field

and taught him to stay up front. The bay found this so much more interesting than eating everyone else's mud at the rear that he now refused to go slowly. This had proved embarrassing, since meanwhile he had been sold to an elderly gentleman who wanted a quiet hunter which would be content to amble along and not take the jumps. So Paddy's son was now bent on re-educating his mount.

I climbed on my chestnut mare. When I asked her name, Paddy told me that he never named his horses, and that she consequently had none. I should think this would prove rather inconvenient; instead of saying "Get so-and-so tacked up" to his stable boy, he must have to say, "Johnny, do you mind the chestnut mare in the fifth stall, the one with the white sock on the near fore? Not the one with the white sock on the off-fore, remember, it's the *near*-fore I'm thinking of, and she has a snip on her nose, as well. Are you sure you know the mare? Then get her tacked up, like a good lad." I would think that this might use up a great deal of spare time, but then the Irish seem to have all they need and more besides, so it makes little difference. Since I don't like to ride a horse to which I have not been properly introduced, I promptly christened her Lady Shamrock in honor of the day, and she answered to it well.

It had been decided that Sydney would follow after us in the car with Paddy Punch, so when we moved off they were right at our heels. A short hack brought us to the first field, where we were supposed to draw. It did not take the harriers long to get on a line and presently we were off at a good speed. This country is varied, with some banks and ditches but mostly stone walls. I was able to get Lady Shamrock to fly the low ones; having been shown the hedge over which she was reputed to have carried Paddy's son I had no compunction in asking her to fly a two-foot-six wall, but she obviously preferred to land on top of it. We had several fast runs. At one point we were accompanied for a mile or so by a riderless horse which no one was able to catch.

Everything was going well when I looked down and noticed that the zipper on my right breeches' leg had come unzipped and the lower part of the leg had worked itself up above my boot. This can be very uncomfortable, so I stopped in a field and tried to remedy it. I was unable to do so and asked a countryman standing nearby to see what he could do. Though he pulled as hard as he could, he couldn't get the stubborn gadget to work. There was but one thing to do: get off and take off my boot. This I did while the man held Lady Shamrock. As I was struggling away, more riders, including Pat, arrived. Of course they thought I must have got into trouble, and were relieved to see it was only a zipper. But even without the boot and on the ground I could do nothing and finally had to pull the boot back on (luckily it wasn't the very tight pair) and climb on again. I tucked the offending breeches' leg in as best I could and hoped I wouldn't come home black and blue. "At least," I said to myself, "it isn't the most important zipper on the breeches," looked down to check and found that that one too had betrayed me! But fortunately it yielded to persuasion or I should have had to keep well to myself.

We were now a bit behind the other riders, but we hopped over a stone wall and started across some fields. Rounding a corner I saw a strange sight. The staff and Field had halted, some on top of a high piece of ground and some below them on the other side of a big ditch. Men were busy as bees digging away in the ditch. "What goes on?" I wondered. "Surely the hare can't have gone to ground. That's a fox's prerogative. And where on earth did they find a shovel way out here, nearly a mile from the nearest farmhouse?"

As I approached I saw the gray head of a horse looking out forlornly over the ditch. It was a beautiful animal that I had been admiring all day, but he had misstepped in coming off the high ground and was now completely trapped in the narrow ditch. It appeared that he was better off than he had been, for I gathered that at first he had been down and now, at least, he was on his feet again. After twenty minutes or so of digging he managed to scramble out, but he was a sad sight, muddy and exhausted.

" 'Tis always the good ones that get in trouble, Doctor," said one man, trying to pierce the unfortunate rider's gloom. "Sure, he was going great 'til he hit that bit of root." The Irish are ever compassionate to anyone in trouble. But the horse was too done in to continue, and after walking him about a bit the rider took him home.

On inquiry I discovered that the tools had come from a distant farmhouse nestled into the side of a hill. It was hardly visible but was probably nearer than it looked, since the Irish atmosphere is often deceiving.

Hounds were now collected and lifted and we were all off again to draw a different field. This entailed jumping over the ditch that had been the cause of the gray's grief and onto the high ground on the other side. It looked a pretty sizable jump, but all the horses took it well. We now came to a rather nasty-looking place, a very wide and deep ditch with somewhat crumbling sides. The Master and the Whip went at it together, and the Master's horse landed on his chest. The Master scrambled out of the saddle and the horse followed him into solid ground.

"You were laughing before ever I hit the damned thing," said the Master in an injured tone, and was mounted and off before there could be a reply.

Not too far from this spot we came to what everyone termed a river, though I couldn't see that it was much bigger than several "drains" we had taken. A number of the horses stopped at this one, including my chestnut, but she changed her mind when she felt my spurs and landed lightly on the far side. Then we had a good gallop over two fields and into a third, where I turned rather sharply to make for a place which was not blocked by other riders. The next minute I was almost thrown by a horse cannonading into Lady Shamrock's quarters while going at a fast gallop. Whether the rider didn't see me, whether I turned so abruptly that I crossed in front of him, or whether his horse was accustomed to "taking a bit of a hold" and could not be stopped in a snaffle I don't know. At all event the rider was most apologetic and no one seemed to be hurt.

The plan was for us to leave the hunt at about two thirty and go on from there to the races at Limerick. It was getting close to that time now, and I was just as glad, for though Lady Shamrock was a fine jumper and a very comfortable ride, she was not in as hard condition as some of the horses and was beginning to tire. Presently one of Paddy's boys rode up to tell me that Pat Scanlan and Sydney were waiting on the roadside.

As usual, Pat had made no definite plans but had counted on Paddy's taking his horse back to his place, where Pat could send for him later. It soon became obvious that Paddy had no such intention.

"Will you put your mind to it, now, Paddy," said Pat, "and see what you can do for me?"

"I'm not thinking," said Paddy.

"But Paddy, will you please think! What ever am I to do with the beast and me twelve miles from home?"

"I'm not able to think," said Paddy, turning his back and climbing into the car.

Sydney and I did not know just

what to do. We did not have our own car here but were depending on Paddy Punch to take us back to it. At the same time we didn't like to leave poor Pat away off in the country. Finally he told us that he would try to get stabling for his horse down the road, and urged us to go along, so we left. Later Paddy told us that he hadn't wanted to take the horse because he was afraid he'd have it for the rest of the summer. I tried to watch the roads carefully so that we could find our way back to pick up Pat. We said goodbye to the Punches at the corner pub, promised Paddy to come back next year and to convey his regards to Jean Slaughter, climbed into the Consul, and started back to look for Pat. Presently we spied him trudging along the road. It looked as though his boots might be a bit tight, and I hoped he hadn't too many blisters. But he was unconcerned and told us he found a fine box-stall for his horse and all was well.

We then drove back to Limerick. The parade, of course, was over, but traffic was being switched around to take care of the race cars. Pat was determined not to be sent into the grounds with the other cars, probably to save the entrance ticket. "Tell the guard you've a horse in the last race and we've to go back by the stables," he told me.

But the guard was obviously skeptical, so Pat took over. I have never heard such a fine flow of words in my life. After the first sentence I completely lost track of the meaning, as did the guard, for after listening a moment he shook his head, muttered something about the guard further along, and waved us ahead. Pat was breathless but triumphant, and Sydney and I were speechless with admiration.

We parked in a narrow street and went into the race grounds on foot. One race had been run but there were several more. It was a beautiful track with a grandstand so placed that one had a full view of every fence. Bookmakers and pari-mutual windows were open for business, and I was given to understand that it was practically illegal to watch a race without betting on it. Now, I have no gambling instincts whatsoever. I really dislike betting on a race, preferring to watch without a favorite, but I was overruled. A race card was thrust into my hands and I found myself agreeing to bet two shillings on "Tutto" both ways—that is, both to win and to place. (I picked Tutto because in Italian his name means "everything," and if I had everything, what could I lose?)

Climbing to the top of the grandstand and looking out the back window, I found I could see the saddling enclosure. One by one the horses were assembled. Then they were blown to their posts and out they filed, led by a man in hunt uniform. Tutto was a chestnut gelding. His jockey wore blue with a yellow hoop on the body of the shirt and a red cap. This augured well, for these are the New Canaan Mounted Troop colors. The horse moved out readily and I had great hopes, not misplaced, as it turned out, for though I appeared to be the only one in the whole grandstand betting on Tutto, he took all the fences in fine style and finished second.

The next race was about three miles, again a steeplechase. I looked down the list and found a horse named Chimney Smoke by one called Soldado. Soldado was owned by the man who had rented me Athlacca, the pearl of a horse that had carried me so nobly on the Scarteen hunt, so on Chimney Smoke I bet. This time I was not alone in my choice for many others had bet on him, but again I was lucky. He too came in second in a very big field.

I cannot remember which horse I bet on in the next race, but I know that again my choice placed second. Evidently whatever I picked was pretty sure to place, though I continued to bet two ways. And then came the end of my luck, just when I thought I had a sure thing. The fifth race listed a horse named "The Fluter," who wore goggles to keep him from shying away from the other horses. Now, Herbie Whitman plays the flute with the No Friends and wears the largest and blackest horn-rimmed spectacles in existence. In fact, he is known to his intimate friends as "Mickey Mouse." Surely the Fluter would not let me down. But he did. He ambled out at the end of the line and got so far behind that before the horses had gone around once his jockey decided it was no use and trotted him home again.

We saw a number of friends in the grandstand and in the paddock. Certainly all of County Limerick must have been there, for it took us nearly an hour to get away in the traffic. Pat, who had lent his car to someone else for the races and counted on picking it up there, was stranded for the second time that day, so we took him home. He had to wait in a shop across the street, however, because his house key was in his car. This didn't seem to faze him at all. He said that he would just have a nice cup of tea and not to worry about him, but to be sure and be back to pick him up at ten o'clock, for he was taking us to a real Irish "Kayly."

XXII

An Irish Kayly—An Irish Point-to-Point—The Midnight Plane to New York

The Kayly (Irish for set or square dance) was lots of fun. We were lucky to get tickets since it was St. Patrick's evening and consequently the most popular dance of the year, but as usual Pat wangled them somehow.

The Irish set dances differ from the American in that there is no caller. Many of them are of the "progressive" type, more common in the South than in New England. In these the dancers, in sets of eight and sometimes more, face each other in two lines. Each line progresses around the hall so that at the end of each figure the opposing lines face different dancers. Because there is no caller the patterns are a little hard to follow, but we soon found ourselves able to manage somehow. If we made mistakes, the good-natured Irish put up with them without a murmur and helped us all they could.

These were the real Irish people at this dance, no Anglo-Irish that I could see. Paddy Punch's sons were there with their girls and I saw several other familiar faces. It was informal, the girls in skirts and blouses or short silk dresses, the boys in tweeds, and there was a wonderful spirit of gaiety and good fun. There was one astounding little man who looked to be pushing ninety. From his hips up one would think that an armchair would have offered about as much activity as he would be capable of, but below the hips he was as agile as an eel. He wore golf trousers and high woolen socks and a beautiful pair of red shoes made of the finest of leathers. Those shoes positively twinkled and flashed as he stepped the measures. Never a mistake did he make, and whereas others were willing to do the ordinary turns and swings, he embroidered his steps with

195

gay little caprioles and extra heel and toe tapping—all this even though it was obvious that he was not one to take the official "closing" of the pubs in honor of the Saint very seriously.

The church was well represented, for a group of seven or eight priests were sitting in one corner, watching the proceedings with much interest. In the middle of the evening one of them got up and made a long speech in Gaelic which, fortunately for me, he then gave again in English. The speech was to the effect that the Irish gala week, "An Tostel," was coming up in April and volunteers were needed for various dramatic, musical, and dancing representations. Apparently many pageants depicting historical and religious events were planned. In addition, there would be various contests in dancing, singing Irish songs, playing Irish instruments, etc. The purpose of the week seemed to be to welcome tourists and show them the best that Ireland has to offer. From the numbers that the good priest said were needed for the exhibition and contests, I would say that no true Irishman or woman would have the opportunity of watching any of the fun; they would all be too busy participating in it.

At about eleven thirty we were treated to an exhibition by one of Ireland's champion tap dancers. She was a young girl dressed in green and white with elaborate gold embroidery on the cape which she wore over one shoulder. Her hair was as black and glistening as a raven's wing. She wore patent-leather slippers with big silver buckles. She danced several dances, all very intricate and beautifully executed, but the Irish conception of tap-dancing seems uninteresting to one accustomed to the American and European styles. To the Irish the dancer's feet are the only thing worth watching; therefore, from the knees up, the body is held as motionless as possible, the arms swing limply close to the torso, and the dancer maintains a completely dead-pan expression, looking straight ahead into space. My own feeling was that if the legs and feet were to be the sole point of interest, then the performer should dance behind a partially lowered curtain that would hide everything except her legs and feet. As it was, accustomed as I am to the engaging expressions and rhythmic use of the whole body characteristic of American dancers, the rather unhappy expression on the lass's face made me want to say, "My dear, you really *don't* have to do this if you don't want to."

I was also told that all the steps are traditional and were composed for each individual piece of music many years ago. I could not find out whether a dancer was ever allowed to invent his own dances or whether the subject was forever closed.

Just after this exhibition, we had a set dance in which there was rather more swinging than usual. Furthermore, it was of the progressive type. Now, though Sydney and I may not know all the steps in the Irish dances, we are accomplished "swingers." As we made our way from one group of dancers to the other down the long hall, our swinging got more and more energetic. The dance was one in which each person swings his partner, swings another member of the set, swings his partner again, swings the remaining member, and then, after a final swing with his partner, goes to the next set. A smooth swing in which each person keeps one foot on the ground and pushes around it with the other is a wonderful movement, but it can develop a good bit of centrifugal force. What was my embarrassment when, just as I had reached the last couple, grasped the elbow and hand of my new partner—a young and very exuberant dancer—and began to whirl, I found that his exuberance did not match his equilibrium. The first thing I knew, he went flying off into space to land in the lap of a young lady sitting on the sidelines!

We returned to the Dunraven Arms at about one o'clock, delighted to have had the opportunity of taking part in the Kayly and ever grateful to Pat. The next day was to be spent taking pictures at the Dunraven Stud with the photographer, Larry Burrows, supplied by *Life;* going to the point-to-point at Kingsland, near Ballinleen; stopping off for tea with Mrs. Hedderman, following the races; then going over to Hospital for a fitting with Mr. Fraser. We hoped to find a moment to run in and say goodbye to the Dunravens and the Fitzgeralds before leaving for the airport at ten o'clock, but as things worked out we had to make our adieus by telephone.

Mr. Burrows had arrived at Dunraven on St. Patrick's Day and was joined by Mr. Montgomery, the nice chap who had taken so much trouble to get my various photographic engagements straightened out when I was in Dublin. He was accompanied by a young lady whose name I don't recall. She was to be the "researcher" and Montgomery had come along to see that everything went smoothly.

Burrows was a long, cool drink of water with great skill at his profession. He found the Irish climate and enthusiasm difficult to deal with. I felt for him when I learned that due to calls on his time he had been able to get back to see his wife and little son for only three days during the previous month. His English reticence and tendency to understatement mixed about as well as oil and vinegar, and I was quite put to it to keep the peace. But he went to no end of trouble to get good pictures, and dear Lord Dunraven, irritated though he obviously was, went to no end of trouble to help him, having his brood mares and their foals paraded around and around the paddock, getting old Panorama and the other noble beasts of his establishment out to be photographed, and posing himself. The day was rather a gray one, and when I saw the finished slides in New York I was astounded at the lovely blue sky that Burrows had miraculously coaxed from nowhere.

Immediately after an early luncheon we set out for the race meeting. I had got directions from the knowledgeable Benny, who gave me a minute description of the route but

A bookie at the County Limerick point-to-point signaling a prospective bettor

failed to mention a final turn to the left which would bring us to our destination. The meeting was way off in the country, and of course there were no posters or markers of any kind to direct us, nor even any road names or signs. But to make up for it, every cottager knew exactly how to direct us, so we eventually got there. We had Pat with us, and Valiant, of course, and Mr. Montgomery and party followed.

An Irish point-to-point is like nothing else on earth. The participants are divided into five categories: First there are the gentry, usually prominent members of the local hunt for the benefit of which the point-to-point is being run. These are the acting stewards, the stewards, the secretaries, the announcers, starter, clerk of the scales, etc. The Clerk of the Course is either a Huntsman or Whip or other member of the hunting staff. He wears a pink coat and escorts the horses to the post. Next we have the owners, trainers, and riders of the competing horses. The owners and trainers are dressed in tweeds; the riders, who may be either men or women, but must be amateurs, wear brilliant racing silks. The bookmakers stand on boxes in a long row with slates beside them on which they write the odds on a given horse. They keep up a continuous chant, usually in a monotone. Each seems to have his own particular song, but I was especially struck with one little chap on the end of the line who kept saying, "Bet your money on the mare, bet your money on the mare, bet your money on the mare," over and over again. He was saying it when we got

Tinkers running games of chance with animals to attract spectators

that there were at least a thousand people, most of whom knew each other and all of whom had tips on what horse was to win what race. Country girls in their best silk dresses and high heels plowed through the mud, children with tickets to sell on the numbers' drawing wormed their way in and out, and men and women right out of Cruikshank's drawings gave a hand here and there when needed.

But the most colorful of all were the tinkers, for, in addition to being a race meeting, a point-to-point is also a small carnival. There were tents and stands of every description. One could spin wheels, throw darts or balls, buy bananas or ice cream, or "pick a number." Why anyone, after looking over the prizes offered to the lucky winners, would ever want to participate in any of the games of chance I cannot imagine. I have seen such prizes before—hideous dolls, metal statuettes, garishly colored objects of every kind, all completely useless—but never in my life have I seen such a collection as was here displayed. The men who ran the "pick a number" game were the most interesting. There were several of these games and the proprietors had different ways of getting the attention of the audience. One had a little white mouse which ran around and around his hat brim; another had a monkey which climbed up his trouser leg, sat on his shoulder, and grimaced at the spectators. Before each of these was a large board ruled into squares, with a number printed in each square.

there and he was still saying it when we left, nor had he stopped, as far as I could tell, even to accept the money of any who cared to follow his advice. Whether he was partial to lady horses or whether a gelding had once let him down I don't know, but I was sorely tempted to go up and offer to bet on a gelding just to get his reaction!

The general public surged back and forth from the saddling paddock (a hastily constructed square inside which fractious animals threw their heels to the sky or tried to lift the stable boys, who were hanging on to the bridles, completely off the ground) to the hillside, from which the races could best be viewed. I would say

Table of gewgaws to be won by spinning a wheel or choosing a pellet out of a box

Notice the religious pictures in the background.

Some of the squares, in addition to the number, stated that the lucky drawer of that number would receive several shillings back for the one he had invested. After a long spiel in which the "barker" told of his honesty and interest in his audience, displayed the antics of his animal, and repeated several times that it was virtually impossible to lose if one joined in his game, a partner passed a box around containing tightly wound scrolls. A shilling gave one the privilege of picking one of these scrolls. On unwinding it one found a number, and if this number corresponded with one of the lucky ones on the board then one received the stated bonus. Alas, though I tried three times, despite the warm assurances of the barker, I always lost my shilling.

The only sad sight was the little tinker and gypsy beggar children who wandered around trying to collect pennies, and the babies, filthily dressed, with pacifiers in their mouths, who were carried by their mothers in hopes that the sight of them would persuade the bystanders to contribute. I took pictures of some and gave copies to the mothers, who were delighted and "God Blessed" me with fervence.

A point-to-point differs from a steeplechase in that the course is over natural jumps and there is no track. Red and white flags mark the riders' path. Originally, of course, the rider was given a series of places, or "points," to which he must go and could choose his own course (hence the name), but that practice has long since been changed. The Limerick Point-to-Point was not considered one of the very best and most spectacular, but it was typical. The jumps were banks, but from where I stood I could not see that they had ditches although there may have been some. My friend Burrows, who had been expressing the hope all morning that there would be some bad spills, decided to place himself and his camera at the most dangerous-looking jump. I could understand his professional interest, but I sort of wished he could have been

An old tinker woman pushing her way through the crowd

Spectators on top of the hill tensely watching races

riding and could experience the feeling of a horse going over on top of him or of being separated from his mount to lie helpless while the horses of more lucky riders galloped over his body. I have had both happen to me and can speak from experience.

The first race had five starters, among them two horses ridden by brothers. One of these riders was the man who had made himself so unpopular by his uncalled-for assault on the "Kentucky Colonel." The other brother, the younger and supposedly less skillful of the two, rode Peg Watt's horse, Golden Tiddles. He had been trained by Mike Fitzgibbons. To the joy of everyone, he won—a feather in the caps of both the young rider and the trainer.

The second race produced a situation which may never have happened before and may easily never occur again. There were nine horses scheduled to start but only four went to the post and only three actually went away. These were Foggy Dew, owned by Mr. J. Green and ridden by K. Coughlan; Muskrat, owned by a Mrs. Farquahar and ridden by Tony Scannell (and oh, what a clever and intrepid rider was Tony!); and Royal Courier, owned by Mrs. E. Williams and ridden by Jerrald Hogan. The race was three miles long, which meant that the riders had to go around the course twice. It looked a much longer three miles than that of the Limerick course the day before.

Presently they were off, and we

Fences

Although these are supposed to be "natural" fences, the bank obviously has been cleared of its "hairy" growth of thorns and the ditch has been filled in.

strained our eyes to see the blue of Foggy Dew's rider, the black of Muskrat, and the dark red of Royal Courier. The horses were bunched together all the way around the first time, and as they passed us it could have been anybody's race. Then suddenly Courier and Muskrat crashed. The crash occurred on the other side of a bank and we could not see exactly what happened but learned later that both riders bit the dust. The Courier's rider had had enough and he let go his horse, who continued on the course in fine style all on his own, but Tony Scannell was not to be defeated by anything so insignificant as a fall. He managed to hang on the neck strap and pulled himself into the saddle again. His horse lost a stride or two but kept boldly on. What was Tony's dismay to find, on remounting, that though he had a willing and able horse under him he had no bridle, for the bridle had come off in his hand when he fell and was now dangling beneath the horse's brisket, threatening to trip him. That would never do, decided Tony, so he reached down, grabbed up the bridle, and held it under one arm while with the other he guided the valiant bay mare by tapping her on the neck. She responded in fine style but was not quite able to make up the distance she had lost in the accident, so she

Muskrat, who fell earlier in the race, finishing without a bridle
The winner who was just ahead was disqualified for going the wrong side of the flag so the bridleless horse won.

finished a length or two behind Foggy Dew. However, the incident was not closed, for a protest was filed, and it was discovered that Foggy Dew had inadvertantly gone on the wrong side of a flag, so Muskrat, with no bridle, won the race!

When I told this story that evening to Mr. Kirkpatrick, manager of Fort Union Stud, this gentleman capped it with two other stories, both equally good. One pertained to a jockey who, like Tony Scannell, was noted for his quick thinking in an emergency. In this case he was riding a horse on which a great deal of money, including his own, had been bet, and found himself coming into the finish line neck and neck with another rider. Both horses were well extended and going stride for stride, so obviously it would be a dead heat, which did not suit the jockey in question at all. He raised his bat and just in the last stride he clonked his mount between the ears. Outraged at the indignity, the poor beast stretched out his neck and so was able to win by a nose.

The other tale concerned a jockey who was known to be far and away the best rider in the country. Moreover, he was riding a horse that, as everyone knew, could beat his opponents with one foot tied up. Unfortunately the horse was not in top condition, the race was a long one, and the jumps were big. The jockey got him away fast and led the field by many lengths throughout the first seven-eighths of the race. But he had taken the animal too fast, and fifty feet from the finish the horse stopped, ridden completely to a standstill and physically unable to move a step further. The crowd was horrified, for, believing the horse to be a sure thing, every last one of them had mortgaged his soul on that horse and that rider. Indignantly they surged onto the course, surrounded the unhappy animal, and half lifted, half pushed him over the finish line. As my informant said, "Even if the other horses hadn't been so far behind they could never have finished because they couldn't have got through the crowd!"

When I went to congratulate Peg Watt on the winning of her race and to get another look at the remarkable horse that had won without benefit of bridle, I found myself watching a lovely fracas between an ice-cream vendor and one of the officials—Major Waller, I think. The vendor in question had parked her car in an undesirable spot and had then firmly refused to move either it or herself, planting her capacious person on top of her ice cream and defying the world. The first reaction of the authorities was the natural one of sending for the guard. But the guard was of little help, preferring to stand with his feet apart and his hands behind his back gazing at the sky rather than take a more active part in the pro-

ceedings. Someone else now had the brilliant idea of starting the motor of the car and moving it off with or without the permission of its owner. This promptly brought action, for the ice-cream lady, ponderous in her wrath, twisted both the arm of her enemy and the key to the car to such an extent that both were bent and put temporarily out of commission. The arm recovered shortly, but the key was so damaged that it could neither be removed from the dashboard nor turned to start the engine. What the outcome was I never learned, though obviously the ice-cream lady had won the first round.

The races continued until about five o'clock, when we all repaired to Mrs. Hedderman's house for tea and drinks. Never have I seen so wonderful a display of tempting delights. There was barely room to move around the table. I met a number of new people and was able to say good-bye to many of the friends who had been so kind to us. They all started making engagements for me for my next visit and no one could understand why we had to leave at a time when so many things were about to happen. Why couldn't we at least stay over for the Dublin Show, which takes place in August, they asked. Among those to whom we said good-bye were the Fitzgeralds, the Watts, and Pat Scanlan, who hinted that we still might see him again. He was most anxious for us to take a small package with us and ship it on to his nephew. That he had not heard from the nephew in many months, that the last address given had been a boarding house in upper New York State, and that he did not know the lad's business bothered him not at all. I am sorry to say that the package, which we duly forwarded on reaching home, was returned to us, and the gay wool scarf still waits to be claimed.

We went on to Hospital, arriving somewhat after seven. Mr. Fraser was all ready for us. In the two days since we had seen him he had cut out both the jacket to my tweed suit and the jacket for Sydney. He now gave us each a careful and most loquacious fitting, pulling out bastings here and putting in pins there. If the garments don't fit to perfection when we get them, it will certainly not be Mr. Fraser's fault.

Our last supper was eaten, our last farewells said, and then we climbed mournfully into the Consul for the last time and drove to Shannon. Here we were met by a whole row of officials, who had been alerted to take care of us, as well as by a gentleman from the Irish *Times,* who wanted details on what I thought of Ireland. In the middle of this came a telephone message from Mr. Tillander, wishing us godspeed and a safe return. Immediately after that Pat arrived, bearing a box of candy, the package for his nephew, and a bunch of forsythia, which we had to refuse since we were not allowed to take plants out of Ireland. There was no set dance going on this time, but I felt around me all the good wishes of the many, many friends Sydney and I had made while in Ireland. We climbed aboard the Flying Dutchman once more with the firm conviction that not many months would pass before we again "came back to Erin."

Postscript

Assuredly it is a foolish thing for a stranger to venture to express an opinion of any country or its inhabitants after only a few weeks' sojourn. But one may be allowed to give impressions. And since everyone whom I met wanted at once to know "what I thought of Ireland," I would like to give a few of these impressions, with the distinct understanding that they are impressions only and not categorical opinions.

First, the Irish temperament. The Irish, as I see them, and the Americans, as I know them to be, have much in common—probably more in common than either has with any other race on earth. They are alike volatile, enthusiastic, generous, democratic, and aggressive. Both have a profound sympathy for the underdog. Neither has the infinite capacity for detail for which the Europeans, especially the Germans, are noted. Neither the American nor the Irishman is malicious by nature or tends to hold a grudge.

But sometimes their mutual characteristics appear in different forms. The American's aggressiveness is demonstrated in his inventiveness, his liking for change, his desire to improve his conditions, and his profound belief in the promise of the future. The Irishman's aggressiveness is exhibited in his general belicoseness and his extreme nationalism. I was amused, for example, to read in a Dublin paper that it would be impossible to broadcast on St. Patrick's Day the results of the hurling match to be played by the Irish National Team against the Welsh National Team; to do so would be unpatriotic, since it would be giving news to do with another nation on a day which should be reserved for Irish events only.

The American's aggression leads him to welcome change; the Irishman's belligerence causes him to resent change and to retreat from it.

The American thinks the only thing worth while in life is to build for the future, to improve his lot, and to give his children a better education and a better start in life than he had himself. The Irish feel that it is today that is important.

If one looks back on the history of the two nations, it is not hard to understand why there is this disparity of attitudes in peoples who really are much alike. In the childhood of her history, Ireland suffered defeat after defeat, invasion after invasion, and treachery after treachery. So she has become like a child who, continually suppressed, continually punished, never winning but always failing, takes what he can at the moment—the child who does not welcome a future which will probably be worse than the bad past he has known.

America, on the other hand, has never known either defeat or invasion. Her sons have been successful in every war. Each generation has known improvements in opportunity and in living conditions over the previous generation. She has never known subservience to a tyrant nor treachery. So is it to be wondered that, like the child who has always met with success and for whom each successive day and year has held out new rewards, she faces the future not with fear but with anticipation, and welcomes change?

From centuries of hardship the Irish people have learned courtesy and a beautiful dignity, whereas many Americans are brash and impatient, like spoiled children. The American is restless and rarely content with what the day may bring. He suffers from emotional disturbances and gastric ulcers. There is no such thing as a psychiatrist in Ireland, at least so far as I could find out. Several times I was asked to explain the meaning of the word and the purpose of psychiatric treatment, especially for children and young people. There may be Irish with stomach ulcers, but I would wager my last dollar that the ulcers come from a bad choice of liquid diet rather than from hypertension.

Though the Irish think of the Americans as lacking in courtesy, the American male is more thoughtful of his wife than is the Irishman. Indeed, it is the poorer-class women in Ireland who really have a hard time, and if the men think *dolce far niente* is a workable philosophy of life, the women don't have much chance to practice it.

To the American, the Irishman who neglects his business or his opportunities for improvement to hunt or fish displays a lack of ambition. But if one accepts the idea that the world might at any minute be rendered barren of life by atomic radiation, perhaps the Irishman is wise to have his fun while he can get it. Who is to say?

As I look back on my trip pictures flash into my mind—that beautiful view from the top of the hill in Oola, where I had the impression that, given a good pair of field-glasses, I could have seen the Empire State in one direction and the Eifel Tower in another . . . the firelight playing on the ivory damask gown of Mrs. Morley . . . the silhouette of a huntsman, balancing on the top of a razor-edged bank set close to a road, and the agile manner in which his horse, catlike, slid his front feet down to the level ground and brought his quarters around under him to avoid slipping on the tarmac . . . the lovely pink of the Miville's Georgian house . . . the feel of Athlacca as he leaped that first great ditch at Mooresville. These impressions I will carry with me forever.

I have said earlier that the physical beauty of many of the Irish and the Anglo-Irish was particularly noticeable, as were their innate friendliness and desire to help. The lovely modulations of their speaking tones fall gracefully on the ear. I should think that to the Irish the American accent must be pure torture, especially the exaggerated Western, Southern, and New England accents, with their ugly nasal quality and flat vowel sounds.

I wish the Irish could be persuaded to flavor their food a little more and to cook both their meat and their vegetables about half the length of time they do now. And I wish, oh, how I wish, that someone would sell them on the idea of adopting route markings for their roads!

The Irishman, seeing the United States for the first time, would, I should think, be struck first by the wide variety in architecture, secondly by the beauty and variety of the shop-window displays, and thirdly by the extreme softness and absorbent quality of that common, plebian necessity, the roll of toilet paper.

I hope to visit Ireland again, not once, but many times. If, in doing so, I am made one half so welcome and have one half as good a time as I did on this, my first Irish Adventure, I shall be more than overjoyed.

INDEX

Abbey Theatre, 140
Abbeyfield, 173
Abernethys, the, 15, 24, 112
   Jane, 17, 18, 24, 25
   Sam, 17, 18, 24, 25
Adare, 15, 23, 31, 32, 33, 43, 50, 71,
    84, 92, 95, 141, 160, 164, 173, 187
   village dance in, 102-03
Aga Khan, 39, 122
Alley, Mr. Peter, 132
Aly Khan, Prince, 122
American Fox Hunter, the, 19
American hunt clubs wanted in Ire-
    land, 45-46
"An Tostel," 196
Appaloosa horse, 149, 150
Ashbourne, 132
Athlacca, 85, 86, 87, 88, 90, 194, 209
Atkinson, Miss, 53

babbler, a, 53
Ballinleen, 197
Ballybeama Pass, the, 170, 172, 173

Ballykeane, 139, 141, 142, 143, 144,
   185
Ballykisteen Stud, 105
Ballymanny, 122
banks, 59-60, 62, 63, 64, 65, 66, 84,
   163, 164
Bantry Bay, 172
Barry, Mr., 121, 122, 129, 131, 133,
   146
Baruch, Bernard, 144
Bass, Jack, 37, 63, 64, 65, 76, 163
   See also Kentucky Colonels
beehive dwellings, 166, 167
Belvoir, the, 50
Benner's Inns, 165
Birr, 108, 110, 111, 182
Black and Tans, the, 83, 90, 109
Blasket Islands, the, 168
Book of Kells, 185
Boroimhe, Brian, 159, 160
Broadley, Mr., 132
Bruff, 173
Burrows, Larry, 119, 145, 197, 200

Cameron, Lieutenant Colonel, 147
capping fees, 49
Cashel, 105, 108, 110
Cashel, Rock of, 74, 76, 185, 186
Cassustown Cross, 69, 71
Castlemain Harbor, 170
Cattle fair, 116
chance, a fox's, in a hunt, 48
Cheltenham, England, 88
Children, Foster Parents Plan for
    War, 14
Chimney Smoke, 194
Circus, The Spring Riding, 14
Clare, 164
Cleeves, Miss, 85
Clogh Jordan, 108, 109, 110
Clonfinlough, 184
Clonmacnoise, 184
collector's items, 96-99
Communism, 130, 151
Conyers, Colonel C. G., 23, 51
Cormac's Chapel, 186
Coughlan, K., 201
County Limerick Harriers, 94
County Limerick Hounds, 23, 37, 50-
    51, 59, 63
coverts, 49, 53, 55, 74, 75, 132, 135,
    136, 177
Croom, 45, 99, 173, 175
Croom Harriers, 59 ff., 67, 163
    Master of, See Watt, Peg
Cruikshank, 61, 151, 199
Curragh, 116, 122, 185

Daley, Mr., 177, 179, 181, 182
dancing, 29-30, 80-81, 195 ff
    See also Kayly
Daresbury, Lord, 50-51, 55, 57
debts, 113, 114
deer, 129, 130, 132, 133, 136, 138
democratic sport, hunting is a, 47-48
Denturius, 42, 105, 106

"Devil's Bit," the, 74
Dingle, 165, 169
ditches, 135, 137, 164
    See also banks
Doncaster, 144
Doon Castle, 183, 184
Doyle, Patrick, 122, 128
Drag Hunt, 17
Dromoland, 140, 141, 145, 155, 156 ff,
    164
Dromoland Castle, 24
Dubber, 132
Dublin, 32, 110, 116, 119, 121, 131,
    132, 139, 140, 146, 147, 153, 154,
    185
    traffic in, 118
Dublin Garrison, 132
Dublin road, 70
Dublin Show, 204
Duhallow, the, 160, 163, 164, 177
Dunbeg, 67
Dunbeg, Fort of, 167, 168
Dunn, Dr., 150, 151, 152
Dunne, D., 147
Dunraven Arms, 24, 32-33, 69, 79, 94,
    95, 141, 160, 164, 172, 175, 177,
    197
Dunraven, Lady, 36, 37, 38, 43, 44,
    187
Dunraven, Lord (Earl of), 23, 32, 36,
    37, 38, 39, 41, 43, 77, 141, 197
Dunraven Stud, 197
Dunravens, the, 197
Durney, D., 147
Durnin, Mr., 20
Dwan, Miss Breda, 71, 75, 76

Elizabeth of Austria, Empress, 121,
    122
Ennis road, 177
equipment, rare old, 96 ff.
escape, a fox's chance of, in a hunt, 48

Farmer's Ball, 92 ff.
Farquahar, Mrs., 201
fences, 18
Fennell, J., 23, 36, 57
Fergus, 135, 136, 137, 138, 140
Field, the, 48, 49, 50, 54, 55, 56, 85, 131, 132, 135, 138, 150, 151, 178, 179, 180, 190, 191
fireplaces, 33
Fitzgerald, Commander, 79, 96
  family of, 80, 102, 197, 204
Fitzgibbons, Mike, 61, 62, 63, 65, 66, 67, 201
Fitzsimons, T., 132, 133
"Fluter, The," 194
"Flying Dutchman, The," 26, 205
Foggy Dew, 201, 202, 203
food, Irish, 209
Fort Etna Stud, 95 ff.
Fort Union Stud, 23, 36, 38 ff., 79, 106, 203
Fosbery, Mr. George, 51
Foster Parents Plan for War Children, 14
Fowler, Brigadier B. J., 148
Fowler, Captain R. H., 147
fox, the, 147, 151, 152, 153, 154, 177 ff.
fox hunting, 16-17, 48 ff., 131, 132
  See also names of individual hunts
Fraser, William, 187, 197, 205

Gallerus Oratory, 168
galtees, 87
Galway, 36, 178
Galway Blazers, 77, 116, 175
Garden State Stakes, 144
Garrison Hounds, 132
Gerrard, Mr., 132
Glengariff, 172, 173
Golden Tiddles, 201
Golden Vale, 67, 76, 82, 86, 105, 108, 180
Golden Vale Hunt, 24, 71, 149

Golden Vale Hunt-Foxhounds, 71
graveyard at Fort Union Stud, 43
Gray, David, 17
Green, Mr. J., 201
Gruenveld, Captain, 26
Guersant, 42, 43
gypsies, 36, 200

habits, 54, 135
  See also livery, uniforms
hackney, a, 73, 75
Haggard, Bill, 37, 64, 65, 76, 77
  See also Kentucky Colonels
half-breed, 54
Hall, Major, 122
Happy Laughter, 122
harrier pack, 71
"Harriers, Master of the Limerick," 81
harriers, 17, 191
Harriman, Lord, 85, 91, 93
Harris, Dr., 84, 148
Harris, George, 60, 105, 106, 107
Harris, Mrs., 108
Healy Pass, 173
  See Tim Healy Pass
Hedderman, Mrs., 99, 101, 197, 204
Hillyhood, 132
Hilmalkedan, 168, 169
"hirelings," 19, 139
His Highness, 43
history, comparison of Irish and American, 208
"Hitchcock pen," 39
Hogan, Jerrald, 201
horn, hunting, 49, 83, 90, 133
"Horse and Hound," the, 82
horse fair, annual, at Galway, 36
horses, 17, 18, 19, 23, 24, 25, 115, 116, 134, 136, 139, 143, 149, 150, 163, 177, 178, 179, 180
  "colored," 34

Hospital, 185, 187, 197, 205

hounds, 47, 48, 49, 50, 52, 53, 55, 56, 57, 60, 73, 74, 81, 83, 85, 86, 87, 88, 90, 132, 133, 135, 136, 138, 153, 160, 177 ff., 180, 181, 192

Howth, Lord, 132

Hunt, Miss, 55, 56

Hunter, Irish, the, 54, 57

hunting clips, 96

hunting field, procedure in the, 48 ff.

"Hunting Holiday in Ireland," 16

"Hunting in Ireland," 16

Huntsman, professional, 49, 132

hurling match, 207

Hyde, Mr. D. W., 122

Hyde, Mr. Tim, 24, 71, 108

Idlewild, 26

Inch, 169

Inchiquin, Lord (Earl of), 24, 157, 159, 160

invitation necessary to hunt in the United States, 51

Ireland, Kings of, 159, 186

Irish, longevity of the, 147

Irish Horse, The, 19

Irish hunts, 20, 23

Irish Kagle, 102

Irish National Anthem, 81

Irish National Stud, 39

Irish Nation l Team, 207

Irish Times, 119, 205

Irish Tourist Association, 19

Irish Tourist Bureau, 23, 25, 69, 146, 159

Jack, 72, 73, 74, 163, 180

James, the valet, 61

Japanese garden, 122, 123, 129, 185

Jorrocks, John, 47, 61, 62

jumping, 73, 74, 85, 86, 115, 137, 143, 163, 164

jumps, 17, 19, 179, 181, 192

Kathleen, 32-33, 60, 61, 94, 109, 189

Kauffman, Mike, 21

Kayly, 194, 195

Kells, Book of, 185

Kenmare, 172, 173

Kennedy, Dr., 24, 72, 73, 75, 163

Kenny, Harry, 25, 95, 109

Kentucky Colonels, 44, 45, 50, 55, 59, 60, 63, 64, 66, 76, 77, 79, 80, 88, 96, 152, 163, 179, 201

Kentucky Derby, 144

Kerry country, 67, 164, 177

Kildare, Earl of, 186

Killarney, 173

Killbride, 142

Killorglin, 36, 170

Kinane, Dr. D., 71

Kingsland, 197

Kirkpatrick, Mr., 203

K. L. M., 27

Knocklong, 173

Lady Shamrock, 190, 191, 192

Lady Ursula, 106

Laidlaw, David, 129, 130

Leamington, 132

Lee, Mr. and Mrs., 80

Lee, Mrs., 94, 164

Life, 119, 145, 197

Liffey, the, 118, 119

Limerick, 15, 18, 31, 32, 53, 70, 75, 76, 80, 81, 84, 92, 93, 95, 170, 178, 182, 187, 189, 190, 193, 194, 201

Limerick Harriers, 81, 102, 189

Limerick Junction, 105

Limerick Point-to-Point, 200

Lippizan horses, 150

livery, 84, 85, 147, 178

See also habits, uniforms

Lloyds, the, 21

Loughrea, 177, 181
Lucinda, 183, 185
Lynch, Stanislaus, 17, 23, 139, 140
Lynch, Tom, 122

MacCarthy, Father, 152
MacCarthys, the, 159
MacGillycudy Mountains, the, 170
Maister-Peece, Markham's, 99
Malcomson, Mr. G. V., 132, 134
Man O' War, 43
mares, 38, 39, 43, 106, 107, 122, 151
Markham's Maister-Peece, 99
Marshall Plan, 130
Master, invitation from the, necessary
   in the United States, 51
Master of Fox Hounds, the, 48, 49
Maxwell, Esther, 24-25, 81, 108, 111,
   112, 113, 114, 116, 182, 183, 184,
   185, 186
Maxwell, Jack, 109, 111, 112, 116, 182,
   183, 185
Maynooth, President of, 121
McAuley, Mr. J. P., 147
McCann (Whip, Ward Union), 133
McCarthy, Joe, 115
McDonalds, the, 165
Meadow of the White Lake
   See Clonfinlough
Meath Fox Hounds, the, 140, 141, 145,
   147, 150
meet, the author's first in Eire, 50
Milesius, King, 159, 184
milk carts, 34, 70
Miller, Joe, 21
Mills, Miss, 67, 164, 166, 167, 168,
   170, 171, 173
Miville, Major, 139, 142, 143, 144
Miville, Mrs., 143, 144, 145
Mivilles, the, 140, 143, 185, 209
Molly, 151
"Monday country," the, 73

monkey puzzle tree, 142, 143
Montgomery, Mr., 119, 121, 141, 142,
   145, 197, 198
"Mooney of the Doon," Mr., 115, 116
Moony, Mrs., 184
Mooresfort, 85
Mooresville, 209
Mordax, 52
Morley, Mr., 30, 45, 46, 69
Morley, Mrs., 45, 209
Munster, Kings of, 186
   See also Ireland, Kings of
"Music, The No Friends of," 13, 25,
   26, 27, 33, 194
Muskrat, 201, 202, 203

National Aga Khan Stud, 119
"National" schools, 113
National Stud, 108, 141, 185
   See. also Japanese garden
needle stones, 168, 184
Nelson's Pillar, 118
Nenagh, 70
New Canaan Mounted Troop, 14, 193
   Spring Exhibition of, 20
New Castle, 173
Newmarket-on-Fergus, 156
"No Friends of Music, The," 13, 25,
   26, 27, 33, 194
Nugenstown, Kells, 147

O'Brian clan, the, 24, 159, 160
obstacles, 17, 64, 74, 88, 90
O'Connors, the, 159
Ogham, 168
O'Hare, Miss, 36, 37, 79, 80, 82, 160
oldest sports, hunting is one of the, 48
O'Malleys, the, 159
O'Neils, the, 159
Oola, 84, 85, 87, 88, 91, 109, 208
O'Reillys, the, 159
Ormund, the, 140

Ormund Hounds, the, 115
O'Sullivan, Mr., 28
outlyers, 129, 132

Panorama, 42, 43, 197
Patrick's Well, 95
"penny, a, for yourself," 170
Perry, Mrs., 109
Perrys, the, 184
Phoenix, 42, 105, 106
pigs, 117, 118
plane trip to Ireland, 26 ff.
point-to-point, 110, 198 ff.
pony, 54, 148, 149
Pratt, Lowell, 15, 16, 19
Puck's Fair, 36, 170
Punch, Paddy, 101-102, 187, 189, 190,
    192, 193, 195

Quinn, Jack, 71, 72, 74, 75

races, 193
Rainsford House, 147
Rathkeale, 23
Red Barn, the, 18, 102
Reeve, Basil, 13
Reeve, Jeanne, 13
Regan, Pat, 53, 55
respiratory ailments, 75
riding clothes, 20-21
Ritchie, Dr., 111, 112
road map, 111, 112
Rocket, 102
Rodes, Jack, 37, 60, 64, 65, 66, 67, 76
    See also Kentucky Colonels
Roscrea, 110, 111, 182
Rossestown Cross, 24, 69, 71
Rothschild, Baron de, 43
Royal Courier, 201, 202
Royal Hibernian, the, 119, 139, 146,
    164, 185
rules of the hunt, 50

Russel, Mr., 190
Ryan, John J., 83
Ryan, Mrs., 86, 87
Ryan, Teddy, 83, 93

St. Matthew, wayside shrine to, 106-
    107
St. Patrick's Day, 187, 189, 195
St. Stephen's Green, 185
Scanlan, Pat, 80, 84, 86, 87, 91, 92,
    93, 94, 99, 109, 152, 177, 181,
    182, 187, 190, 191, 192, 193, 198,
    204, 205
    See also Valiant
Scannell, Tony, 201, 202, 203
Scarteen country, 178
Scarteen Hounds, 83
Scarteen Hunt, 92, 148, 194
    evening dress, 93
Scarteen territory, 163
school children, 34-35
Shannon, 16, 27, 28, 30, 32, 44, 146,
    156, 158, 159, 205
Shannon Travel Agency, 30, 45
Shannon Travel Bureau, 30
Sheehy, Mr., 20
Sheelamagig, 183, 184, 185, 186
sheep, 116, 117, 144, 170, 185
Shorty, 52, 53, 55, 57, 63
signposts, 70-71
Silvermines, 87
sin, fox-hunter's, 56
sires, outstanding, 42
Slaughter, Jean, 18, 102, 193
Slea Head, 165, 168
Slieve, 165
Smith, Mr. Lancelot, 178
Smith, Mrs., 180
Soldado, 194
speech, Irish, 209
Spring Riding Circus, The, 14
stag, 133, 135, 136, 138

staghunt, 17

staghunting, 131 ff.

stallions, 41, 42, 105, 106

stone walls, Irish horses do not fly, 53

"stud," definition of, 38

stud farms, 139, 144

stud fees, 39, 42

Supple, Benny, 37, 50, 55, 60, 61, 67, 69, 197

surnames, 160

telephone book, the Irish, 36-37

telephone, difficulties encountered in use of, 79, 140, 142

temperament, comparison of Irish and American, 207 ff.

Thoroughbreds, 73, 96, 135, 136, 149, 178

Thurles, 70, 71, 75, 110

Thurles and Kilshane Foxhounds, 71

Tillander, Mr., 79, 80, 96, 99, 160, 164, 205

Tim Healy Pass, 172

  See also Healy Pass

Time, Inc., 141

tinkers, 116, 117, 142, 199, 200

  carts, 35-36

Tipperary, 32, 92, 93

Tipperary Road, 84, 105

traffic, 31-32, 69-70, 155

Trafford, Major Raymond de, 61, 63, 64, 65, 66, 67, 80, 86, 87, 91, 105, 109, 161, 164, 175

Trafford, Mrs. de, 84, 105, 109, 110, 139, 141, 142, 144, 146, 161, 164, 175, 187

Tralee, 165

Trinity College, 119

tuberculosis, prevalence of, 34, 75

Tulyar, 39, 108, 122

Turn To, 144

Tutto, 193, 194

tweeds, 172, 173, 185, 187

uniforms, hunt

  County Limerick Hounds, 51

valet service, 61

Valiant, 84, 94, 177, 182, 198

Van Wyck, Katie, 13, 14, 15, 101

Van Wyck, Philip, 13, 14, 15, 18, 24, 101

Victor Cola, 60, 63, 64, 65, 66

Victor Stud, 105, 106, 107

Wakely, Major General, 24, 69, 71, 72

Waller, Major, 80, 204

Waller, Mrs., 80

Ward Hounds, 132

Ward Union, 147, 152, 178

Ward Union Hounds, 129, 131, 132

Ward Union Kennels, 132

Watt, Major, 173, 175, 204

Watt, Mrs. Peg, 59, 60, 61, 62, 63, 64, 65, 66, 67, 72, 80, 81, 82, 85, 87, 88, 101, 137, 163, 173, 175, 201, 204

weather, 28, 33, 72, 165

Webb, Major, 67

Wellington, Duke of, 152

Welsh National Team, 207

Wheelock, Ralph, 25

whips, the, 48, 49

White Lake, Meadow of the

  See Clonfinlough

Whitman, Herbie, 27, 194

Whitman's "Picken Chicken" party, 13

Whitmore, Miss, 185

Williams, Mrs. E., 201

yearlings, 39, 106, 122